RESEARCHING

CW00801962

Researching Prisons provides an overview of the processes, practices, and challenges involved in undertaking prison research. The chapters look at the different practical, theoretical, and emotional considerations required at the various stages of the research process, drawing on the reflections and challenges experienced by over 40 other prison researchers both in England and Wales, and across the world.

After introducing the rationale for prison research, its methodological and critical context, and covering basic practicalities, this book offers a range of tips and tricks for the prison researcher. It covers key topics such as ethics, the process of choosing methods, and looks at researching prisons around the world. It provides an overview of the key elements when undertaking a piece of prison research from start to completion, and draws on the experiences of a broad selection of global prison researchers. In doing so, it acts as a guide to those working in prison research and brings the prison research community to them.

It is essential reading for students engaged with prison research methods and for early career researchers.

Jennifer Anne Rainbow is Senior Lecturer in Criminology at Sheffield Hallam University.

RESEARCHING PRISONS

Jennifer Anne Rainbow

Routledge
Taylor & Francis Group

LONDON AND NEW YORK

Designed cover image: © Shutterstock Images / ASTA Concept

First published 2024
by Routledge
4 Park Square, Milton Park, Abingdon, Oxon OX14 4RN

and by Routledge
605 Third Avenue, New York, NY 10158

Routledge is an imprint of the Taylor & Francis Group, an informa business

British Library Cataloguing-in-Publication Data
A catalogue record for this book is available from the British Library

Library of Congress Cataloging-in-Publication Data
Names: Rainbow, Jennifer Anne, author.
Title: Researching prisons / Jennifer Anne Rainbow.
Description: Abingdon, Oxon; New York, NY : Routledge, 2024. |
Includes bibliographical references and index.
Identifiers: LCCN 2023044813 | ISBN 9781138238626 (hardback) |
ISBN 9781138238640 (paperback) | ISBN 9781315297217 (ebook)
Subjects: LCSH: Prisons—Study and teaching. | Prisons—Resarch.
Classification: LCC HV8754.R35 2024 |
DDC 365.072—dc23/eng/20230928
LC record available at https://lccn.loc.gov/2023044813

ISBN: 978-1-138-23862-6 (hbk)
ISBN: 978-1-138-23864-0 (pbk)
ISBN: 978-1-315-29721-7 (ebk)

DOI: 10.4324/9781315297217

Typeset in Sabon
by codeMantra

In loving memory of my beloved Dad,
Kevin Sloan.
I still can't believe you're not here.

CONTENTS

ACKNOWLEDGMENTS

Many thanks to all the prison researchers who made suggestions for content, particularly all the contributors to the vignettes, for your honesty, integrity, and insightful reflections, many of which I felt incredibly moved by; and to those who took part in the 2014 survey about their experiences of the process, and tips for future researchers – your suggestions and reflections have been invaluable (and highly reassuring!). In particular, thanks to Dr Serena Wright who started the journey with me, for her suggestions, enthusiasm, editing, and all her work on our first chapter together (Sloan and Wright, 2015) and the 2014 survey. Special thanks also to Professor David Best for teaching me how to write quickly and effectively, Dr Abigail Stark for all her patient emails and incredibly helpful suggestions; and Dr Victoria Lavis for inspiring me so much by talking about Appreciative Inquiry that it gave me goosebumps!

Many thanks to the most amazing colleagues at Sheffield Hallam University, for their support, suggestions, and patience in listening to my rants, and for giving me the time to write. Thanks also to my students, for asking the questions that helped to form some of the answers in this book! To everyone involved in the publishing process – to Tom Sutton for the idea in the first place, and to Hannah Catterall, Jessica Phillips and Helen Birchall for their endless patience and belief in the project – thank you for your kindness and for pushing me to get this done!

As always, Mum, Dad and James, Isla, and Toby – thank you.

In the course of writing this book, I have lost a lot of extremely special people, not least my beloved Dad – this book is dedicated to him.

In loving memory of Robin Jones. You always believed in me. Chris Pote, Surrogate Grandmother Supreme. Marjorie Mol, a wonderful Nana-in-Law. Margaret Rainbow, a loving Grandmother-in-Law. Philip Sloan, a beloved Uncle. Marian Reyner, a beloved Aunt.

Additional Contributors

When I was asked to write this book, I was both honoured and daunted – the world of prison research is so big, and there are so many different aspects to it! I started asking for advice on what to include from fellow prison researchers, and it occurred to me that it was important to draw on a range of voices, experiences, and approaches, in order to try to give a bigger picture of the breadth of possibilities when it comes to researching prisons. I am indebted to all the prison researchers who agreed to include their own reflections on their prison research journeys in this book, and am in awe of each and every one of you for what you are achieving. You are all amazing!

Katherine Albertson
Heather Anderson
Ben Nevis Barron
Colette Barry
Shereen Baz
Jamie Bennett
Charlotte Bilby
Lauren Bradford-Clarke
Alexandria Bradley
Louise Brangan
Nichola Cadet
Ben Crewe
Sacha Darke
Lukáš Dirga
Anita Dockley

Rod Earle
Rachel Fayter
Liv S. Gaborit
Richard Gee
Hannah Gilman
Carl Gordon
Jason Heeley
Kate Herrity
Marie Hutton
Alice Ievins
Andrew Jefferson
Robert Johnson
Chris Kay
Laura Kelly-Corless
Shadd Maruna
Matthew Maycock
Tony Murphy
Conor Murray
Madhumita Pandey
Rosemary Ricciardelli
Ashley Rubin
Jennifer A. Schlosser
Abigail Stark
Alisa Stevens
Aoife Watters
James Woodall
Serena Wright

And to the Members of the NRC who very generously gave me their time!

CONTRIBUTORS

Serena Wright, formerly Lecturer in Criminology in the Department of Law & Criminology at Royal Holloway, University of London (2016–2023), is an independent researcher. An experienced prisons researcher, Serena conducted a series of studies focusing on lived experience of the penal system between 2009 and 2023, before leaving academia. The largest of these projects, a longitudinal study with colleagues at the University of Cambridge, involved more than 250 in-depth interviews over 10 years with women and men serving life imprisonment from a young age. She has conducted research with people in prisons of all security categories, and across both the female and male estates, as well as within National Probation Service sites across the UK. In addition to her work on life-sentenced men and women, Serena has also published on the experiences of repeatedly criminalised women, a critical reflection on 'trauma-informed' prisons for women, and an evaluation of a support service for women in prison with traumatic brain injuries, funded by the Disabilities Trust. She has also developed a series of creative outputs, including podcasts and two graphic novel-style representations of research findings. She has also taught in prisons, creating and facilitating three Learning Together courses at HMP/YOI Bronzefield and HMYOI Feltham. Since escaping academia, she has worked in the third sector, and is currently Lead Researcher at Scope, the national disability equalities charity.

Dr Katherine Albertson is Associate Professor in Criminology at Sheffield Hallam University, England.

Dr Heather Anderson is a Senior Lecturer in the School of Humanities, Language and Social Science at Griffith University in Queensland, Australia.

Ben Nevis Barron is a PhD student in Geography at the University of Colorado Boulder, USA.

Dr Colette Barry is Assistant Professor in Criminology at University College Dublin, Ireland.

Dr Shereen Baz is a Doctor in Criminology, formerly working towards prison reform in the Middle East.

Dr Jamie Bennett is Deputy Director for Security, Order and Counter Terrorism in HM Prison & Probation Service in England and Wales.

Charlotte Bilby is a Researcher at Northumbria University, Newcastle, England.

Dr Alexandria Bradley is a Senior Lecturer at the School of Humanities and Social Sciences at Leeds Beckett University, England.

Dr Lauren Bradford-Clarke is Assistant Professor at the School of Sociology and Social Policy at the University of Nottingham, England.

Dr Louise Brangan is a Senior Lecturer and Chancellor's Fellow in Social Work and Social Policy at the University of Strathclyde, Glasgow, Scotland.

Nichola Cadet is a Senior Lecturer in Criminology at Sheffield Hallam University, England.

Professor Ben Crewe is Professor of Penology and Criminal Justice and Deputy Director of the Prisons Research Centre at the University of Cambridge, England.

Dr Sacha Darke is Reader in Social Sciences at the University of Westminster, England.

Dr Lukáš Dirga is Assistant Professor in the Department of Sociology and Social Work at the University of West Bohemia and Head of the Science and Project Realization Department at the Institute for the Study of Totalitarian Regimes, Czechia.

Anita Dockley is an independent consultant specialising in criminal justice and research impact. She was formerly the Research Director at the Howard League for Penal Reform.

Dr Rod Earle is a Senior Lecturer in Youth Justice in the Faculty of Health and Social Care at The Open University, England.

Rachel Fayter is a PhD student in the Department of Criminology at the University of Ottawa, Canada.

Dr Liv Gaborit did her research at DIGNITY – Danish Institute Against Torture, Roskilde University and Lund University. She has now left academia to work as a psychologist and advocate for the people of Myanmar as an activist.

Dr Richard Gee is Associate Professor in the College of Arts and Human Sciences at the University of Wisconsin-Stout, USA.

Hannah Gilman is a PhD student in Law and Criminology at Sheffield Hallam University, England.

Carl Gordon is studying for a PhD in Criminology at the University of Westminster, England.

Jason Heeley is a former undergraduate student in Criminology at Sheffield Hallam University, England.

Dr Kate Herrity is a Research Fellow in Punishment at Kings College, University of Cambridge, England.

Dr Marie Hutton is a Lecturer in Criminology at the University of Sheffield, England.

Dr Alice Ievins is a Lecturer in Criminology at the University of Liverpool, England.

Dr Andrew M. Jefferson is a Senior Researcher at DIGNITY – Danish Institute Against Torture, Denmark.

Professor Robert Johnson is Professor of Justice, Law and Criminology at American University, Washington D.C., USA.

Dr Chris Kay is a Senior Lecturer in Criminology at Loughborough University, England.

Dr Laura Kelly-Corless is a Senior Lecturer in Criminology at the University of Central Lancashire, England.

Professor Shadd Maruna is a Professor in the School of Social Sciences, Education and Social Work at Queen's University Belfast, Northern Ireland.

Dr Matthew Maycock is a Senior Lecturer in Criminology at Monash University, Melbourne, Australia.

Tony Murphy is a Staff Tutor and Lecturer in Criminology at the School of Social Sciences and Global Studies, Faculty of Arts and Social Sciences at The Open University, England.

Dr Conor Murray is a Lecturer in Criminology at Ulster University, Northern Ireland.

Dr Madhumita Pandey is a Senior Lecturer in Criminology at Sheffield Hallam University, England.

Professor Rosemary Ricciardelli is Professor and Research Chair in Safety, Security, and Wellness at Memorial University of Newfoundland, Canada.

Dr Ashley Rubin is Associate Professor in Sociology at the University of Hawai'i at Mānoa, USA.

Dr Jennifer Schlosser is Associate Professor and the Director of the Incarcerated VOICE Initiative at Coastal Carolina University, USA.

Dr Abigail Stark is a Lecturer in Criminology at the University of Central Lancashire, England.

Dr Alisa Stevens is a Senior Lecturer in Criminology at Cardiff University, Wales.

Dr Aoife Watters is a Lecturer in the Department of Management and Financial Studies at Dundalk Institute of Technology, Ireland.

Professor James Woodall is Professor in Health Promotion at Leeds Beckett University, England.

One

INTRODUCTION

My mother once expressed to me her wish that I had chosen a happier topic to research, like butterflies. Putting to one side the fact that some butterflies are poisonous, others cannibals in their caterpillar phase, and that there is even a thing called 'pupal rape' (Engelhaupt, 2016), I understand her sentiment (and have sometimes thought the same thing). Prisons can be sad, violent, hopeless places. They can be – but they are not always. Many prisons contain joy, laughter, friendship, and hope – it all depends on where and how you look. Prison research is not easy, and arguably it is unlike any other form of research in the criminal justice system. In addition to everyone seemingly being an expert on prisons after watching one episode of *America's Toughest Prisons* (for those in need, there are numerous texts explaining the problematic nature of representations of prisons vs reality – Eigenberg and Baro, 2003; Fiddler, 2007; Mason, 1995; 2006a; 2002b; Sloan, 2013; Wilson and O'Sullivan, 2004; 2005), which other field of research has such extreme challenges at every step of the process? The prison researcher must negotiate how to access closed and often secretive institutions; state power and restrictive access policies surrounding dimensions of national security; mental health and vulnerability of participants; and the emotional labour experienced by both participants, others present in the institution, and the researcher. Prisons are central to implications for notions of identity, representation, and oppression within individuals and groups, both living and working within (and alongside) them. Even the definition of prison research is extensive – as a

DOI: 10.4324/9781315297217-1

community we are highly inclusive: you don't have to have been in a prison before to be a prison scholar, or you could be a former resident. The central tenet of prison research is the prison – but its reach and influence (and scope for academic interest) is enormous.

As such, prison research is an extremely important undertaking, and imposes serious responsibilities on the researcher. In today's troubled times, the challenges faced by those doing such work are extensive. In addition to the topics of the prison, how it works, prisoners, and prison staff, it is vital to consider the importance of prisoners' lives before and after the prison, their families and friends (or enemies), the local communities on the fringe of the prison estate, victims, and even the general population who judge and influence penal populism (Pratt, 2007) which shapes the institution. The impact of the prison extends far beyond the walls and bars themselves. Research from the Joseph Rowntree Foundation, for instance, showed the financial costs of imprisonment to extend far beyond the immediate money for incarcerating an individual (Smith, Grimshaw, Romeo and Knapp, 2007). It is important to take all these elements into account when considering undertaking prison research – if nothing else, the wider issues can generate little gems of research insight which add depth and context to the primary subject of inquiry.

The imposition of impermeable borders both tangible and intangible generates substantive challenges to the research process in comparison to other research settings. Researching settings of incarceration places the researcher into a relationship with the state which is unlike any other and can have consequences for the way such research is undertaken. Where research reports on state practices within closed sites, for instance, there is often a level of control placed upon (a) access and (b) reporting of the results, which can be 'justified' in terms of preserving security and maintaining the effective functioning of the institution regarding resourcing and staff implications. Whilst such implications are inherent in researching other criminal justice institutions, rarely elsewhere can the state control the subjects of investigation to such an all-encompassing degree.

Such dimensions of control often have implications in terms of the mental health of those subjected to it. Families of prisoners also suffer hugely in different ways, be they the children of prisoners, spouses, parents or others, visiting or not (see Condry, 2007; Condry and Scharff Smith, 2018; Murray, 2005; Smith, Grimshaw, Romeo and Knapp, 2007). There is also an increasing trend of prison researchers openly discussing the emotional labour associated with undertaking work within the prison estate (see Garrihy and Watters, 2020; Sloan and Wright, 2015; Drake and Harvey, 2014). Behan (2002) reports that 'prison damages people' – including those who visit and work in these institutions (see, for example, Barry, 2017; 2020; Crawley, 2002; 2004; Nylander, Lindberg and Bruhn, 2011; Humblet, 2020), and including prison researchers. It is important that this is taken into consideration by anyone thinking of taking on such a piece of work. The reflexive process discussed in Chapter Seven can be helpful for some, and everyone experiences the prison setting in a different way – sharing such experiences and coping mechanisms is an important element in the research process, and highlights the importance of situating oneself within a research community with some element of prison experience – be that within an HE institution, within a regional network such as the British Society of Criminology Prisons Network, or within an international group such as the Global Prisons Research Network (GPRN).

There have been numerous discussions regarding how to undertake prison research, and some of the key epistemological and philosophical questions of the process; not least the work of Professor Alison Liebling: it certainly played a huge part in my development as a prison researcher. Liebling's piece 'Doing Research in Prison: Breaking the Silence' (1999) has been of fundamental importance to many a research scholar. In it, she argues that there are numerous questions that have arisen from her reflections with others on her extensive fieldwork experiences:

> For example, how can prison research be carried out in an environment which changes, reacts to internal and external dynamics or external political pressures, where the research by its presence affects that which is to be researched (a prison version of Heisenberg's principle)? How can prison research be carried out on people by people who by their nature

must interact (influenced by gender, age, class, politics, identity, psyche, etc.) with those being studied? Can we achieve 'objectivity' through method? Should we be aiming to do this at all? How can one separate theory from practice in the human sciences? What status have generalizations got and what intellectual purchase can they claim? And finally (but perhaps most interestingly), what role does experience (and emotion) play in the formulation of knowledge?

(1999: 151)

In 2001, Liebling went on to discuss some of the issues with neutrality and objectivity in research in her key piece 'Whose Side Are We On? Theory, Practice and Allegiances in Prisons Research,' in which she argues that 'it *is* possible to take more than one side seriously, to find merit in more than one perspective, and to do this without causing outrage on the side of officials or prisoners, but this is a precarious business with a high emotional price to pay' (2001: 473), going on to note the importance of empathy:

The capacity to feel, relate, and become 'involved' is a key part of the overall research task. Research is after all, an act of human engagement. To achieve criminological *Verstehen* – subjective understanding of situated meanings and emotions – researchers have to be *affectively* present as well as physically present in a social situation.

(2001: 474)

In 2015, she developed this argument further:

We change the world by "right description". We achieve this through outstanding and humanistic methods, generative theory, and the determination to encounter, in a I–Thou manner, whole people as they are, via attentiveness to detail. We often have to work against what others seem determined to misunderstand, including what questions to ask. This overall task takes both humility and courage.

(Liebling, 2015: 30)

Liebling hits the nail on the head here. Research design, methods, and integrity in its completion, is vital to any attempt to change the world.[1] Similarly, Jewkes (2011: 63) makes the point that 'a more frank acknowledgment of the convergence of subject–object roles does not necessarily threaten the validity of social science, or at least "it is a threat with a corresponding gain," ' arguing for the importance of emotion as an 'intellectual resource' in the prison context – this was developed by numerous other prison researchers discussing the importance of emotion and autoethnography in the special edition of *Qualitative Inquiry* (2014: 20(4)).[2]

In terms of practical considerations, Roy King's chapter in the first edition of *Doing Research on Crime and Justice* (King and Wincup, 2000) is another excellent piece of work to guide prison researchers. King lists ten nostrums for doing field research in prisons, these being: 1. You have to be there; 2. You have to do your time; 3. You should not work alone unless you have to; 4. You have to know why you are there; 5. You must always remember that research has costs for staff and prisoners; 6. You must know when to open your mouth and when to keep it closed; 7. You must do whatever you have to do to observe but do not go native; 8. You should triangulate your data collection wherever possible; 9. You must strike a balance between publicity and anonymity; and 10. You should try to leave the site as clean as possible (King and Wincup, 2000: 297–308). This is some of the most useful and valuable advice that I have ever read – I would strongly recommend its consideration. For those spending more time within the prison setting, the *Handbook of Prison Ethnography* (Drake, Earle and Sloan, 2015) also contains numerous chapters discussing the challenges and experiences of undertaking prison ethnography (with skills that apply to many areas of fieldwork beyond 'pure' ethnographic practice). There are also numerous books on criminal justice/criminological research more broadly (Rubin, 2021; Crow and Semmens, 2008; King and Wincup, 2000; 2007).

What *this* book aims to do is to provide an overview of the key elements of undertaking a piece of prison research from start to completion. It begins in Chapter Two by discussing the landscape of prison research, and highlighting some of the issues with seminal pieces of prison research, as well as looking at some of the developments in prison research methodologies since then. In Chapters Three and Four, consideration is given to the practicalities of prison research running up to the moment of walking through the gates, including the politics of access, gatekeepers, prison typology, and researcher identity. In particular, consideration is given to the English and Welsh context and the processes required by His Majesty's Prisons and Probation Service (HMPPS) to gain entry to the carceral estate via the National Research Committee. It also gives some key 'tips and tricks' developed from a survey undertaken with fellow prison researchers about their experiences (see also Sloan and Wright, 2015). In Chapter Five, consideration is given to the ethical issues and ethicality of undertaking such a project – a topic which often goes under-examined in all methodological texts.

Chapters Six and Seven look at the key choices made in a prison research project including methods and participants, thinking also about the importance of *reflecting* in the prison research project – a process which is increasingly popular (and important) in prison research in the twenty-first century. Chapter Eight looks further afield, considering the global context of researching prisons, and establishing some of the 'universal truths' which run throughout prison research projects across the world. Finally, Chapter Nine concludes the book with some key thoughts regarding the future of prison research and some potential forthcoming challenges – not least the impact of living in a Covid-19 world. At the back of the book, there is also a basic (and by no means conclusive) checklist to assist anyone starting out fieldwork in the prison.

When I began work on the book, I have to admit feeling extremely daunted by the prospect of detailing such a broad topic. I have undertaken prison research, I have visited numerous prisons, and I have taught students about prisons and research methods. Yet my experiences are from one perspective, and I certainly don't see myself as an expert in everything about researching prisons – far from it. It then occurred to me that I have met so many incredibly talented prison researchers over the years – that their voices, experiences and perspectives needed to be shared. As such, throughout the book there are case studies/testimonies from a host of other prison researchers about their own methodological experiences, challenges, and reflections from a broad spectrum of perspectives and methodologies. I hope you find them as fascinating and useful as I have!

Whilst consideration is given to prison research being undertaken in other jurisdictions, and whilst notions of ethnocentrism are given particular attention, it should be noted that this book is being primarily written from the perspective of a white, female, British researcher, whose main research has been situated within the English prison context (Sloan, 2011; Sloan, 2016). Whilst I have tried very hard to produce a book that will be useful to prison researchers from across the globe, and included testimonies from researchers working worldwide, I must provide the caveat that some of the specifics regarding process and policy around access and ethical processes are focused on a British (England and Wales specifically) context.

I started writing this book prior to going on maternity leave in 2018, and learning to work and look after twins. I returned to the project in the summer of 2020 – a time that will be raw in all our minds, with the trauma of a global pandemic, widespread lockdowns, hundreds of thousands dead, and pointless political rhetoric left, right and centre. There were heated arguments about social distancing, mask wearing, and what the 'new normal' might look like, yet very little public discussion looked at the prison context in this regard, even though Covid-19 featured heavily within the prison setting. Lockdowns have had a tremendous impact upon prison life and prison research, and later in the book I give consideration to researching in the Covid-19 era and beyond.

As I say, throughout, I defer to examples from other prison researchers working on a broad range of topics within the discipline. There is so much vibrant and exciting work emerging within the field of prison research, and I am truly honoured that so many people have been able to contribute their experiences to this book to help those that want to learn more about the research process. I hope any prospective prison researcher can see that there is a place for you in the prison research community.

Conclusion

I began this chapter by stating that prison research is hard. It undoubtedly is. Indeed, I once gave a presentation talking about the stresses of prison research, after which a valued colleague came to me and said 'don't scare the students!'[3] I did not, and do not, intend to scare, but I do want the realities of prison research to be known to those thinking of embarking upon the journey, and it would be disingenuous of me to say it was all sunshine and daisies (or butterflies). Svallfors notes that he is increasingly frustrated by the fact that 'university scholars do not teach about the realities of research... we should at least talk about what we do and how it feels' (2020: xii). Jewkes similarly says that

> doctoral students and novice prison researchers frequently experience considerable anxiety about entering the field and particularly about observing and interviewing prisoners. [...] a more honest and reflexive approach to qualitative prison research would provide a benchmark for others trying to process their experiences and feelings about the research they undertake (Ellis, 2009: 230).
>
> *(Jewkes, 2011: 72)*

That said, doing research in/on prisons is also fascinating, empowering, life changing and, at times, great fun. It is vital that anyone considering starting such a journey knows some speck of what to expect, and that there is an awareness of the need for planning and potential problem solving, and self care. Yet in fact, every prison researcher's experience is very different, as prisons speak to us all in varying ways. The key is to keep your ears open, and try to work out what the prison is saying to you.

Notes

1 I was talking with a colleague the other day about the feelings of guilt that we can feel as prison researchers. In Western neoliberal and retributive cultures of punishment, we are often made to feel that we have to 'pick a side,' and that if we sympathise with prisoners, we are, in some way, 'against' victims. It is important to acknowledge and dispense with this enforced dichotomy that is a product of a criminal justice system that is founded on adversarial and side-taking, and results in the problematic policies emanating from penal populism, which ultimately often spirals into anti-prisoner rights rhetoric. For anyone who needs to hear this – I would argue that it is NOT the case that researching prisoners, and advocating for prisoner rights means

that you are against the victim, or undermining the seriousness of the offence committed by said prisoners. Researching prisons helps us to understand people who do (or who are accused of doing) bad things; as well as the people who work with them; the people who love them; the people who live alongside them; the policies, institutions, and structures that create and shape them; and sometimes, how to help them, and to try to stop further bad things from happening.

2 A FANTASTIC collection of articles!
3 When I returned to the hotel after, I called my (now) husband and confessed that I might have just ruined my career with my frankness. Fortunately not – it has led me to this point and writing this book.

References

Barry, C. (2017) Encountering death in the prison: An exploration of Irish prison staff experiences, emotions and engagements with support. Doctoral thesis, Dublin Institute of Technology. doi:10.21427/D7QH65

Barry, C. (2020) 'You can't tell anyone how you really feel': Exploring emotion management and performance among prison staff who have experienced the death of a prisoner. *International Journal of Law, Crime and Justice*, 61, 100364.

Behan, C. (2002) Transformative learning in a total institution. Unpublished MA dissertation, National University of Ireland, Maynooth.

Condry, R. (2007) *Families Shamed: The Consequences of Crime for Relatives of Serious Offenders*. Cullompton: Willan Publishing.

Condry, R., & Scharff Smith, P. (2018) *Prisons, Punishment, and the Family: Towards a New Sociology of Punishment?* Oxford University Press.

Crawley, E. (2002) Bringing it all back home? The impact of prison officers' work on their families. *Probation Journal*, 49(4), 277–286.

Crawley, E. M. (2004) Emotion and performance: Prison officers and the presentation of self in prisons. *Punishment & Society*, 6(4), 411–427.

Crow, I., & Semmens, N. (2008) *Researching Criminology*. Maidenhead: Open University Press.

Drake, D. H., & Harvey, J. (2014) Performing the role of ethnographer: Processing and managing the emotional dimensions of prison research. *International Journal of Social Research Methodology*, 17(5), 489–501.

Drake, D., Earle, R., & Sloan, J. (eds) (2015) *The Palgrave Handbook of Prison Ethnography*. Basingstoke: Palgrave Macmillan.

Eigenberg, H., & Baro, A. (2003) If you drop the soap in the shower you are on your own: Images of male rape in selected prison movies. *Sexuality & Culture*, 7(4), 56–89.

Ellis, C. (2009) *ReVision: Autoethnographic Reflections on Life and Work*. Walnut Creek, CA: Left Coast Press.

Engelhaupt, E. (2016) Butterflies behaving badly: What they don't want you to know. *National Geographic*, available at https://www.nationalgeographic.com/science/phenomena/2016/03/14/butterflies-behaving-badly-what-they-dont-want-you-to-know/

Fiddler, M. (2007) Projecting the prison: The depiction of the uncanny in The Shawshank Redemption. *Crime Media Culture*, 3, 192–206.

Garrihy, J., & Watters, A. (2020) Emotions and agency in prison research. *Methodological Innovations*, 13(2), 1–14.

Humblet, D. (2020) Locking out emotions in locking up older prisoners? Emotional labour of Belgian prison officers and prison nurses. *International Journal of Law, Crime and Justice*, 61, 100376.

Jewkes, Y. (2011) Autoethnography and emotion as intellectual resources: Doing prison research differently. *Qualitative Inquiry*, 18(1), 63–75.

King, R. D. (2007) Doing research in prisons. In King, R. D. & Wincup, E. (eds) *Doing Research on Crime and Justice*, 2nd edn. Oxford University Press.

King, R. D., & Wincup, E. (eds) (2000) *Doing Research on Crime and Justice*. Oxford University Press.

King, R. D., & Wincup, E. (eds) (2007) *Doing Research on Crime and Justice*. 2nd edn. Oxford University Press.

Liebling, A. (1999) Doing research in prison: Breaking the silence? *Theoretical Criminology*, 3(2), 147–173.

Liebling, A. (2001) Whose side are we on? Theory, practice and allegiances in prisons research. *British Journal of Criminology*, 41(3), 472–484.

Liebling, A. (2015) Description at the edge? 'I–It/I–Thou' relations and action in prisons research. *International Journal for Crime, Justice and Social Democracy*, 4(1), 18–32.

Liebling, A., & Stanko, B. (2001) Allegiance and ambivalence: Some dilemmas in researching disorder and violence. *British Journal of Criminology*, 41(2), 421–430.

Mason, P. (1995) Prime time punishment: The British prison and television. In Kidd Hewitt, D. & Osborn, R. (eds) *Crime and the Media: The Postmodern Spectacle*, pp. 215–233. London and Chicago: Pluto Press.

Mason, P. (2006a) Prison decayed: Cinematic penal discourse and populism 1995–2005. *Social Semiotics*, 16(4), 607–626.

Mason, P. (2006b) Lies, distortion and what doesn't work: Monitoring prison stories in the British media. *Crime, Media, Culture*, 2(3), 251–267.

Murray, J. (2005) The effects of imprisonment on families of prisoners. In Liebling, A. M. & Maruna, S. (eds) *The Effects of Imprisonment*, pp. 442–462. Cullompton, Devon: Willan.

Nylander, P. Å., Lindberg, O., & Bruhn, A. (2011) Emotional labour and emotional strain among Swedish prison officers. *European Journal of Criminology*, *8*(6), 469–483.

Pratt, J. (2007) *Penal Populism*. London and New York: Routledge.

Rubin, A. (2021) *Rocking Qualitative Social Science: An Irreverent Guide to Rigorous Research*. Stanford, CA: Stanford University Press.

Sloan, J. (2011) Men inside: Masculinities and the adult male prison experience. Unpublished doctoral thesis, University of Sheffield.

Sloan, J. (2013) Inter-prisoner sexual harm: Representation vs reality. In Meško, G., Sotlar, A. & Greene, J. R. (eds) *Criminal Justice and Security: Contemporary Criminal Justice Practice and Research*. Conference Proceedings, University of Maribor.

Sloan, J. (2016) *Masculinities and the Adult Male Prison Experience*. London: Palgrave Macmillan.

Sloan, J., & Wright, S. (2015) Going in green: Reflections on the challenges of 'getting in, getting on, and getting out' for doctoral prisons researchers. In Drake, D., Earle, R. & Sloan, J. (eds) *The Palgrave Handbook of Prison Ethnography*, pp. 143–163. Basingstoke: Palgrave Macmillan.

Smith, R. Grimshaw, R., Romeo, R., & Knapp, M. (2007) *Poverty and Disadvantage among Prisoners' Families*. York: Joseph Rowntree Foundation, Centre for Crime and Justice Studies.

Svallfors, S. (2020) *The Inner World of Research: On Academic Labor*. London and New York: Anthem Press.

Wilson, D., & O'Sullivan, S. (2004) *Images of Incarceration*. Winchester: Waterside Press.

Wilson, D., & O'Sullivan, S. (2005) Re-theorizing the penal reform functions of the prison film: Revelation, humanisation, empathy and benchmarking. *Theoretical Criminology*, *9*(4), 471–491.

Two

THE LANDSCAPE OF PRISON RESEARCH

Prisons have been sites of contention since their beginnings, and observers have been fascinated with how they function as a result. In the British context, penal reformers who have written about their work have gone on to become historic names within public discourse: John Howard and Elizabeth Fry being just two. Indeed, the need for greater investigation into carceral conditions has lasted throughout the decades. I am not going to attempt to document the long lineage of the development of prisons and incarceration, not least because others have already been there and done that better than I ever could. For those interested in a historical account of prison development, I would recommend a number of different texts; in particular within the UK context, I have enjoyed Wilson's *Pain and Retribution* (2014); Marston's *Prison: Five Hundred Years of Life Behind Bars* (2009); and there is an excellent special edition of the *Prison Service Journal* focusing on 'Understanding from the past' (no. 249, November 2019). In addition, Morris and Rothman (1995) have compiled an excellent collection of chapters on punishment in Western society; and the Shire Library Classics book by May, *Victorian and Edwardian Prisons* (2010) is particularly rich in contextual imagery.

There are also texts looking at the development of the prison in the USA (Rothman, 1995; Rubin, 2014; 2018) and a number of other jurisdictions, such as the gulags in the former Soviet Union (Applebaum, 2007), Colonial Hong Kong (Holdsworth and Munn, 2020), and Australian colonies (Hirst, 1995), although there appears to be a dearth of published work considering the

DOI: 10.4324/9781315297217-2

history of the prison in the 'global South'[1] other than consideration of the development of penal colonies following transportation (see Anderson, 2020), or the impact of colonialism on
punishment. Again, the majority of these texts focus upon the
male closed prison estate, although there are some prominent
penal historical works considering the development of women's
incarceration, such as Zedner (1991; 1995); Johnston and Turner
(2015); and Johnston (2019). The methodologies used in these
texts (where stated) tend to be aligned with the historical research
methodologies of archival research and documentary-based
analyses – clearly some of the more interactive social science methodologies are inappropriate here (bring on the time machine!).
Such 'desk-based'[2] and archival work will be discussed further in
Chapter Six.

In addition to learning about the histories of prisons, it is
important to look at the methodological issues that are associated
with comparing the past to the present, so that we may be able
to learn lessons and understand penological development over
time. In addition to archival and documentary research, one
way in which an immediate comparison is often attempted between 'now' and 'then' is through visiting historic prisons and
prison museums, part of the growing realm of penal tourism. Penal tourism has become an increasing topic within the academic
context – more and more, historic prison settings are being used
for purposes of education, tourism, and titillation. You can take
trips to Robben Island in South Africa, Auschwitz in Poland, Alc-
atraz in the USA, Patarei in Estonia, Karosta in Latvia.[3] Such sites
offer a different perspective on the prison experience, allowing a
degree of semi-immersion into the physical building of the prison.

It should be remembered that such experiences are generally
heavily manufactured and will lack many realities and perspectives of the experience, as well as there being ethical issues with
the objectification processes, and lack of depth and engagement
fostered by a simple prison visit (see Kennedy, 2017; Piche and
Walby, 2010). I would never say that entering a prison museum
or prison 'experience' could be compared to being a real prisoner
(or count as a valid or reliable research method), but it does sometimes give the hint of a flavour of how prison might be for some,

and can allow us to see some of the impacts of history on penal developments. Those making such visits also ought to remember the seriousness of the locations: prisons are sites of sadness, pain, illness, regret, and harm. They are the culmination of some victims' pains, and the current source of others' such as prisoners and their friends and families. They are sites of punishment, not theme parks or zoos.

I have been lucky enough to be involved with a Comparative Criminal Justice Summer School hosted by the University of Tampere in Finland and run by Dr Ikponwosa Ekunwe, where we have experienced a range of forms of penal tourism and 'experiential learning' (Meisel, 2008) – visiting functioning prisons across the Baltic States; as well as non-functioning former institutions (e.g. Patarei in Estonia); prison 'experiences' (e.g. Karosta in Latvia); and prison museums (e.g. the Riga Soviet Museum in Latvia). Such experiences have been fascinating and enlightening when thinking comparatively (both temporally and spatially), about prisons (see also Chapter Eight), but, as another of the Summer School's regular member's, Dr Richard Gee, notes, the historical comparisons do need to be made with a dose of caution:

HISTORICAL RESEARCH ON PRISONS

Richard Gee

Most texts in the United States that I have used for courses in corrections, or in general penology begin with a brief description of the two predominant philosophies and practice: Pennsylvania Model and The Auburn Model. Both of these models had at their core the positivistic rehabilitation of the offender even if their methods differed. If we look further back in history, we see the inhumanity of corporeal and capital punishment (see Foucault, 1975). In light of this, as society has progressed, we tend to perceive the previous conceptions of punishment as outdated and the new as better than what was. The comparisons are a critical part of the student experience during the comparative criminal justice course held at Tampere University. In the experiences of being treated as a prisoner in a former Soviet military prison, to touring historical prisons where the atrocities that occurred within are described, the students tend to have a sense that the current operations of the prison system and the way prisoners are treated is better than it was back then. But have we come full circle and expanded the collateral damage of the prison system?

The 8th amendment to the US Constitution guarantees the right against cruel and unusual punishment. This was passed in 1791 and amended in 1992. It was a direct rebuke of the previous practices of punishment. Progress towards a better society, a more humane and rational one. Cruel and unusual punishment prior to passage would have been primarily corporeal. It is interesting that the passage of the 8th amendment is a little less than 100 years from the Salem Witch Trials.

It took nearly 200 more years for the US to determine that the death penalty was unconstitutional in the Furman v. Georgia (1972) case. It was determined to be cruel and unusual punishment. It would seem that corporeal and capital punishment were progress towards a more just and humane society. Four years later, Gregg v. Georgia (1976) reversed the Furman decision. Between these two cases, an article was published that declared the rehabilitative model to be "not working" (see Martinson 1974). This shifted sufficient public opinion, and policy makers were quick to jump on. It was progress away from something that was seen as ineffective.

This ushered in the punitiveness of the US system. If rehabilitation wasn't working, then making serving time longer and tougher conditions may deter crime. Sentence lengths increased, mandatory minimums were imposed, three strikes legislation was passed and prisons were being built at an astounding rate to keep up with the new influx of prisoners. Even with the rapidity of construction, prisons continued to be over-crowded. Punishment was no longer corporeal so long as the mind is not contained in the body. Prisoners suffer psychological harm as a result of their incarceration. Thumb screws of the Spanish Inquisition weren't being used, so better than that time. Progress.

This was just in the institutional setting of the prison; however, post-release was riddled with additional sanctions and hurdles. Job applications with felony tick-boxes, credit checks when renting an apartment, and lack of access to any social service were just some of the continuing punishments that were meted out. But these were not isolated to the ex-prisoner. Their family, an important factor in desistence, if receiving social services could not continue to get them if those services went to support their formerly incarcerated family member.

One additional aspect of punishment that continues to this day is the stigma of incarceration. Unfortunately, this is not limited to the convicted person, but also is applied to family members through social marginalisation *vis-à-vis* 'honorary stigma,' or in common parlance, guilt by association.

After almost ten years of visiting historical prisons around the world, one thing that seems to be consistent in all of the descriptions provided by plaques, literature, and tour guides is that the conditions back then were awful. The creation of a false dichotomy of then and now has set a very low bar for prison operations. Researching the history of prisons and corrections tends to set the progress ideology in motion, and yet to ignore the current state of affairs and create the cognitive and temporal distance in saying progress does a disservice to the research in penology.

Indeed, as Meisel notes, 'though there are numerous educational benefits to adopting experiential learning activities, the rewards must be evaluated in light of the potential harms to non-student participants. Student observations of criminal justice settings can reinforce common stereotypes of prisoners as scary and dangerous while reifying the legitimacy of state power exercised through agents of social control' (2008: 196). Many of the actual experiences of prisoners can be lost through the scripting of the carceral tour (Piche and Walby, 2010), and there is a risk of 'prison voyeurism' (Ross, 2015) whereby misrepresentation and stereotype combine with a process of gaining pleasure through the observation of the hidden world. When entering such sites of tourism/voyeurism/experiential learning, it is vital to consider who has framed or scripted the experience, and, more importantly, which voices and perspectives are missing from the view that you are seeing.

Thurston (2017) offers some guidance to data collection within the prison museum as 'environments of narrativity,' and explains her use of an 'eclectic approach to data collection – photographs, interviews, observation, audio recordings' (Thurston, 2017: 4) and making use of the spaces when interviewing staff or volunteers: 'walking and talking enabled me to follow the curator or staff member (literally around the exhibits) while asking questions and seeking elaboration' (Thurston, 2017: 4). When looking at visual media in the prison museum context, Thurston discusses looking to the 'internal content of the narrative in detail' (ibid.), after which she would consider 'the meanings within the stories which had been documented' looking to theory, place, and significance within the story of the prison museum (ibid.). She also considers the examination of the 'narrative structure' as well as the 'interactional context' and how prison museum narratives are performed with regard to 'evoked authenticity, tour story dynamics and narrative tensions' (2017: 7). As such, for those using prison museums within their methodological toolkits, it is vital that a critical understanding of the limitations, fabrications, and creative liberties is achieved in the display of such materials and stories.

Research Methods in 'Seminal' Penal Texts

There are, arguably, some 'seminal[4] texts' in prison research. Sykes (1958), Clemmer (1940), Toch (1992; 2007), Irwin and Cressey (1962), Morris and Morris (1963), Cohen and Taylor (1972; 1977; 1976) – the names litter our literature reviews and fill many of our bookshelves. The majority of these researchers drew upon key sociological research methods including interviews, observations, and ethnography – in fact many of the most influential of the older prison research texts are seated within (generally male) sociologists' immersions within the (generally male and closed) prison setting for sustained periods of time. Yet many of these texts have important elements missing: in addition to being considerably ethnocentric and lacking the voice of the global South, most of these texts have a tendency to leave out any detailed critical discussion of the methods employed. Although Sykes (1958) does discuss the methods employed in his research, they have been relegated to the realm of the appendix and consists of only two pages, with certain elements that would be said to be central to contemporary methodological discourses – ethical processes, access negotiation, exemplars of questionnaire and in-terview instruments – conspicuous in their absence.

This is not unusual. These elements that our social science methods courses have taught us are requirements to prove valid-ity and reliability; the aspects that, when missing, have caused many of us to give students a lesser grade on their assessments and proposals, and which are often central to funding bids and grants, have historically not been seen to be that important. Which is an interesting message to send to those reading: it's about what the findings are, more than the processes. Whilst many of us might find that somewhat reassuring, at the same time it speaks of an unsettling absence: in a field where processes and procedures are so stringent; where rules and regulations are a centre-point; and where the potential for exploitation of a potentially vulnerable group is high, this is a fundamental dearth in the discussion.

It is true that, certainly in the past, methodological discussions have not been favoured by editors and publishers – in books and journal articles alike, words are money, and research findings are the 'sex, drugs and rock'n'roll' of the academic publishing world: they sell. Yet more and more we are seeing a demand for – and an in-terest in – questions of methodology within the prison research field (I hope so at least, for this book's sake!). This aligns with the shift to greater prioritisation of ethical processes in journal publications, and a move to open publishing and data-set sharing that is highly influential within academic publishing. Where data is open for use by others, the user needs to know how and why it was collected.

Changes in the Prison Research Process

Since the creation of such seminal texts, prison research methods have come quite a long way, and even more influential scholars have developed the prison research sphere, giving methodology a much more prominent position within the discourse. Professor Alison Liebling has had a particularly important role to play in the interrogation of research processes in and of themselves, asking questions such as 'who's side are we on?' (Liebling, 2001) and actively describing coping with the emotional labour which comes with prison research (Liebling, 1999) – this notion of emotional labour has become much more prominent in methodological discussions (Drake and Harvey, 2014; Sloan and Drake, 2013), as has the importance of situating oneself within the research process in a more ethnographic or autoethnographic approach (see Drake, Earle and Sloan, 2015; Jewkes, 2014).

In addition to the change in the prominence of the researcher in the acknowledgement of the research process, there has been a huge development in the tools and methods used to research behind prison walls in general. The move towards using new and inventive methods of prison research will be discussed more in Chapter Six – suffice to say, there has been a considerable shift in approach, including a move towards more feminist approaches of bringing forward the voices of prisoners, as well as the use of creative methodologies such as images (Gariglio, 2016), arts and crafts (Bilby, Caulfield and Ridley, 2013), TikTok videos (Schlosser and Feldman, 2022), and the broader senses (Herrity, 2020; Herrity, Schmidt and Warr, 2021) to gather alternative interpretations of the carceral world.

When comparing the 'old' with the 'new,' there are a few apparent developments. Whilst one might expect changes in methodologies to reflect technological advances, this is not always the case with prison research. The limitations placed upon technologies within the prison estate place considerable restrictions upon the researcher. Whilst technology may aid the analytical process through programmes such as *SPSS* and *NVivo*, it rarely plays a large role within the prison itself. Indeed, advances in prison methods seem to reflect a greater 'simplicity' as it were – stripping things back and going to the prisoners and their voices, emotions, stories, feelings, and interpretations. There is something rather beautiful about the negation of technology bringing the individual's voice to the fore in a place where the removal of such technology is intended to do the opposite.

In addition to practical developments, there has been increasing recognition of the wider stakeholders in the prison process – the potential participants who are arguably on the 'periphery' of the prison. Indeed, if prison research participants were a topic on (arguably very niche episodes of) *Family Fortunes* or *Pointless*, 'prisoners' would arguably be the high scoring answer, followed by 'prison officers.' There are, arguably, others who feature within the realm of prison experience more broadly who are often left out, including families and friends of prisoners, enemies, local communities, the general population, and even the prisoner's victims. These are all key stakeholders in the prison process, and have increasingly become the subject of greater inquiry – although not in all cases, and often only for certain groups of prisoners. There are many more routes of inquiry for the future prison researcher to meander down.

My initial thought was that other advances within research demonstrate the evolution of social problems within the modern-day context. Yet, in reality, the same social problems have pervaded the prison since those seminal texts were written: drugs, sex, violence, gangs, suicide and self harm: very little has changed. Even the development of human rights and legislation has not changed much: when it comes to prisoners, protective developments tend not to be the main priority, as has been seen in the tussle between the UK government and the European Court of Human Rights on such issues as prisoners' voting rights, to name but one example.

That said, there are key elements missing, or certainly severely under researched, within the global prison research field. Although prominent in some jurisdictions, notions of race and ethnicity are not always given the prominence in analytical discussions that they perhaps should be, and neither are notions of gender and sexuality – other than when they are problematised. Indeed the 'prominence of problematisation' is a seemingly normalised status within much prison research: prisons are rarely recognised for any potential positives. Arguably this is understandable for the prison abolitionist arguments – but there can also be moments of joy, hilarity, love, and friendship (see Straub, 2021) within the prison, which run the risk of going unseen or unacknowledged.

One developing area within prison research methods is the growth in research within the 'global South' – not a term that

I particularly like, when what is really being referred to is 'not the continents of North America or Europe (and by Europe, we don't mean everywhere in Europe).' But the point stands – while the research has been happening for a long time, we are finally seeing the publication and dissemination of such research being given the respect it so thoroughly deserves. In Chapter Eight I will look more at the global context of prison research, but in terms of the methodological landscape, the varied methods and findings coming from 'non-Western' (another unsatisfactory term) jurisdictions is only just starting to be explored and seen, not least with the growing acknowledgment of the need to decolonise the research process (see, amongst others, Q'um Q'um Xiiem, Lee-Morgan and De Santolo, 2019), and address the elephant in the room that is ethnocentrism (again, discussed further in Chapter Eight).

As such, while there have been interesting developments within the methodological field of the prison setting, ultimately we must always start with the literature and a critical analysis of what has gone before – at present, prison research history tends to be dominated by white, male, Western (English-speaking) academics looking at traditional notions of the (adult male) prison. That said, the growth in the community of female academics undertaking such work is extremely encouraging – *Prison Stories: Women Scholars' Experiences Doing Research Behind Bars* (Schlosser, 2020a) is a phenomenal anthology of work that directly engages with the gendered nature of prison research experiences honestly and openly:

> The experience of doing prison research [...] is not the kind of work that can be put aside when the day ends and laptops are closed, field notes are piled neatly (or not) on the edge of the desk, and the kids are ready for dinner [...] As researchers, prison gets inside us – it takes up space, it makes itself known. The experiences we have had in the prison research field are such that the weight of simply being a party to the incarceration experiences of our fellow humans buoys us, anchors us, and sometimes, if we're not careful, can drown us.
>
> *(Schlosser, 2020b: ix)*

Such acute observations of the gendered challenges of prison research within the book are essential for understanding the gendered nature of prisons more broadly, and the ways in which our academic knowledge of them is fundamentally shaped by the positionality and identity of the researcher.

Whilst some prison researchers will go on to undertake further empirical work following this critical analysis, others will be able to do marvellous things with documents alone. This is another field which tends to go somewhat overlooked in the prison research discussions: archival and documentary analysis (discussed further in Chapter Six) plays a fundamental role in aiding our understanding of the current penal problems, yet is arguably not given the respect and admiration it deserves, nor always seen as truly prison research, as opposed to history. In the same vein that criminology is defined as parasitic (Cohen, 1988) or 'stealing from our friends' (Osgood, 1998), it is vital that we take a more inclusive approach to 'seeing' prison research, in order to benefit from the extensive range of methods and findings being used across a mass of disciplines – sociology, law, history, geography, education, medicine, architecture, and so on (although I would advocate inclusive interdisciplinarity and a combining of efforts, rather than thievery and consumption, but each to their own). Even my father, a civil engineer, was able to tell me stories of the time he was involved in a building project within a prison, and the security and practical issues that accompanied it.

Conclusion

In this chapter, I have given brief consideration to the historical traditions of prison research in terms of the methodological similarities and, arguably, potential weaknesses of the 'seminal' prison texts, as well as addressing the importance of considering the past (albeit with serious critical consideration given to the manner in which such history is represented in terms of curated museums and experiences). The ways in which prison research has developed since those key texts, in terms of more attention given to the role of the researcher; the impact (or not) of technology that might be expected; the consideration of wider stakeholders; and the need for inclusivity of perspective and interdisciplinary working: all of these examples of progress show how prison research has become so much more. The landscape of prison research methods is by no means barren or boring – or simple, as the following chapters will show – and hopefully help with!

Notes

1 I do not like this term, particularly when it is code for 'non predominantly white Western' states. Because that is what we generally mean here.
2 Another overused term, particularly when there can be a lot of travel and movement associated with this area of work – see Rubin (2021).
3 Where you can also stay the night undergoing a Soviet prison experience – I did this in 2017 as part of an international summer school that I was attending accompanying my students. It was utterly terrifying – I ended up sleeping in my cell with my luggage jamming the door open to make sure it could not be shut on me without my knowledge. When those of us who had spent the night emerged the next day and reboarded the coach (the majority had declined the offer and opted for a local hotel with its own idiosyncrasies), I was told by a colleague that we emerged with a look of trauma and shame.
4 From a gendered perspective, this term is scarily accurate.

References

Anderson, C. (ed.) (2020) *A Global History of Convicts and Penal Colonies*. London: Bloomsbury Publishing.

Applebaum, A. (2007) *Gulag: A History*. New York: Anchor.

Bilby, C., Caulfield, L., & Ridley, L. (2013) Re-imagining futures: Exploring arts interventions and the process of desistance. Available at: https://nrl.northumbria.ac.uk/id/eprint/16846/1/Re-imagining_Futures_Research_Report_Final.pdf

Clemmer, D. (1940) *The Prison Community*. Boston, MA: Christopher Publishing House.

Cohen, S. (1988) *Against Criminology*. Oxford and New Brunswick, NJ: Transaction Books.

Cohen, S. (2017) *Against Criminology*. Abingdon: Routledge.

Cohen, S., & Taylor, L. (1972) *Psychological Survival: The Experience of Long-term Imprisonment*. London: Penguin.

Cohen, S., & Taylor, L. (1976) *Prison Secrets*. London: National Council for Civil Liberties, Radical Alternatives to Prison.

Cohen, S., & Taylor, L. (1977) Talking about prison blues. In *Doing Sociological Research*. London: George Allen and Unwin.

Drake, D. H., & Harvey, J. (2014) Performing the role of ethnographer: Processing and managing the emotional dimensions of prison research. *International Journal of Social Research Methodology*, 17(5), 489–501.

Drake, D. H., Earle, R. & Sloan, J. (eds) (2015) *The Palgrave Handbook of Prison Ethnography*. Basingstoke: Palgrave Macmillan.

Foucault, M. (1975) *Discipline and Punish: The Birth of the Prison*. New York and London: Vintage.

Gariglio, L. (2016) Photo-elicitation in prison ethnography: Breaking the ice in the field and unpacking prison officers' use of force. *Crime, Media, Culture*, 12(3), 367–379.

Herrity, K. (2020) Hearing behind the door: The cell as a portal to prison life. In Turner, J. & Knight, V. (eds) *The Prison Cell*, pp. 239–259. Cham, Switzerland: Palgrave Macmillan.

Herrity, K., Schmidt, B. E., & Warr, J. (2021) *Sensory Penalities: Exploring the Senses in Spaces of Punishment and Social Control.* Leeds: Emerald Publishing.

Hirst, J. (1995) The Australian experience: The convict colony. In Morris, N. & Rothman, D. J. (eds) *The Oxford History of the Prison: The Practice of Punishment in Western Society*. Oxford University Press.

Holdsworth, M., & Munn, C. (2020) *Crime, Justice and Punishment in Colonial Hong Kong: Central Police Station, Central Magistracy and Victoria Gaol*. Hong Kong: HKU Press.

Irwin, J., & Cressey, D. R. (1962) Thieves, convicts and the inmate culture. *Social Problems*, 10(2), 142–155.

Jewkes, Y. (2014) An introduction to 'doing prison research differently.' *Qualitative Inquiry*, 20(4), 387–391.

Johnston, H. (2019) Imprisoned mothers in Victorian England, 1853–1900: Motherhood, identity and the convict prison. *Criminology & Criminal Justice*, 19(2), 215–231.

Johnston, H., & Turner, J. (2015) Female prisoners, aftercare and release: Residential provision and support in late nineteenth century England. *British Journal of Community Justice*, 13(3), 35–50.

Kennedy, L. (2017) 'Today they kill with the chair instead of the tree': Forgetting and remembering slavery at a plantation prison. *Theoretical Criminology*, 21(2), 133–150.

Liebling, A. (1999) Doing research in prison: Breaking the silence? *Theoretical Criminology*, 3(2), 147–173.

Liebling, A. (2001) Whose side are we on? Theory, practice and allegiances in prisons research. *British Journal of Criminology*, 41(3), 472–484.

Marston, E. (2009) *Prison: Five Hundred Years of Life Behind Bars*. Kew: The National Archives.

Martinson, R. (1974) What works? Questions and answers about prison reform. *The Public Interest*, 35, 22.

Matfin, C. (2000) Doing research in a prison setting. In Jupp, V., Davies, P. & Francis, P. (eds) *Doing Criminological Research*, pp. 215–233. London: Sage.

May, T. (2010) *Victorian and Edwardian Prisons*. Oxford: Shire Publications.

Meisel, J. S. (2008) The ethics of observing: Confronting the harm of experiential learning. *Teaching Sociology*, 36, 196–210.

Morris, N. and Rothman, D. J. (1995) *The Oxford History of the Prison: The Practice of Punishment in Western Society*. Oxford University Press.

Morris, T., & Morris, P. (1963) *Pentonville: A Sociological Study of an English Prison*. Routledge.

Osgood, D. W. (1998) Interdisciplinary integration: Building criminology by stealing from our friends. *The Criminologist: The Official Newsletter of the American Society of Criminology*, 23(4), 1–44.

Piche, J., & Walby, K. (2010) Problematizing carceral tours. *British Journal of Criminology*, 50, 570–581.

Q'um Q'um Xiiem, J. A., Lee-Morgan, J. B. J., & De Santolo, J. (2019) Decolonising research: Indigenous storywork as methodology. London: Zed Books.

Rothman, D. J. (1995) Perfecting the prison: United States, 1789–1865. In Morris, N. & Rothman, D. J. (eds) *The Oxford History of the Prison: The Practice of Punishment in Western Society*. Oxford University Press.

Ross, J. I. (2015) Varieties of prison voyeurism: An analytic/interpretive framework. *The Prison Journal*, 95(3), 397–417.

Rubin, A. T. (2014) Three waves of American prison development, 1790–1920. In *Punishment and Incarceration: A Global Perspective*, pp. 139–158. Leeds: Emerald.

Rubin, A. T. (2018) Prison history. In *Oxford Research Encyclopedia of Criminology and Criminal Justice*. Oxford University Press.

Rubin, A. T. (2021) *Rocking Qualitative Social Science: An Irreverent, Practical Guide to Rigorous Research*. Stanford, CA: Stanford University Press.

Schlosser, J. (ed.) (2020a) *Prison Stories: Women's Experiences Doing Research Behind Bars*. Lanham, MD: Rowman & Littlefield.

Schlosser, J. (2020b) Introduction. In Schlosser, J. (ed.) *Prison Stories: Women's Experiences Doing Research Behind Bars*. Lanham, MD: Rowman & Littlefield.

Schlosser, J. A., & Feldman, L. R. (2022) Doing time online: Prison TikTok as social reclamation. *Incarceration*, 3(2), 1–17. doi:10.1177/26326663221095400

Sloan, J., & Drake, D. H. (2013) Emotional engagements: On sinking and swimming in prison research and ethnography: Jennifer Sloan and Deborah H. Drake consider the importance of processing the emotional dimensions of prisons research. *Criminal Justice Matters*, *91*(1), 24–25.

Straub, C. V. (2021) *Love as Human Virtue and Human Need and Its Role in the Lives of Long-term Prisoners*. Wilmington, DE: Vernon Press.

Sykes, G. M. (1958) *The Society of Captives: A Study of a Maximum Security Prison*. Princeton, NJ: Princeton University Press.

Thurston, H. (2017) Don't mess with Texas: Stories of punishment from Lone Star museums. In *The Palgrave Handbook of Prison Tourism*, pp. 583–606.

Toch, H. (1992) *Living in Prison: The Ecology of Survival*. Washington DC: American Psychological Association.

Toch, H. (2007) *Men in Crisis: Human Breakdowns in Prison*. Piscataway, NJ: Transaction.

Wilson, D. (2014) *Pain and Retribution: A Short History of British Prisons, 1066 to the Present*. London: Reaktion Books.

Zedner, L. (1991) *Women, Crime, and Custody in Victorian England*, p. 102. Oxford: Clarendon Press.

Zedner, L. (1995) Wayward sisters: The prison for women. In Morris, N. & Rothman, D. J. (eds) *The Oxford History of the Prison: The Practice of Punishment in Western Society*. Oxford University Press.

Three

DOING PRISON RESEARCH

Practicalities

As has been noted, undertaking prison research is unlike any other form of empirical fieldwork. Most methods texts fail to engage directly with the distinct challenges that working within a prison brings – yet when speaking to those who have done such work, it is clear that there are many shared experiences that run across the discipline. Indeed, I regularly see a look of pure relief when talking to those newly experiencing a prison research project and sharing in challenges and 'solutions.' For the 'green' prison researcher (see Sloan and Wright, 2015), knowing that you are not the only one to experience such abnormalities can be highly reassuring! It was for that reason that Dr Serena Wright and I wrote the chapter 'Going in Green: Reflections on the Challenges of "Getting In, Getting On, and Getting Out" for Doctoral Prisons Researchers' (2015) – indeed, we met and shared a bond through just such a process of sharing trials and tribulations in the doctoral prison research process. In that chapter, we refer to some research that we undertook asking more experienced prison researchers about their own prison research processes, and tips and tricks that they had for others – these will be discussed further in this and the following chapter. The key take-home message for those experiencing prison research challenges is (a) you are not alone, and (b) write it down for others to learn from.

Access and Accessibility

One of the most challenging practical aspects of undertaking any form of research – but particularly in a closed institutional setting,

DOI: 10.4324/9781315297217-3

is that of gaining access to the research site, gatekeepers, and potential participants. Sometimes constraints such as time, security, or simply participant disinterest can mean that we have to think creatively about how to get the information we are interested in, and how to represent the voices that we want to be heard.

COURTESIES WITHIN PRISON RESEARCH

Alexandria Bradley

For my Ph.D. research I wanted to explore the voices of individuals who may benefit from a trauma-informed approach. Although I was not successful in getting access to individuals serving current sentences, I was able to speak to uniformed officers and senior leaders in the prison service. I spent a lot of time with prison officers during my data collection and I found that my research benefitted from the relationships and trust I built up with staff. This seems obvious, doesn't it. However, the small gestures actually went a long way for me. I did this out of decency as I was aware that my presence would likely be a disruption or seen as a 'resource issue.' Having also worked in a prison, I was aware how I might be perceived, and treats are always a welcome addition to any office.

I started off by sending each prison governor an information pack. In this I briefly explained that I was completing the official Her Majesty's Prison and Probation Service ethical clearance (formerly NOMS); gave an introduction to who I was; explained what my research would consider and asked if they would like to talk to me about the research in advance. I was really interested to know if looking at the implementation of trauma-informed practice would benefit their prison site. Within a couple of weeks I had secured access with three out of four of my 'first choice' prisons. I had spoken to either governors or members of the senior leadership team, who were arranging a point of contact for me to support my research.

This was not 'luck.' It was explained to me that many applications fall onto a governor's desk and researchers often do not introduce themselves while expecting instant access. These small courtesies fundamentally supported my access to notoriously difficult environments. One prison governor even contacted my fourth prison to speed up my access, which was wonderful.

With prison officers I took in small treats and spent time getting to know everyone and chatting about all sorts of random things in wing offices. Eventually I was invited to the prison staff canteen with groups of officers (instead of being locked in an office with my packed lunch) and included in a lot more interesting discussions, including daily wing meetings and walk-throughs of the prison. My advice would always be, first, be authentic (because if not this can be smelt a mile off), but second, be genuinely kind and courteous to staff in prisons when conducting research. They can support you in so many ways which can really enhance your experience, but also their insights are valuable to aid your understanding of the issues tackled in your research.

PRISON RESEARCH AND NEGOTIATING ACCESS

Aoife Watters

Accessing prisons for research purposes invariably involves a lengthy dialogue between the researcher and the prison authorities. This reflection draws on the author's experience of negotiating access to prisons in Ireland during her Ph.D. research.

Traditionally, the Irish Prison Service (IPS) had been reticent to engage with researchers and allow them access to prisons. At the time the researcher was seeking access, it was still very much uncharted territory. The author's experience of negotiating access will be familiar to prison researchers.

Negotiating access and applying for ethical approval to undertake research in prisons are interdependent. Prior to, and during the ethics approval process, contact was made with the

Director General of the IPS, the governors of the prisons where the proposed research would take place, the National Executive of the Prison Officers' Association (POA) and the local branches of the POA. Prisons and criminal justice organisations may be distrustful of 'outsiders' so introducing yourself and your research allows a conversation to develop around the aims of the research and how the research may be of benefit to the prison system, prisoners, staff, etc. Building a relationship of trust is also essential to what may be a long, emotionally taxing journey of negotiating access. My research was welcomed by the aforementioned interested parties, which was of benefit during the research process.

Obtaining ethical approval can be a lengthy process. In the author's case, ethical approval took over one year to obtain, which was marked by a number of bureaucratic delays, such as having to resubmit the same application on a new form five months after submitting it. To the researcher, these bureaucratic impediments may feel like an attempt to thwart the research from ever taking place. Researchers are in a precarious position in such situations and may feel the burden of dealing with the 'system' as a power imbalance, which as Naylor observes, is not always discussed in prison research (Naylor, 2015: 82).

Once the researcher has received ethical approval and enters the prison to undertake the research, the struggle to access data, participants, and the prison itself may resurface. The gatekeepers to prisons wield the power to refuse entry and so the researcher may find themselves subject to a renegotiation of access upon each arrival at the prison gates. The familiar conversation of 'who are you, a psychologist? What are you here for?' repeated itself on many occasions, with the same officers. There were times when the author couldn't enter the prison as there was no officer available to escort her, or times when she was waiting to enter for what seemed like an endless period of time. These predicaments are to be expected in prison research, where the prison climate can rapidly change. For the researcher, they are easiest to deal with when

> you are prepared for the eventuality that they are likely in the un-
> predictable prison environment.
>
> > Preparation is important for the prison researcher; being pre-
> > pared to change plans at short notice, acknowledging that
> > there are likely to be delays along the way and this may even
> > extend to revising your methodology if data isn't available or
> > forthcoming. These all form part of the prison research pro-
> > cess. Ultimately, they can be of benefit to the researcher if re-
> > flexivity is employed throughout the research process, which
> > allows for further insight into the data under exploration
> >
> > (Garrihy and Watters, 2020).

As can be seen from Dr Bradley's and Dr Watters' reflections, accessing a prison is very much about personal relationship building and trust and rapport development. Gaining access
to the prison setting is one of the most challenging aspects of
the research process. Foucault's recognition of punishment being
'the most hidden part of the penal process,' and the notion that
'justice no longer takes public responsibility for the violence that
is bound up with its practice' (1977: 9) recognises the closed nature of the prison estate (worldwide). Prisons are not often open
for scrutiny – in some instances, scrutiny is actively discouraged,
with visits being somewhat curated to show certain perspectives
(Zhang, 2019). Such secrecy (for secrecy is what it is) has led to
substantial public curiosity – often fed through under cover filming of particularly negative prison experiences for television.

Academic access to the prison is not easy and should never
be taken for granted. In the US context, Reiter blames 'a multitude of substantial barriers, from institutional inaccessibility[1] to
bureaucratic idiosyncrasies and insufficient public accountability' (2014: 420). In England and Wales, access is dependent on
the completion of a centralised application process, which must
be approved by HMPPS National Research Committee. In the

course of writing this book, I was able to speak to key members of the National Research Committee, which was fascinating. At the time (late 2020), they were still operating within the research hiatus that was brought in with the Covid-19 lockdown of March 2020, wherein all research in prisons in England and Wales was put on hold. No new applications were being reviewed, and so no new research could be done. From a humanitarian perspective, this made perfect sense, and was actually a sign of great consideration within this area of government: if people in prison were not allowed to have family or friends come to visit them for months on end, then the idea of allowing researchers in was distasteful. That said, it made life extremely difficult for those who were just starting their particular prison research journey as the pandemic hit. One academic in particular who I am in complete awe of is Hannah Gilman, a Ph.D. student at Sheffield Hallam University, who was just starting her doctoral research on whole life prisoners as lockdown hit.

RESEARCHING PRISONS IN THE TIME OF COVID-19

Hannah Gilman

When I started studying for my doctorate, I was admittedly somewhat naïve to the complexities of conducting prison-based research within England and Wales. I had spent years researching and networking prior to commencing my study and believed that I had prepared for every eventuality. In truth, nothing could have prepared me for the reality of conducting (or endeavouring to conduct) such research, particularly during a global pandemic.

I had originally proposed and endeavoured to consider 'The Psychosocial Experiences of Whole Life Prisoners within England and Wales' and was aiming to conduct a series of face-to-face semi-structured qualitative interviews with a small sample of male whole life prisoners within England and Wales. These interviews would have focused primarily upon themes such as adaptation, hope, and legitimacy so as to consider whether (and/or how) whole life prisoners adapt – or possibly struggle and/or fail to adapt – to the psychological stressors which are presumably experienced during the primary (and later) stages of incarceration, and whether receiving a whole life order also condemns a person to a life devoid of hope.

I was collaborating with a colleague from the University of Nottingham who had actually submitted a research application to the National Research Committee in February 2020. Nevertheless, just a few short weeks after the research application was received, my study was completely upended by Covid-19 and the subsequent government guidelines.

In March 2020, the National Research Committee decided – in response to Covid-19 – to restrict research within Her Majesty's Prison and Probation Service and subsequently closed to new applications for primary research. This announcement essentially eradicated every contingency proposal that I had previously prepared – such as conducting my interviews via video conferencing software (such as Skype or Zoom) or via phone and or corresponding with my participants – as only applications involving secondary data analysis which did not pose any risk of (potential) harm to individuals and or impact negatively upon resources were going to be considered by the National Research Committee for the foreseeable future.

I was initially hopeful that the government guidelines and the National Research Committee's subsequent closure were temporary measures and consequently continued to work on the (incorrect) assumption that my study would resume shortly thereafter, albeit slightly behind schedule. However, the government guidelines persevered and, as the weeks became months, it became apparent that my original study and contingency proposals would no longer be feasible within the prospective timeframe of my study. Unfortunately, at a certain point – even if the National Research Committee had reopened – my research simply could not have been completed within the timeframe of my study due to the already significant delays incurred, as well as the prospective backlog of research applications.

Thus, nine months into my degree, I had no choice but to entirely redesign my study. I spent months researching and considering a variety of alternative avenues which would remain feasible irrespective of any ongoing or future government guidelines. I eventually chose to consider the way(s) in which whole life sentences have been and are being used in England and Wales and particularly why the imposition of whole life sentences in England and Wales has changed so considerably within recent years, as well as the perceived experiences of whole life prisoners in England and Wales and particularly if (and/or how) whole life prisoners navigate whole life imprisonment. I am subsequently employing a mixed-methods approach involving secondary data analysis alongside primary research comprising qualitative interviews with former prison staff members; as such an approach requires only my university's research ethics committee's authorisation, which has essentially allowed me to circumvent the National Research Committee's closure.

Since receiving the authorisation required from my university's research ethics committee, I have submitted (and am continuing to submit) a series of Freedom of Information requests to the Ministry of Justice within which an array of demographic information was requested so as to address my aforementioned research aims whilst also considering themes such as health and access to health care, mental health and access to mental health programmes, self-harm, and suicide.

I also received the authorisation required to conduct a series of semi-structured qualitative interviews with a variety of former prison staff members – such as prison governors, prison directors, prison officers, psychologists, psychiatrists, health care providers and or chaplains, etc. – in England and Wales. These interviews will focus on their own experiences of working with whole life prisoners in England and Wales, as well as their observations of the whole life prisoners' day-to-day and longer-term experiences of whole life imprisonment so as to consider the perceived

experiences of whole life prisoners in England and Wales and particularly if (and/or how) whole life prisoners navigate whole life
imprisonment.

I have advertised my study on various social media sites and
am currently pursuing participants via any available means. Indeed, the National Research Committee reopened, albeit tem-
porarily. Thus I immediately submitted a screening form to the
National Research Committee which requested the authorisation
to conduct a series of semi-structured qualitative phone interviews
with a small number of current prison staff members, as such an
approach would significantly increase the quantity of participants
available to partake in my study. Nevertheless, my screening form
was 'on hold' for four months as a consequence of the latest government guidelines.

Subsequently (at the time of writing), until government restrictions ease, I will persevere with my Freedom of Information
requests and interviews with former prison staff members. Nevertheless, I will reassess whether to submit a research application to
the National Research Committee (within which I will request the
authorisation required to conduct a series of semi-structured qualitative phone interviews with a small number of current prison staff
members) if and or when restrictions start to ease and the National
Research Committee reopens, depending largely upon the predicted duration of the application process and my stage of study.

The experiences I have had thus far have taught me that (pandemic aside) conducting prison-based research is certainly a complex process; regardless of how much research and preparation is
done, any study is highly unlikely to go ahead as planned without any amendments, complications or delays and may not, for
whatever reason, come to fruition, as researchers can only work
within the confines of what is permitted by governing bodies such
as His Majesty's Prison and Probation Service, the Ministry of Justice, the National Research Committee, funding bodies, and universities. My study has had to continually evolve in accordance
with government guidelines and the National Research Committee's regulations in order to remain feasible and, whilst this has

unquestionably complicated matters, I have acquired a greater understanding of my area of study and have learned valuable skills which will continue to benefit me for the remainder of my academic career. Thus, whilst I am disappointed that my original study was affected by Covid-19, I am incredibly grateful for everything that I have learned and achieved whilst continuing to pursue my doctorate during a global pandemic.

Even in non pandemic times, accessing the prison setting has numerous restrictions applied to it for the prison researcher. In addition to negotiations with numerous complex gatekeepers (to be discussed at a later point in this chapter), there are certain restrictions which can impact on the accessibility an individual may have regarding the prison setting in the context of England and Wales. It should be noted that this level of bureaucracy differs hugely depending on the geographical context an individual is looking to research. Not only do ethics (and thus access[2]) processes differ from educational institution to educational institution, but those working in non-educational organisations may have no formal ethics processes at all. It is important to familiarise oneself with the requirements at the local level of the setting in which you as a researcher are based with regard to access *out* of your institution, *and* the local bureaucratic processes that give you access *into* the research world.

In England and Wales, HMPPS requires researchers to apply to it to undertake any research within their settings (i.e. prisons and probation). The National Research Committee (NRC) for Prisons Research in England and Wales is responsible for the approval of research in HMPPS, in the majority around offenders and prison staff, but any prison research must attain NRC approval. I was lucky enough to be able to discuss the NRC with two of its members (it is made up of a small number of staff within the Ministry of Justice – numbers on the actual committee reviewing applications vary, but it is a team approach, with a lead reviewer within that group). There are set criteria in the process of NRC application evaluation in the guidance provided online; however, it was emphasised that some of the key issues considered when looking at applications were as follows:

1. The importance of the proposed research to HMPPS and the Ministry of Justice – is it worthwhile, does it add to the existing body of evidence and knowledge? Does it align with MoJ evidence priorities outlined in their Areas of Research Interest (2020)?[3]
2. The specified methodology and methodological appropriateness – will the proposed methodology help to answer the questions posed? What are the plans for sampling and data collection? And what are the considerations with regard to ethical issues and data protection? Exactly what is the researcher planning to do and how?
3. The skills and experience of the proposed researcher(s).

Some of the key sensitivities noted when undertaking prison research were issues around learning and literacy with regard to participants, and the need to ensure that tools and research materials were designed with these factors given appropriate consideration; and consent. I was struck in my discussions by the high importance assigned to the wellbeing of research participants by NRC members – they were very against the idea of 'research for research's sake,' and the moratorium on research that they established in the time of Covid lockdowns emphasised this. As frustrating as it may have been for prison researchers, the fact that the wellbeing of people in prisons was given ultimate priority demonstrates a sense of care and integrity that is reassuring.

When research applications are being considered, there is no set list of topics that are allowed/disallowed, although there are HMPPS and MoJ priority areas which may be looked on more favourably. In fact, rarely is the topic area the reason for rejection: usually there are other issues, including those concerning the fact that certain groups are difficult to access and may result in potentially very small cohorts. In this situation, care must be given to ensure there is not an issue of responder fatigue from individuals being over researched (and of course one must consider if an individual may become identifiable by virtue of being part of a small cohort, which raises issues concerning confidentiality). Other pitfalls include applications that don't really think through access and sample selection and imply NRC facilitation of this most complex part of the process. The NRC is not there to provide samples, data sets or specific access: this is something that the researcher has to work out for themselves!

In actuality, data sets tend to be owned by different parts of the organisation – as such, researchers should allow time to attain clearances from these other departments and to establish data sharing agreements. Although the NRC may give approval in principle for a proposed secondary analysis of data, they are not the ultimate decision makers about whether a researcher can or cannot use that data – that depends on which department or organisation 'owns' that information, and cannot be assumed. There is some data that is open to researchers to use: the Office of National Statistics often releases data sets, and the Ministry of Justice has made some key data sets available to 'accredited researchers, from within government and academia, to access the data in an ethical and responsible way' through the programme 'Data First' (https://www.gov.uk/guidance/ministry-of-justice-data-first). This still entails a hefty application form to attain secure access to such data, and is subject to rejection, but still provides access to data that was not previously 'open.'

I asked the NRC about what they would recommend to anyone thinking of submitting an application. It was noted that it is sensible to speak to the relevant prison(s) to check if they would be supportive in principle, and that you should get any relevant funding *first*. When writing the application, make things easy to understand and not too complex for the reader (consider language), and make sure the methodology is detailed and explicit about how you plan to undertake this work (but not too long!). The sampling frame/identification of participants should be given clear consideration, as should ethics, although the NRC is not an ethics board, and applicants must get institutional ethical approval (i.e. from the relevant university). There is an expectation that ethical approval should be attained before (or at least in parallel) to the NRC application process, and any approvals will be subject to ethical approval.

It was interesting (and a bit disheartening as someone who teaches research methods, if I'm honest) to see how many suggestions given for success by the NRC were actually simple research methods issues, rather than being prison context specific. Ideas noted included 'does your methodology fit the questions that you are asking?'; 'think about your research questions'; is it 'focussed and easy to understand?'; and avoid bias – it was noted that some applicants already 'know' what they are trying to show in the research (i.e. conclusions have been drawn before even setting foot in the prison or opening a data set).

As always, the position of any government department is subject to change overnight, but this NRC (spoken to in December 2020) was very reassuring in its support and knowledge of the important issues at the heart of its role. It was a pleasure talking to them!

In addition to methodological and practical requirements, HMPPS explicitly states that those applying from academic institutions are limited as follows:

All student applications below doctoral level need to be supported by an MOJ/HMPPS business lead in order to be considered. This business support needs to come from a senior member of staff, working in MOJ/HMPPS Headquarters who is willing to state that they believe the research is going to be of benefit to MOJ/HMPPS and will have minimal resource demands. Due to the potential volume of student applications, the NRC is not able to assist with student applications below doctoral level that do not have this business support.

(HMPPS, 2023)

As such, unless there is business support from within, undergraduate and master's students cannot undertake first-hand empirical prison research independently within England and Wales – there must be a lead researcher at doctoral level or above, even in instances where the student may have buy-in from the individuals they plan to speak to. Whilst this does not completely preclude undergraduate- and master's-level students from completing a piece of research within the prison, it does place certain limitations on what they can do, and ensures a level of supervision from the academic institution in the form of a lead researcher for any empirical studies. This is a positive aspect of the restriction, and does provide a degree of protection for the institution in terms of limiting the engagement of researchers to those with academic and/or HMPPS/MoJ support, and to established research projects (at the same time, addressing the potential problems associated with the short length of time an undergraduate/master's students has in order to gain access sitting in conflict with the long length of time it can take to achieve access in reality). It does create challenges though, and is not encouraging for those students not embarking on a full Ph.D. journey who may still be able to ask interesting questions of prisons.

For undergraduate and master's students who are unable to work within the parameters of a higher level project, many will have to opt for a critical appraisal of the existing literature and policy, or undertake secondary analysis of existing data sets. This is not, as some students sometimes think, the 'easier option' – indeed, finding, selecting, and critically analysing the relevant literature is a challenge that many of us find daunting! For those who do it well, some fascinating conclusions can be drawn and recommendations made, without even setting foot within a prison. For example, one of my students came up with this compelling argument for a change in policy:

> The ongoing Covid-19 pandemic has hugely impacted daily routines of prisons. Face-to-face visits were suspended in March 2020, meaning that video calling was alternatively implemented (PRT, 2020). As all prisons in England and Wales now have internet calling facilities, it could be suggested that these become a permanent feature of prison after the pandemic as an alternative for women on short-term sentences to maintain relationships with children who either do not want to visit due to fear (Condry et al., 2016), do not want children to visit or cannot visit due to distance (Masson, 2019) and school

hours (Minson, 2019). This would allow children to see their mother, alleviating some of the worries they may have without having to experience the invasive visiting procedure.

(Smith, 2021: 21)

Simple, yet highly effective. I do hope this actually happens – as Heard notes, 'the "new normal" as we move out of the pandemic should therefore mean that prison systems provide and promote in-person visits and real-life activities to the widest extent possible, *and* make wider use of remote technology-enabled communication and learning' (2020: 859).

There are other options for undergraduates. In 2020–21 I was dissertation supervisor for an undergraduate student who wanted to investigate toxic masculinities in prison (Heeley, 2021). Knowing he would not be able to talk to prisoners himself, he opted for an interesting approach: interviewing prison researchers who focused on masculinities as a key theme, and trying to understand their experiences of researching in this area – yet even this was not an 'easy' option:

UNDERGRADUATE PRISON RESEARCH

Jason Heeley

In 2020 I undertook my dissertation research during the height of Covid-19 lockdown, investigating the extent to which prison perpetuates a culture of toxic masculinity that reinforces negative personality and gender stereotypes. I conducted online semi-structured interviews with academics specialising in prison research to gain invaluable insights into prison environments and individual mindsets creating a host of problematic discourses regarding toxic masculinity. The performances of masculinity stemmed and were reinforced from a multitude of complexities within the prison environments: offender age, toxic masculinity expectations, relationships, gendered precedence, environments, and hierarchies which resulted in inauthentic characteristics and performances; frontstage–backstage identity and masculinity portrayals. This research provided several unique opportunities to interview leading academics from all over the world and gain knowledge that presented the opportunity to investigate toxic masculinity from a new perspective.

This was an incredibly difficult time to be a student, leading many, including myself, to struggle to adapt to the new standard of teaching and complete a dissertation; upon completing my studies it had occurred to me that I had lost the previously underappreciated luxury of face-to-face teaching, contact, or support to which we were once accustomed. Students wanted individual support mechanisms whilst teachers were forced to adapt learning curriculum and teaching approaches to fit the new abrupt online techniques that presented challenges to meet the requirements of providing individual discussions. This presented several obstacles when completing, participating, and conducting primary research. The dissertation involved video calling as opposed to on-campus meetings which continued across the whole process, leaving myself often feeling a false sense of reality within my studies and academic work as whilst the work was important, it often felt like an alternative reality in which my room became imprisonment; I can't even begin to imagine what the prison population must feel like. Confined to solely work-related boundaries until my interviews, thematic analysis, and discussion were completed, all whilst having to communicate with academics who existed in some other form of reality guiding what felt to me like obscure and imaginable experiences and academic studies. This was detrimental to my mental health alongside the fears and uncertainties of Covid-19, that I'm still struggling with more than ever today. Anxiety and paranoia combined with isolation and lockdowns created a situation in which I never left my room, presenting new difficulties in overcoming the challenges of conducting research in a new environment of zoom meetings and online learning approaches. I was unable to access various support resources that were normally accessible and available at a moment's notice; family, friends, university support measures, which left me reliant on my amazing dissertation supervisor and girlfriend to overcome these boundaries and gain the confidence to conduct research and complete my dissertation studies.

Online interviews allowed me to conduct this research safely and develop important correlations and information that might have gone un-noted in other academic articles and research papers. Overall, the ongoing pandemic has been far from fantastic, causing several problems such as mental health issues, but it is important to recognise and find the positives whilst conducting primary research data collection. The online meetings, whilst great for overcoming Covid-19 barriers safely and securely, also quickly gave rise to problems such as lack of personal connection between the interviewer and interviewee, and it was important to overcome this; otherwise presenting possible negative implications for the clarity and overall quality of the work. Whilst this was stressful, it emphasised the importance of video conversation. Video conversation established a greater degree of personal rapport between the involved parties, from which derived a better understanding of the information shared.

This was an incredibly challenging year, providing an opportunity for personal growth and confidence in one's academic ability, and overcoming these obstacles allowed for significant personal growth throughout the year. These achievements, whilst enduring endless breakdowns and justifications for dropping out, made it worth sticking to the project to the end and completing my dissertation research to the best of my ability, as this was important to me. Completing a degree during this time highlighted the importance of family, friends, and supervisor relations to completing the work and remaining confident and motivated to continue studying. My supervisor, girlfriend, and family made this module interesting and most importantly possible, providing motivational and emotional support when needed alongside the important academic guidance that resulted in successful primary data collection and analysis.

For those applying to the NRC, it could be tempting to state objectives and mechanisms to attempt to reduce the amount of time or staff contact/supervision required in order to make the project appear more appealing to those granting access: keys, for example. If a researcher has their own set of keys, this allows them to move freely within most prisons without taking up staff time. Yet this can also have implications for relationships within prisons in terms of the shift in power dimensions that accompanies being a key-holder in a world of locks (Carr, 2015; Mills, 2004; King, 2000). Other ways in which resources could be reduced include spending less time in the prison – yet spending time in the prison allows the researcher to get a distinct picture of the organisation and institution, as well as getting to know participants and gaining trust and rapport. The fear of not getting access can make it tempting to make such decisions, which could have potentially negative implications in terms of the data gathered, relationships developed (or not), lessons learned, or conclusions made. That said, it is important not to underestimate the resources you may need: it is arguably better to need less than to have to ask for more, and allows the institution to make realistic plans to enable the research.

Access: Security

Security and access to the prison go hand in hand. In order to enter a prison, certain security checks must be undertaken. Sometimes this can be security by association – if you know the right people, they will allow you to come into the prison with minimal security investigations (depending on what you want to do/see). This can be seen particularly in jurisdictions that do not subject researchers to severe application processes and requirements. In the majority of instances, however, some degree of security procedure will need to be completed, whether that is pre-visit vetting (especially if you are to be given a set of keys), searches at the gate, or even sometimes signing the Official Secrets Act (in England and Wales). Such processes can take time (and are a potential administrative burden on the prison service, so need to be factored into the planning of any project.

Not only will you have to go through a security process to get into the prison in the first place, this may be even more detailed (and so longer) if you are given a set of keys. The security department of the prison may give a briefing to ensure that you are aware of the key issues, how to use your keys, and risks and responsibilities. Deciding whether to take on keys is not something to be taken lightly: whilst it can ease access within the prison, and reduce the potential burden that you may cause through needing to be escorted, it comes with a different degree of power over your participants, and has serious responsibilities attached: you will (at least in outward appearance) become a part of the security fabric of the institution (for more on keys, see Sloan, 2016; King and Liebling, 2008; Sloan and Wright, 2015). The intertwined nature of power and security can have serious implications for the experiences of the researcher too.

THE PRISON RESEARCH EXPERIENCE

Jennifer A. Schlosser

I first started working and researching in prisons when I was a doctoral candidate in 2006. As a young woman with no prior experience in correctional settings and no real advisors or mentors with similar experience, I had to learn on the job. Prior to my first time entering prison I did my best to prepare as much as possible without knowing what I would encounter. Like most people (I imagine) I thought prison would be a place where I was unwelcome, where I would be seen as a trespasser coming in to disrupt the status quo, a disruption and a distraction to the normal operations. It took quite a bit of work to convince the prison warden to let me conduct research at his facility and, once approval was finally granted, it took even more work to convince my university's IRB to allow me to proceed.

Before I entered prison that first day, I'd been provided with some instructions: don't wear my hair in a ponytail, don't wear revealing clothing, no jewellery, don't speak to any incarcerated person if they approached me outside of the interviews, wear shoes I could easily run in. I expected the worst – 'cat calls,' untoward remarks, and other gestures designed to make me uncomfortable. But what I didn't expect was for those displays of power and disapproval to come almost solely from the prison staff. Not once in the many months I was there collecting my data (or, for that matter in all the years I've spent working in prisons since) was I ever threatened, dehumanised, or objectified by any incarcerated person the way I was (and continue to be) by guards, officers, and prison employees.

For me, that mainstay has been the most surprising thing about doing prison research. At first, I thought perhaps it was only those guards at that prison who acted the way they did. But, over the course of the next 16 years I've found no other theme to be more constant across different levels, types, and institutional locations across the US.

Most recently, just this year, I encountered a prison chaplain who made a point to sit me down before I began teaching my class in his prison to warn me that 'these guys – they don't give a fuck who you are or how many Ph.Ds you have. They will manipulate you, use you, and do it all with a smile on their face.' Based on my prior experiences encountering people like this chaplain in different prisons, I know that his posturing was designed not only to shock, scare me and assert his power and position over me (here was a chaplain swearing and denigrating prison inmates), but also to indicate the power he held over the incarcerated people in his charge.

Certainly, prisons are places where outsiders like researchers or teachers can disrupt the established order and whose mere presence can threaten the hierarchy of power that exists there. In my experience, those embedded in prisons will go to great lengths to protect their position and power in the presence of an outsider. In my case, however, my focus was on the wrong actors – I assumed the people who would be disrupted most by the presence of an outsider are those living their lives behind bars when, instead, it has proven time and again that those who have reacted most negatively to the perceived threat of my presence are the agents of the institution themselves.

Access: Equipment

Whilst technology is central to many researchers' toolkits, it is important to recognise that this is often highly restricted within the prison setting. This is inclusive of recording equipment and cameras. As such, prison researcher can *never* assume that they can take any of these items into the prison with them without explicit, written permission from the governor of the prison (see also Reiter, 2014; Byrne, 2005). This should be carried with the equipment at all times to ensure no confusion regarding the legality of the equipment can occur. When I was carrying my Dictaphone in the prison for my doctoral research, I was pretty terrified that someone might think I was smuggling it in! I would carry the letter from the governor with me all the time, and checked with the gate when I entered the prison *every* time (I think they got a bit sick of me waving this letter at them every day!). Still, better safe than sorry.

Such restrictions play an important part in shaping what a researcher can and cannot do within the prison. Photographic methods of narrative research (Gariglio, 2016), or the use of online resources can be heavily restricted (if allowed at all), and mean that the researcher needs to be quite inventive when attempting to do something a bit different within prisons (although just wait until Chapter Six!). Even within the open prison estate, technology (laptops, USB sticks, etc.) cannot be guaranteed to be freely brought within the confines of the prison, which can make the differences between prisons and the real world extremely stark.

Access: Gatekeepers

In addition to getting physical access to prisons, there are other 'accessibility' issues that need to be considered, such as the more symbolic access granted by gatekeepers in prisons. Contrary to other forms of research, where institutional buy-in may encourage individuals to engage with a research project, prisons are much more political institutions, and individuals working/living in them are not necessarily going to engage merely because HMPPS's National Research Committee has given you the 'OK'. As noted at the beginning of the chapter, diplomacy and respect is required at numerous steps in the process of getting 'real' access to prisons and those in them.

Gatekeepers: Funders and Research Commissioners

Whilst funding is an almost essential aspect of undertaking a piece of research, funders must also be viewed as a form of gatekeeper. Funders will often place requirements upon their researchers – whether that is to comply with certain institutional health and safety policies, ethical scrutiny, and risk assessments (as in the case of most academic institutions); or whether it is placing restrictions on what is looked for and in what ways. Charities and NGOs, for example, have certain priorities in their constitutions and terms of reference, which may well shape the research that they fund. Indeed, it is much more likely that these groups will be looking to fund projects aimed at addressing specific problems that they encounter, or evaluating interventions that they run, as opposed to exploratory studies with a wider focus. In addition, such groups may have access to specific prisons, given their own working relationships, which will also shape the research population.

If the research is funded by an external body such as the Ministry of Justice or HMPPS HQ, there may be restrictions again on the project's terms of reference (indeed, much of that work is instituted through calls to tender for specific research work). Although having the backing of these governmental departments can make getting literal access much easier, given the institutional buy-in, it can result in a restrictive research protocol, often in short time periods, as well as potentially limiting what can subsequently be disseminated. Always check the terms of your contract to determine who has intellectual property rights over the data collected – you may need to negotiate (if you can) in order to have the right to use that data in academic publications.

HMPPS and Psychologists

As noted already, the standard HMPPS application must be completed in order to gain access to prisons in England and Wales. This is then sent to HMPPS NRC, who will either judge the proposal themselves, or who will require it to be approved by the institution under research. In the latter case, this is often the role of the prison psychologist. It should immediately be noted that prison psychologists have a myriad of roles within the prison institution. Harvey notes the abundance of different tasks within psychologists' roles, including to 'deliver psychological therapy, carrying out risk assessments, train staff, offer consultation' and so on (Harvey, 2015: 396). Reviewing applications for researchers to come in takes time, and may have implications in terms of giving them future responsibilities – for example, for my time during my doctoral research project I was put under the supervision of the psychology department. Although I hope I was helpful in doing bits of administrative paperwork and filing, I was yet another thing to think about for an already overworked team.

The Prison: The Prison Governor

The ultimate gatekeeper of any prison is undoubtedly the prison governor (or, in the case of private prisons in England and Wales, the director). In addition to getting permission from HMPPS to undertake the research project, the governor is the ultimate gatekeeper for the prison under study: they are the person who will grant access and start negotiations with other staff; they are the ones who need to approve any equipment coming into the prison; they can make or break a research project before it even begins.

Governors are experts in the prison administration process, and will undoubtedly be the experts regarding certain dimensions of their own prison, its context, fabric, inhabitants and challenges (although see Bryans, 2008: 220). Indeed, prison governors themselves may well have priorities for what they would like to be researched in order to help them to manage the prison and address context-specific challenges. Prison governors have been recognised as being policy-makers in their own right (Dubois, 2018), so are an extremely important gatekeeper within the prison, and may well be able to make practical use of the research findings you create (those of us immersed in REF-culture academics can hear the ever present whispering of 'impact'). Similarly to the point made regarding funders, it is vital that the researcher is careful to maintain their integrity *vis-à-vis* the project they are undertaking, as well as managing the expectations of the governor (see also Reiter, 2014: 423) – hopefully resulting in both the researcher and the governor getting the knowledge they need. The researcher may also have to undertake some elucidating of certain key principles behind their research (see Ismail and de Viggiani, 2018) – it cannot be assumed that the governor will share the values, priorities or understanding of the researcher.

The governor may also be the subject of the research in itself – increasing attention is being given by researchers to prison managers (see Bryans, 2008; Bryans, 2013; Crewe, Bennett and Wahidin, 2008). The sheer volume of tasks that governors undertake is mind-blowing – from budgetary accountability, to staff recruitment, to regime setting, funding generation, relationship and partnership management, and being the figurehead of the prison, amongst other things (Bryans, 2008). As such, they are very, very busy people, which can pose an access issue in itself!

The Prison: Prison Security

As has already been noted, negotiating with prison security will be an important part of gaining access to the institution proper – these individuals will be making judgments and risk assessments regarding whether you have keys or not, as well as the literal process of getting in and out of the prison itself – to gain entry, you must go through some degree of security process. Security is at the heart of the prison process – how secure a prison is will influence the population within, as well as the institutional regime and how easy it is to undertake research there. In England and Wales, the security categorisation of a prison varies according to sex: men's prisons are categorised differently to women's (not least because there are substantially more of them!). Indeed, security categorisation varies hugely from jurisdiction to jurisdiction, adding an extra dimension of complexity to comparative research (as will be discussed further in Chapter Eight) or the transferability of results across contexts. In the Czech Republic, there are also four levels of prison, but these are 'flipped' in comparison to England and Wales: 'A-type prison – minimum security, B-type prison – medium security, C-type prison – high security, D-type prison – maximum security' (Dirga, 2015: 118). In the USA there are jails and prisons – jails for those individuals who have been convicted of misdemeanours, prisons for those who have committed felony crimes (and 'supermax' prisons for extremely high risk offenders (Shalev, 2013)). In Pakistan, the classification system follows more socioeconomic and class-based lines, and in the Philippines, the system is based on sentence length. In fact, the UN Standard Minimum Rules for the Treatment of Prisoners (otherwise referred to as the Nelson Mandela Rules), sets down certain criteria for the separation of categories of prisoners:

> Rule 11: The different categories of prisoners shall be kept in separate institutions or parts of institutions, taking account of their sex, age, criminal record, the legal reason for their detention and the necessities of their treatment; thus:
> (a) Men and women shall so far as possible be detained in separate institutions; in an institution which receives both men and women, the whole of the premises allocated to women shall be entirely separate;
> (b) Untried prisoners shall be kept separate from convicted prisoners;
> (c) Persons imprisoned for debt and other civil prisoners shall be kept separate from persons imprisoned by reason of a criminal offence;
> (d) Young prisoners shall be kept separate from adults.
> *(UNODC, 2015: 5)*

The Rules were created under General Assembly Resolution 70/175.[4] As such, although voted into force by UN member states, they are not, per se, enforceable legal instruments, but they may be linked to other legal human rights obligations which *are* legal instruments, and have some persuasive value as targets and aspirations (see also Prais, 2020).[5] As such, comparative prison research can often require much greater understanding of the legal contexts of the nations under study in order to understand the particular requirements and obligations of the setting.

On a more practical note, the security of the prison will also have implications in terms of resources: it is more expensive to keep a prisoner in higher security conditions due to the needs for more staff and physical security resources, for instance. Such wider implications of the incarceration setting need to be borne in mind when thinking about which setting to access – it is much harder to get access to prisons of a higher security category due to resources, risks, and other restrictions. It is not, however, impossible, and there have been some fascinating studies which have spent considerable time within high security prisons, undertaking ethnographies, interviews, and observations (see Williams and Liebling, 2018; Liebling and Williams, 2018; Liebling, Arnold and Straub, 2011; Liebling and Arnold, 2012; Drake, 2012).

The Prison: Other Prison Staff

Within the prison, other members of prison staff play a vital role in the prison research project. In addition to being potential participants in themselves, they play a key role in acting as gatekeepers both physically and symbolically for men and women in prisons. Remember, prison staff are not merely those in uniform – they can also contain those working on the Offender Management Unit; psychologists; probation officers; health care workers; religious professionals; offending behaviour programme deliverers; library staff; education workers; gym staff; those working in the training/prison work areas; non prison-facing staff such as secretaries and administrators (who may never come into direct contact with prisoners); or those working within the Senior Management Team. The roles and experiences of those working within prisons are extensive and hugely varied, and provide a wealth of knowledge from many different perspectives.

If you are not given a set of keys, prison staff members will need to facilitate your movement around the prison (and even if you have keys, you will still be subject to certain restrictions regarding where you can and cannot go without staff help). Prison staff know the routine of the prison – where prisoners will be and when, and how to find out. They may also know of suitable candidates to speak to to start recruiting participants, as well as being able to talk about you and your work to the prisoners and other members of staff you meet. As an unknown entity within the prison, such introductions and groundwork are vital for a successful project (particularly when working within time limits).

In terms of practicalities, prison staff can be vital allies. They can find spaces for research interviews, or point out areas in the prison which might be of most use for observations. Such help must be reflected on – are the prisoners they suggest representative of the general community? Are the things that they point you towards observing telling you the whole story? Particularly as a novice researcher, this must be thought about carefully – prison staff do have inside knowledge, but may also not 'see' what you are looking for, or look at it in quite the same way – although this is not necessarily a bad thing, and is a level of understanding that is of great significance to those undertaking 'insider research.'

INSIDER RESEARCH BY PRISON STAFF

Matthew Maycock

Research within or about a particular social setting by someone from that setting (otherwise known as insider research) raises a number of ethical challenges (Toy-Cronin, 2018). Within criminology, insider research has tended to have been undertaken from the perspective of people with a particular lived experience of prison, largely relating to the prisoner experience of prison. This comes together within 'convict criminology,' which has made a significant contribution to contemporary criminology (Earle, 2014; 2016; Ross and Richards, 2003). Convict criminology has foregrounded the experiences of those who have first-hand experience of prison settings, although these perspectives have not included insider perspectives from people who are or who have worked within prisons or perhaps spent time in prisons in some kind of professional capacity. Taking Scotland as an example, in 2019/20 the average daily prison population was 8,198 (www.sps.gov.uk/Corporate/Publications/Publication-6615.aspx) and the Scottish Prison Service (SPS) employs over 4000 people (https://www.sps.gov.uk/Careers/WorkingfortheSPS/Working-for-the-SPS.aspx). Additionally, there are further staff not employed directly by the SPS who are not included in this figure. Given the relative lack of research about and by prison staff, the views, experiences, and research potential of around a third of the people regularly within prison spaces are largely not realised. This omission in and of itself constitutes a significant ethical challenge for penology, given that so many potential perspectives and experiences of everyday life in prison are missing from what we know about everyday life in prison.

This contribution advocates for the development of a different and in some senses complementary insider research to convict criminology, a body of research created by prison staff. This would have a number of benefits and potentially create a space for prison staff to critically reflect about everyday life in prison. There are few notable examples of such approaches, including Lucy Carr's important chapter in the *Palgrave Handbook of Prison Ethnography* (2015). That there has been so little research about prison from the perspective of prison staff is surprising, and has resulted in gaps in the evidence around life in prison and some of the influences shaping this. For example, relatively little is currently known about the influence of prison officer trade unions within prison settings, despite the high levels of unionisation within prisons internationally. Empirically, penology would be enrichened by insider research from the perspective of prison staff, although this would open up the same sorts of ethical challenges encountered by insider research in other contexts. It is hoped that the important and often neglected views of prison staff are the focus of greater academic attention in future, and that prison staff themselves are able to contribute to the evidence base relating to prisons.

One academic who is an 'insider researcher' from a staff per-spective, is Dr Jamie Bennett:

INSIDER ETHNOGRAPHY

Jamie Bennett

Traditionally, ethnography has involved researchers venturing into unfamiliar worlds, originally remote colonial societies, but later communities closer to home. The participant observer attempted to attain sufficient intimacy in order to understand the social rules and processes of these groups. In contrast, the insider researcher comes from a position of direct, lived experience but seeks to gain sufficient distance and perspective in order to apply a more analyt-ical lens to their own social world. From different starting points, both insider and outsider ethnographers are navigating a space between intimacy and detachment.

I have worked in prisons for over two decades, and for most of that time have also been conducting research on the working lives of prison managers. This is a complex, messy, and some-times uncomfortable combination. The position of an insider re-searcher has raised challenging issues around identity, power, and confidentiality.

Research shifted my own identity. I felt uncomfortable and un-certain in my role as a researcher and only over time felt less of an imposter. At the same time, critically examining my working world prompted sometimes troubling questions about my profession and my complicity with wider power structures. Although I con-tinued to work in prisons, I did not feel like the same person who had gone into the research. I felt more questioning, less attached to the organisation for its own sake, more conscious of the social web that imprisonment formed part of, and more conscious of the strengths and limitations of managerial practices. This made me a different prison manager, although I make no claims to be a more effective one, but that after all was never the purpose.

Prison managers, the subjects of my research, responded to me and sought to understand my identity in different ways. Many attempted to position me within a social and organisational hierarchy, where I was a colleague, a superior, or mentee. Such responses were revealing about the occupational power dynamics but also illustrated how an insider researcher never discards their insider position. There were also attempts by the people I was researching to understand my research role. Was I there as an expert judging their work? An auditor observing their level of compliance? A social scientist completing an academic tome? Or was I an enigma with unfathomable motives and undertaking a bemusing task? These responses revealed how research is understood in the context of the managerial cultures of contemporary prisons.

As an 'insider' I potentially hold power, but I am also the subject of power. This gives rise to issues about the potential effects of the research for myself and for others. Gaining access and research approval were straightforward and there were not any serious attempts to control or shape my research. The absence of control rather than the exercise of it was notable. This may have been because I was assumed to be trustworthy, compliant or self-regulating. In conducting the research I had to be sensitive to the ways in which I carried residual power and how this may have an influence on consent and disclosure. For example, some people may have perceived a need to comply with my requests to observe their work or participate in interviews or have been concerned about the implications of not participating.

As with many researchers, I faced situations in which I was exposed to problematic behaviours or disclosures. There is a balance between gaining an authentic insight into the social world, and challenging or reporting misconduct. As an insider, I was particularly concerned that my organisational status may have conferred a degree of tacit approval when I did not intervene or challenge. Generally, the balance seemed to lie in maintaining openness rather than shutting down and breaching confidentiality. On one occasion I felt that the balance lay differently, where a prisoner made an allegation that he had been assaulted by prison staff at his previous prison. Initially it was not clear that there was going to be any follow up on this. I decided that the risk was serious and immediate and therefore wanted to be assured that the prisoner was receiving medical attention and that the matter was properly reported. In the event, the manager I was shadowing did ensure that these things happened without the need for me to overtly intervene, but my questions betrayed that I had more than a research interest at the time and that my concern was clear. Dilemmas about when to stand back, when to intervene, when to keep confidentiality and when to break it are always presented in the field. As with other issues, my dual role had an influence in framing the nature and context of these problems

The Prison: The Prisoner

The prisoners themselves act as fundamental gatekeepers in the prison research process. As participants, prisoners have the ultimate choice in whether or not to take part (although this can be limited in some cases if individuals do not fully understand that they can say no). In addition, prisoners can play an incredibly important role in gaining access to others and snowballing the sample: they can (and often will!) talk about their time spent with you with other prisoners, who may also be interested in being involved. As such, there is an important responsibility for prison researchers to make the prison research experience a positive one – in addition to any emotional or mental damage that may result, a bad experience could stop a prisoner (and those he/she talks to about it) from taking part in any future work.

Step by Step

Whilst not all prison research will follow the same sequence, there are some key processes in the planning and development of a prison research project that must be given consideration:

1. Picking and Planning the Right Project, and Posing the 'Right' Central Research Question(s)

The choice of research project is both simple and complex together. Simply, does the project interest you and seem achievable? If the answer to either of these questions is no, then perhaps a rethink is in order. On a more complex level, a researcher needs to think about whether the project they are looking at is suitable at this point in time, in the prison system in question, and looking at the issues at hand. Research in general goes through different 'fashions' – research councils are more likely to fund certain projects than others according to key priorities occurring at the time, and priorities and strategy can change swiftly according to current politics and pressures.

One of the key decisions that needs to be made in any piece of research is that of the central research question – what is it you actually want to find out? This should be your anchor in planning a piece of research: your central research question will help you decide on the research design of choice[6]; the time scale needed to complete the work; questions of sample (and subsequently considerations of access); and ultimately your methodological and analytical approach. As I say, it is the anchor that you can keep returning to when you face methodological decisions and questions: What do I need to do to answer the question?

2. Choosing the Right Site

Once a project has been developed on paper, and has been granted access, one of the first considerations and negotiations required is with a prison site itself. Decisions need to be made regarding a multitude of questions:

Q: Where in the country (and which country)? Is it easy for you to get to (which in turn tells you something about what prisoners may experience when it comes to receiving visitors or being released!)?

Q: Which sex of prison? Male? Female? Both? Prisons with transgender prisoners?

Q: Which security category of prison?

Q: What age category of prison? Juvenile? Young Offender? Adult? Older Prisoners? What do these categories actually mean in the jurisdiction under examination?

Q: What is going on in that prison? Are there particular initiatives/programmes/ideas going on that might make it more or less suitable for exploration?

Q: Has a lot of prison research already been done there? This can be both beneficial in terms of prior knowledge, but also potentially risks over-researching a particular site.

Q: Do you have existing relationships with that prison that you can draw on?

Q: Is the prison representative of the wider estate, or will it make an individualistic case study?

Q: Do you want to look at more than one prison?

Q: What was the prison's last inspection report like? This may have implications in terms of the availability of resources to facilitate your research, as well as the inclination of the prison to let you in (they might see your research as something that could assist them in addressing key issues that were raised in their last inspection, or they may need time without researchers there to try to deal with challenges they currently face).

3. Choosing the Right Sample

Alongside choosing the type of prison, you will be thinking about the sample of participants that you wish to investigate.[7] Choosing the prison site will help to narrow the sample according to broad age and sex categories, but if you are interested in key characteristics, this may need further exploration. For example, does the prison have a racially representative population? Are there key offence/sentence types that you are interested in, and will those individuals be situated in those prisons? If looking at prison staff, will the types of staff you are interested in be there? Inspection reports can help with some of these questions – they give some basic prisoner-based information regarding socio-demographic characteristics, although these may be out of date when it comes to reading them.

You may be undertaking prison research which is interested in those other than the prisoners themselves. Prison staff are not generally recorded in the same way as prisoners, so there is unlikely to be a freely available breakdown of staff characteristics from jail to jail (which might also have security implications). Who do you really want to speak to?

4. Choosing the Right Method

In Chapter Six, we will be looking in more detail at the choice of methods available and suitable for prison research, but it is also important to consider this selection when negotiating access with gatekeepers – not least as it may have implications of the amount of resources required of the prison. When choosing methods, it is important to accept that how a method works outside the prison setting is not how it will necessarily translate within the prison. Thought needs to be given about how appropriate that method may be for a group of people who live and/or work behind bars. Will it be overly intrusive? Will it ask questions that we already know the answers to? Will it cause reflections or thoughts that could be harmful once the researcher leaves the setting? Does it need to be done in the prison? Will it (albeit potentially) make a difference, and will that difference be positive or negative? Will participants understand the research? Once you have collected the data, can you keep it secure? All of these questions have practical and ethical dimensions to them which are important to consider at an early stage.

5. Choosing the Right Analytical Path

One thing that many do not think about at an early stage is how they plan to make sense of the data. True, such decisions are seated within the data itself, and so sometimes need to be made once you can see what you have got, but it is important to think about the final product and what sense might be able to be made from what you have collected. Will quantitative/qualitative data be enough? Would qualitative/quantitative data be better? If mixing your methods, how will you put these together to get the most from the project? Thinking through the sense-making process can be very helpful before you start, as it allows you to think about the big picture end-result and how you are actually going to achieve this in reality.

6. Choosing the Right Means of Dissemination

Another important consideration is the process of dissemination and feedback. In an HE setting which is increasingly publication-focussed, such dissemination is central to any research project. Whilst academic publications are given regular thought, it must be remembered that the prison should be fed back to as well, and how to do this can take some diplomacy. If your research finds some uncomfortable truths within the prison, how do you plan to feed these back? Recommendations for problem-solving can be helpful in this case. In addition, who will be able to access your disseminative product? If prisoners were involved, is a report the best way to tell them the results? Care should be taken to ensure that dissemination is accessible to those involved where possible, taking into account literacy and learning difficulties, and this may require some more creative approaches to be thought through.

In addition to all of these, there are some practical elements of the process which need to be remembered when actually on the ground and doing the research – these have been put into a checklist which can be found at the end of the book. It is by no means an exhaustive list, but something to get the prison researcher thinking before entering the site (particularly if you have a memory like mine!).

Contingency Plans

As can be gleaned from Hannah Gilman's reflections earlier, and from the discussion above, prison research is anything but simple, and almost never goes completely according to plan. As such, contingency plans are essential at each stage of the research process. If you can't get into the prison that you want to (which is not unusual), where could you get the equivalent data instead?

What are your options? Remember to look at the big picture of what you are trying to find out – there is almost always another way! This was certainly the approach that had to be embraced by Dr Alisa Stevens when attempting to undertake research for the Howard League for Penal Reform.

RESEARCHING SEX IN PRISON

Alisa Stevens

Sex research presents special difficulties. Sex research with prisoners, even more so. As I discovered when advising the Howard League for Penal Reform's Commission on Sex in Prison (2012–15), there are numerous challenges, methodologically and ethically, to obtaining such highly confidential and sensitive data, in a custodial environment antithetical to confidentiality and sensitivity.

The Commission's focus was upon understanding the phenomenon of prison sex, rather than estimating its prevalence or incidence. We wanted to hear from people who felt able to share their knowledge or experiences of consensual or coercive sexual relationships, sexual health care services, or support following sexual violence. In order to avoid inadvertently 'outing' prisoners in same-sex relationships or re-traumatising assault survivors, we thought it essential that people volunteered to participate and had confidence they could 'speak out' anonymously and in private. Postal surveys, for example, were discounted because of the impossibility of ensuring their return to the researcher without being intercepted by prison staff or other prisoners. Pragmatically too, with just one researcher and a limited budget, the Commission had neither the human nor financial resources to replicate the quantitative and mixed method research designs used, in particular, in the United States and Australia. These typically involve a team of researchers and thousands of randomly sampled prisoners at multiple correctional facilities.

The qualitative research design we accordingly proposed to institutional gatekeepers involved short periods of fieldwork in

six closed prisons for men and women, with self-selecting participants found through distributing leaflets to prisoners on the wings,
at health care, and other strategic venues such as LGTB support
groups. To preserve participants' anonymity, prisoners would be
offered a one-to-one interview, held off-wing under the plausible
guise of a legal visit or probation meeting. Alternatively, they could
choose to complete a questionnaire, handed out and collected back
in a sealed envelope on the same day by the researcher. At each
prison visited, we would also seek to collect pertinent institutional
data and interview prison managers with relevant responsibilities.

When this proposal was rejected, we adapted the design to remove the need for fieldwork by advertising for interviewees in the
newspaper for British prisoners, *Inside Time*, freely available in every
establishment. If necessary to keep the project manageable, we
would purposively sample across prisoner and prison 'types.' But this
proposal was also rejected; thwarted, it seemed to the Commission,
by fundamental differences in opinion about what data, obtained
how, and predominantly from whom, was important, and the political difficulties the research findings might cause (Stevens, 2020).

Undeterred, by advertising with two charities whose clients
had experienced imprisonment, we recruited 26 people from
across Britain for telephone or face-to-face interviews. Their testimonies raised significant and troubling issues about both the realities of, and institutional responses to, prison sex (Stevens, 2017).
The moral of the story? When seeking to secure access, be resilient,
be creative, and remember that 'prisons research' need not require
the involvement of serving prisoners. When trying to illuminate
the opaque world of prisons, formerly imprisoned people also
have much to contribute.

When in the prison, security measures can also call for second thoughts – what if you can't take recording equipment in
one day? What if you can but your batteries run out halfway
through an interview (which has happened to me, and resulted
in a mass scribble for the rest of the interview, and certainly
changed the dynamic of the discussions and the data I was able to

use – particularly in terms of verbatim quotes)? Having such contingency plans in place means that the panic that comes from actually encountering such challenges loses its intensity somewhat. It is also important to remember that all prison researchers face challenges – that's what makes this type of research (a) so interesting, and (b) so respected within the prison research community!

Conclusion

In this chapter, I have tried to consider some of the practical challenges associated with prison research, particularly regarding access, accessibility, security, and negotiating gatekeepers. The key element to all these dimensions is the importance of relationship building, diplomacy, and thoughtfulness: these are busy, potentially traumatised people that you are attempting negotiations with, and one needs to remember the importance of context and timing. I have tried to give some ideas for a step-by-step thought process for planning a prison research project – undoubtedly there will be other considerations that I have missed, or potential challenges that are never faced, but throughout your planning, it is important to try to consider every eventuality, and to come up with contingencies so that your time and attention when in the research context can be focussed on the important things that you really want to see, hear, smell, feel, read, and understand.

Notes

1 The NIMBYism associated with the building of many prisons means that this physical inaccessibility is a pervasive problem. I remember one visit to a prison on the outskirts of a city: I did not at that time have a car, so I booked a taxi to take me. Not only did the driver not know where the prison exactly was, but we actually drove past it on our way – the lack of signage and physically hidden nature of the prison was bizarre, and must make life exceptionally hard for those attempting to visit as family and friends.
2 Ethics and access have hugely overlapping remits: not least because if you fail to get ethical approval, your access to research external organisations is denied – from the university perspective, without ethical approval, you aren't getting access to the research world. The door 'out' is shut.

3 https://www.gov.uk/government/publications/ministry-of-justice-areas-of-research-interest-2020
4 In fact, they date back much earlier than this to 1955, however, the amended 'Nelson Mandela Rules' were adopted in 2015 (McCall-Smith, 2016).
5 Many thanks to Dr Thomas Bundschuh and Dr Sevie Magill for their advice on this matter!
6 For example, cross-sectional, longitudinal, comparative, experimental or case study (see Bryman, 2016: ch. 3).
7 I will not even begin to discuss the intricacies and methodological options available with regard to probability and non-probability sampling and the like – for that detail I would strongly recommend the work of Bryman (2016: chs 8 and 18) and Heap and Waters (2019).

References

Bryans, S. (2008) Prison governors: New public managers? In Crewe, B., Bennett, J. & Wahidin, A. (eds) (2008) *Understanding Prison Staff*. Cullompton: Willan.

Bryans, S. (2013) *Prison Governors*. Cullompton: Willan.

Bryman, A. (2016) *Social Research Methods*. Oxford University Press.

Bureau of Jail Management and Penology (2015) *BJMP Comprehensive Operations Manual 2015 Edition*. Available at https://www.bjmp.gov.ph/images/files/Downloads/BJMP_OPERATIONAL_MANUAL_2015.pdf

Byrne, M. W. (2005) Conducting research as a visiting scientist in a women's prison. *Journal of Professional Nursing*, 21(4), 223–230.

Carr, L. (2015) Re-entry to prison: Transition from HMP researcher to independent researcher. In Drake, D. H., Earle, R. & Sloan, J. (eds) *The Palgrave Handbook of Prison Ethnography*. Basingstoke: Palgrave Macmillan.

Condry, R., Kotova, A., & Minson, S. (2016) Social injustice and collateral damage: The families and children of prisoners. In Jewkes, Y., Bennett, J. & Crewe, B. (eds) *Handbook on Prisons*, 2nd edn. Abingdon: Routledge.

Crewe, B., Bennett, J., & Wahidin, A. (2008) *Understanding Prison Staff*. Cullompton: Willan.

Dirga, L. (2015) The possible applications of the guard's world concept in the analysis of the Czech prison system. *Acta Fakulty Filozofické Západočeské Univerzity v Plzni*, 7(3), 115–131.

Drake, D. (2012) *Prisons, Punishment and the Pursuit of Security*. Cham: Springer.

Dubois, C. (2018) Prison governors as policymakers, phronetic practices as enacted knowledge. *The Howard Journal of Crime and Justice*, 57(3), 363–378.

Earle, R. (2014) Insider and out: Making sense of a prison experience and a research experience. *Qualitative Inquiry*, *20*, 429–438.

Earle, R. (2016) *Convict Criminology: Inside and Out*. London: Policy Press.

Earle, R. (2017) *Convict Criminology: Inside and Out*, 2nd edn. London: Policy Press.

Foucault, M. (1977 [1975]) *Discipline and Punish: The Birth of the Prison*. London and New York: Vintage.

Gariglio, L. (2016) Photo-elicitation in prison ethnography: Breaking the ice in the field and unpacking prison officers' use of force. *Crime, Media, Culture*, *12*(3), 367–379.

Garrihy, J., & Watters, A. (2020) Emotions and agency in prison research. *Methodological Innovations*, *13*(2). Doi:10.1177/2059799120926341

Harvey, J. (2015) The ethnographic practitioner. In Drake, D. H., Earle, R. & Sloan, J. (eds) *The Palgrave Handbook of Prison Ethnography*, pp. 390–402. Basingstoke: Palgrave Macmillan.

Heap, V., & Waters, J. (2019) *Mixed Methods in Criminology*. Abingdon: Routledge.

Heard, C. (2020) Commentary: Assessing the global impact of the COVID-19 pandemic on prison populations. *Victims & Offenders*, *15*(7–8), 848–861.

Heeley, J. (2021) An investigation exploring the extent to which prison perpetuates a culture of toxic masculinity that reinforces negative personality and gender stereotypes. Unpublished undergraduate dissertation, Sheffield Hallam University.

His Majesty's Prison and Probation Service (HMPPS) (2023) Research at HMPPS. Available at https://www.gov.uk/government/organisations/hm-prison-and-probation-service/about/research

Ismail, N., & De Viggiani, N. (2018) How do policymakers interpret and implement the principle of equivalence with regard to prison health? A qualitative study among key policymakers in England. *Journal of Medical Ethics*, *44*(11), 746–750.

King, R. D. (2000) Doing research in prisons. In King, R. D. & Wincup, E. (eds) *Doing Research on Crime and Justice*. Oxford University Press.

King, R. D., & Liebling, A. (2008) Doing research in prisons. In King, R. D. & Wincup, E. (eds) *Doing Research on Crime and Justice*, 2nd edn. Oxford and New York: Oxford University Press.

Liebling, A., & Arnold, H. (2012) Social relationships between prisoners in a maximum security prison violence faith and the declining nature of trust. *Journal of Criminal Justice*, *40*, 413–424.

Liebling, A., Arnold, H., & Straub, C. (2011) *An Exploration of Staff–Prisoner Relationships at HMP Whitemoor: 12 Years On*. Cambridge: Cambridge Institute of Criminology, Prisons Research Centre.

Liebling, A., & Williams, R. J. (2018) The new subversive geranium: Some notes on the management of additional troubles in maximum security prisons. *British Journal of Sociology*, 69(4), 1194–1219.

Masson, I. (2019) *Incarcerating Motherhood: The Enduring Harms of First Short Periods of Imprisonment on Mothers*. Abingdon: Routledge.

McCall-Smith, K. (2016) United Nations standard minimum rules for the treatment of prisoners (Nelson Mandela Rules). *International Legal Materials*, 55(6), 1180–1205.

Mills, J. (2004) *There's a Lot in Those Keys Isn't There?' The Experience of a Female Researcher Researching Rape in a Male Prison Undertaking the Research as a Key Holder*. Washington DC: National Criminal Justice Reference Service, US Department of Justice.

Ministry of Justice and HM Prison and Probation Service (MoJ and HMPPS) (2020) *Security Categorisation Policy Framework*. Available at https://assets.publishing.service.gov.uk/government/uploads/system/uploads/attachment_data/file/1011502/security-categorisation-pf.pdf

Ministry of Justice and National Offender Management Service (MoJ and NOMS) (2011) *Categorisation And Recategorisation of Women Prisoners, Prison Service Instruction 39–2011*. Available at https://assets.publishing.service.gov.uk/government/uploads/system/uploads/attachment_data/file/1028815/psi-39-2011-cat-women-prisoners.pdf

Minson, S. (2019) Direct harms and social consequences: An analysis of the impact of maternal imprisonment on dependent children in England and Wales. *Criminology & Criminal Justice*, 19(5), 519–536.

Naylor, B. (2015) Researching human rights in prisons. *International Journal for Crime, Justice and Social Democracy*, 4(1), 79–95.

Prais, V. (2020) The implementation in Canada of the UN Standard Minimum Rules for the Treatment of Prisoners: A practitioner's perspective. *Journal of Human Rights Practice*, 12, 730–767.

Prison Reform Trust (2020) *CAPPTIVE: Covid-19 Action Prisons Project: Tracking Innovation, Valuing Experience: How Prisons Are Responding to Covid-19; Briefing #1: Families and Communications*. Prison Reform Trust. Available at http://prisonreformtrust.org.uk/wp-content/uploads/old_files/Documents/CAPPTIVE_families_webfinal.pdf

Prison Service Instruction (PSI) 40–2011 (2011).

Reiter, K. (2014) Making windows in walls: Strategies for prison research. *Qualitative Inquiry*, 20(4), 417–428.

Ross, J. I., & Richards, S. C. (2003) *Convict Criminology*. Belmont, CA: Wadsworth/Thomson Learning.

Shalev, S. (2013) *Supermax: Controlling Risk through Solitary Confinement*. Cullompton: Willan.

Sloan, J. (2016) *Masculinities and the Adult Male Prison Experience.* Basingstoke: Palgrave Macmillan.

Sloan, J., & Wright, S. (2015) Going in green: Reflections on the challenges of 'getting in, getting on, and getting out' for doctoral prisons researchers. In Drake, D. H., Earle, R. & Sloan, J. (eds) *The Palgrave Handbook of Prison Ethnography*, pp. 143–163. Basingstoke: Palgrave Macmillan.

Smith, L. (2021) Women in prison: The effects of using short-term custodial sentences. Unpublished undergraduate dissertation, Sheffield Hallam University.

Stevens, A. (2017) Sexual activity in British men's prisons: A culture of denial. *British Journal of Criminology*, 57(6), 1379–1397.

Stevens, A. (2020). Access denied: Research on sex in prison and the subjugation of 'deviant knowledge.' *Criminology & Criminal Justice*, 20(4), 451–470.

Toy-Cronin, B. (2018) Ethical issues in insider-outsider research. In Iphofen, R. & Tolich, M. (eds) *The SAGE Handbook of Qualitative Research Ethics*. Thousand Oaks, CA: Sage.

UNODC (2015) The United Nations Standard Minimum Rules for the Treatment of Prisoners (the Nelson Mandela Rules), General Assembly resolution 70/175, annex, adopted on 17 December 2015.

Williams, R. J., & Liebling, A. (2018) Faith provision, institutional power and meaning among Muslim prisoners in two English high security prisons. In *Finding Freedom in Confinement: The Role of Religion in Prison Life*, pp. 269–291. Westport, CT: Praeger.

Zhang, S. (2019) Unresolvable tensions and ethical dilemmas: Reflecting on the experience of doing 'prison research' in China – a research note. *The Prison Journal*, 99(6), 662–682.

Four

DOING PRISON RESEARCH

Tips and Tricks

Jennifer Anne Rainbow and Serena Wright

In April 2014, Serena Wright and I undertook a small piece of research with established prison researchers, entitled 'Reflections on the challenges of "getting in, getting on, and getting out" for prisons researchers.' In addition to asking about respondents' first time in a prison setting, they were asked about how they generally get into prisons, their reflections on self-conduct in the prison, leaving the prison setting, and the perceived impacts of prisons research on them.

> *Q: Have you experienced any obstacles to undertaking prisons research? And Q: What would you say is the most difficult obstacle that needs to be overcome to undertake prisons research today?*

In response to these questions, the majority of researchers referred to the time consuming and complex nature of gaining access through the HMPPS (formerly NOMS) National Research Committee (NRC), in addition to gaining permission to publish findings. Staff gatekeeping and misunderstandings can get in the way of getting full access, and participants referred to the need to gain the trust of staff (in balance with the trust of prisoners). Those writing from an international perspective suggested that the access processes (and university ethical scrutiny) in the UK tended to be perceived as much more complex and time consuming in comparison to that of other jurisdictions, highlighting the need for 'diplomacy skills.' It was noted by one participant that 'access

DOI: 10.4324/9781315297217-4

seems to be becoming more restrictive and linked to organisational need rather than academic curiosity and scrutiny,' an issue that is evident when examining the need to establish links to policy and strategy within the HMPPS application, as demonstrated above. Indeed, with the benefit of hindsight (and a reflection of how the process has changed in the years since we conducted this small study), linking research aims and objectives to HMPPS policy and strategy is now probably *the* most important and most persuasive element of the application.

Prison researchers were also asked *What three tips would you offer to new prisons researchers planning to do prisons research in 2014?* Some of the suggestions were related to areas of research and how to understand the research context:

Don't forget staff and management
Don't forget the interrelation between society and prisons
Do fieldwork[1]
Do extensive homework ahead of time about the administration, trying to meet gatekeepers
Keep in mind that institutions need to be approached as systems, not as containers of individuals
Have a balanced approach so you are not seen to be 'taking sides' or favouring any one group over another
All research is political – choose the right side

As can be seen, some of the advice that was given by different academics was somewhat contradictory!

Others spoke in terms of the practicalities in planning and undertaking research:

Be patient and persistent and prepare for the unexpected
Try to make your topic seem relevant and interesting to [HMPPS] i.e. consistent with their strategic priorities
Think about resources implications for the prison you want to study. Be realistic about this.
Allow far more time than you think you will need
Take time to build trust with staff and prisoners within the prison
Write down EVERYTHING
Allow plenty of time for securing permission

Develop networks within the prison system
Consult informally first
Build support for the topic
Be well informed
Be open
Look and listen very carefully
Enjoy yourself
Early application to [HMPPS]
Read prison biographies
Read ethnographic material[2]
Do it with another researcher, if possible
Question and observe as much as you can with a critical eye

Whilst most participants evidently focused on practicalities, there was mention of the emotional aspect of the process, with one participant stating:

> You just have to find a way to have a reasonably good time doing it. That's the most important issue. As a researcher, you just can't do your job properly if you're miserable all the time. Even though there's a lot of awkwardness and even tough experiences, you have to be able to enjoy yourself doing it.

Other comments in this vein included the need to have a 'back-up team of trusted people you can turn to if necessary for debriefing' and the importance of 'taking time off from the field work when you feel you need it.' One respondent also reflected on feeling 'a sense of fear and vulnerability, which is not physical or personal, but structural' (a feeling that many of us in the field can associate with). When researching in prisons, there is an underlying tension that pervades the institutional fabric of the prison itself (arguably a manifestation of its innate deterrent function). Feelings of safety for researchers can often depend a lot on gender (of researcher and research site), security category, and a lack of staff presence in understaffed and overpopulated prisons, amongst other things. Indeed, personal experience and trauma feeds into this – for example, Serena felt much less safe going into prisons to conduct research after her friend Jack Merritt and fellow Learning Together colleague Saskia Jones were killed by a man recently released from prison at Fishmongers' Hall in London. Prior to this, she could convince herself (and her loved ones) that there was little risk to herself (compared to, say, other prisoners or prison staff), because she was doing work aimed at amplifying the voices of criminalised people – after that, she no longer felt that to be true, because of what she stood for.

With hindsight (and given that Serena has now left prison research, and academia more generally, in part as a consequence of the affective impact of this work), we feel it is important to reflect at this point on the fact that the tips and tricks given that related to emotional wellbeing and mental 'resilience' in our 2014 survey were few and far between (indeed, those which we were provided with tended to take the form of multiple comments from one or two individuals, rather than spread across the sample). This absence appears starker when compared to the multitude of detailed responses focused on issues such as access and personal conduct and presentation in research sites. Historically, prison sociologists have tended to eschew reflexivity; indeed, at the time we conducted this small study, discussions in this field were heavily concerned with the reflexive turn, with academics fearful of appearing narcissistic or 'naval gazing' for engaging with the emotional aspects of their research (see Jewkes, 2014). As we noted almost a decade ago (see Sloan and Wright, 2015), prison researchers are often keen to ensure that they do not appear more concerned with their own mental wellbeing than that of staff and residents within their carceral research sites. Even now, in a society that is flooded (in the UK and the United States, at least) with notions of wellness and mindfulness in the workplace, the field of criminology continues to send doctoral students and researchers into the field with no real provision of meaningful support, and with little recognition of the 'vicarious trauma' that can evidently arise (for example, see Dr Shona Minson's discussions on the *Locked Up Living* podcast). We therefore felt it was remiss not to extend these tips and tricks with a few of our own, which apply to novice and experienced prison researchers alike:

Be prepared that deeply personal interviews can raise difficult ethical and emotional responses, some of which may be linked to your own personal experiences in ways that can be challenging.

Always ensure that you have someone – your doctoral supervisor, a co-researcher or a trained professional – to debrief with following an interview, and to discuss any potential safeguarding concerns.

Understand the signs of vicarious trauma and seek out support if needed.

Where possible, cost in access to a professional supervisor or counsellor to any research funding bid where extensive lone-worker fieldwork in prisons (or similar sites) are planned.

When planning prison research, try to limit the number of interviews you are conducting in a day or week, so that you have adequate time to process and decompress in between.

If you are a doctoral, early career or junior researcher, speak openly about any challenges you face with your supervisor or primary investigator/principal researcher – your wellbeing is partially their responsibility.

Another issue that many new prison researchers face when entering the prison is the question of how to present yourself – how do you want to appear to potential participants or others within the context? If you dress too formally, you run the risk of appearing like a member of senior management or the psychology team (for instance, when Jennifer went into one of her first meetings in prison, she wore a suit. She was later told that people thought she must be a new governor). If you dress less formally, you risk being mistaken for other types of staff members (a bereavement or substance misuse counsellor, as happened to Serena), an undergraduate or college student (also Serena, as a thirty-something year-old lecturer!), or a new resident on the landing (also Serena, at various women's prisons). Dressing too informally may also give an indication that you are not serious or respectful.

There is, of course, a strongly gendered aspect to this; women in men's prisons often feel a disproportionately keen need to police their behaviour and dress (Genders and Player, 1995) (although male prison sociologists are not necessarily immune from this; see Crewe, 2014). Given our own experiences, we asked the following question in our survey to find out more about this issue: *Given that some of the most frequently asked questions form new prison researchers relate to the presentation of self, what advice*

do you have on conducting oneself in the prison environment?
Responses were as follows:

See if you can establish some sort of role for yourself that fits with
  both the way you see yourself and with the particular prison
  you are researching. It doesn't have to be too prescribed, just
  a way of understanding yourself and a way of making yourself
  understandable to others in a prison setting. Something like
  'independent observer,' 'researcher in residence,' 'student,' or
  even 'member of the public' might suffice.
Be yourself.
You have to be yourself, but at the same time, you have to manage your presentation of self to a certain degree. Even though
  it may be difficult, you have to remember that you have a professional role to play. Striking the balance between being too
  distant and too close is difficult, and often down to gut feeling.
  It will get easier with time. Be friendly, but not a friend.
Be authentic, careful, respectful to all.
Presentation is, in my view, less important than reflection. Understand how you present yourself, who you are, how people
  perceive you and interact with you.
That is a hard question! From the obvious dress appropriately
  [which we would argue is an ambiguous and gendered observation!] to the less obvious and ambiguous advice to be
  authentic.
It's helpful to be both friendly and self-contained and to align with
  the concerns of those you meet - in other words, to explore
  what difficulties your presence creates for prisoners and staff.
Be respectful. Be as authentic as possible. Don't try too hard to 'fit
  in' with any particular sub-group, or stratum. In the end, this
  will make you seem phoney to another sub-group or stratum,
  and that's bad news for your personal and professional integrity. Don't be loose lipped – information moves very quickly.
  Wear warm and comfortable shoes.
Be attentive to the signals the institution and its occupants send;
  don't imagine that because you have familiarised yourself with
  a place that it will be the same always.

Give some thought to how you will handle the need to compromise, to withhold, to perform an identity you may not be entirely comfortable with.
Be patient and flexible and persistent.

As such, it can clearly be seen that even the most experienced prison researchers have had their challenges!

Finally, we would recommend that anyone wanting to conduct research in prisons, or with people being supervised by the National Probation Service, familiarise themselves with the advice and protocols of the HMPPS NRC website (as of July 2023, this could be found at: https://www.gov.uk/government/organisations/hm-prison-and-probation-service/about/research). This page also provides up to date information about any current 'blocks' or 'caps' on applications, which should help potential prison researchers to plan their application accordingly.

Conclusion

Whilst there is no single way to approach undertaking prisons research, this chapter has attempted to lay out some of the main practicalities and tips for the process of preparing to 'do' prisons research. At the same time, it is important to recognise the somewhat organic process that negotiating access and interacting with gatekeepers consists of. Similarly, it is vital to accept that the process of applying for access via the NRC might not be successful the first time, and will require contingency plans to be thought of. Such processes are time-intensive, and can have substantial implications for the length of such projects – as such, a back-up can help to save time and allay the almost constant fear of 'this isn't going to happen' that precedes almost every prison research project!

Remember also that conducting research in prisons can be mentally challenging, particularly for those with lived experience and/or other personal experiences which may shape the degree to which research sites or interview disclosures affect individuals. To this end, ensure that your plan for prison research includes time, space and the opportunity to debrief and discuss safeguarding issues during fieldwork.

Notes

1 Of course, survey respondents in 2014 could not have predicted the global Covid-19 pandemic, which shut down prison- and probation-based research for the best part of 18 months between March 2020 and the autumn of 2021. Indeed, as of July 2023, when this book was submitted for publication, the HMPPS NRC website not only continues to list adherence to Covid-19 protocols as a key part of any research application, but has also (since March 2023) put a 'cap' on the number of applications for multi-site research (14 per month) on a first-come, first-served basis. This policy is due for review at the time of writing.

2 We would also strongly suggest reading the 'methods' chapters of books detailing prison research, such as Crewe, Hulley and Wright (2020); and Jewkes and Wright (2016).

References

Crewe, B. (2014) Not looking hard enough: Masculinity, emotion, and prison research. *Qualitative Inquiry*, 20(4), 392–403.

Crewe, B., Hulley, S., & Wright, S. (2020) *Life Imprisonment from Young Adulthood*. Basingstoke: Palgrave Macmillan.

Genders, E., & Player, E. (1995) *Grendon: A Therapeutic Prison*. Oxford University Press.

Jewkes, Y. (2014) An introduction to 'doing prison research differently.' *Qualitative Inquiry*, 20(4), 387–391.

Jewkes, Y., & Wright, S. (2016) Researching the prison. In Jewkes, Y., Crewe, B. & Bennett, J. (eds) *Handbook of Prisons*, 2nd edn, pp. 659–676. Abingdon: Routledge.

Locked Up Living (May 2023). *Shona Minson: Are You at Risk of Vicarious Trauma?* (episode 126). Available from: https://www.podbean.com/ew/pb-hy4im-1398644

Sloan, J., & Wright, S. (2015) Going in green: Reflections on the challenges of 'getting in, getting on, and getting out' for doctoral prisons researchers. In Drake, D. H., Earle, R. & Sloan, J. (eds) *The Palgrave Handbook of Prison Ethnography*, pp. 143–163. Basingstoke: Palgrave Macmillan.

Five

THE ETHICS AND ETHICALITY OF PRISON RESEARCH

Sociological research is fraught with ethical issues, but when in the context of the prison these are amplified. Prisons are spaces of restriction, security, and control. In this chapter, consideration is given to the ethical issues surrounding researching prisons, along with the ethicality of undertaking such a project. Whilst the ethical issues of researching people can be managed through achieving informed consent, maintaining confidentiality, and conforming to institutional regulations, it may still not be ethical to do the work in the prison context, where choice and autonomy are limited (see Sykes, 1958), and where the individuals under consideration may be vulnerable (or not, as will be discussed), or unable to understand sufficiently to be able to give truly informed consent to anything (and this applies to both prisoners, staff and others engaged with the carceral institution). In addition, the growth of interest in undertaking prison research can lead to over-researching this population, which also has ethical implications and problems. Just because we can, does not mean that we always should. It is these such issues that researchers need to consider and grapple with when planning their projects and thinking about the practicalities. It should always be remembered that, whilst your research may be important, the integrity and wellbeing of the research participant is supreme.

What Are Ethics and Why Do They Matter?

Beauchamp and Childress (2001) discuss the definition of ethics being 'a generic term for various ways of understanding and

DOI: 10.4324/9781315297217-5

examining the moral life' (2001: 1), which can be normative or non-normative. In this context, we are arguably most interested with normative ethics, which Beauchamp and Childress argue consists of 'general normative ethics [...] a form of inquiry that attempts to answer the question "Which general moral norms for the guidance and evaluation of conduct should we accept and why?"' (2001: 2) and 'Practical ethics (often called applied ethics) [...] the attempt to implement general norms and theories for particular problems and contexts' (ibid.) – i.e. the problem and context of prisons. The fact that this issue is normative highlights something of key importance when discussing ethics in the context of prisons – that is, this issue *matters* and has real-life consequences. As prison researchers, we have a real and substantial responsibility to ensure that we are considering these ethical questions carefully and thoroughly, as the implications of 'getting it wrong'[1] can be highly significant to an individual's life. Schlosser notes that 'The standards and requirements for studying inmates are different from other types of human subjects research. Interviewing in prison presents unique sets of obstacles and "methodological landmines" of which inexperienced researchers may be unaware' (2008: 1501). As such, the principles of 'Nonmaleficence' ('an obligation not to inflict harm on others' (Beauchamp and Childress, 2001: 113)) and 'Beneficence' ('a moral obligation to act for the benefit of others' (Beauchamp and Childress, 2001: 166)) can be important considerations.

For those undertaking research with human participants, ethical considerations and processes can be trying and complex. It can often feel like there are endless hoops to jump through and hurdles to clear before we can get to doing the 'real' work. For example, within most higher educational establishments, one must have their potential project scrutinised by ethics committees or Institutional Review Boards (USA) comprised of academic peers, who then offer suggestions for improvements or can completely put a stop to the whole project, in a process which can feel like a huge impingement on academic freedom. After achieving acceptance from the HE institution, further ethical scrutiny can be undertaken by the gatekeepers of the potential participants, which again can bring the project to a complete standstill or throw the application back for further amendments, which then may need to go through the HE process again. The cycle can appear endless, time consuming, and laborious, particularly when faced with tight deadlines by funders or doctoral studies timescales.

What one needs to consider, however, is that these processes are here for a number of reasons:

1. To Protect the Potential Participants from Harm

The most well recognised reasoning behind ethics and scrutiny processes comes down to the protection of those who are the focus of the research. In the prison research context, this is generally people living or working in prison, although it can also be staff or families/friends of those incarcerated. The problematic nature of the application of labels of vulnerability will be discussed later in this chapter, but in essence the main function of the ethical scrutiny process is to protect those who may be vulnerable from being over-researched, exploited, or harmed through inappropriate research. This can be through various means of 'protection,' such as ensuring fully informed consent, confidentiality, using pseudonyms, debriefing and referral to further support if required; but in essence the key is treating the participant as an active, autonomous agent who should be respected as such. If someone does not want to take part in research, regardless of how interesting they are, or how valuable their story is, their wishes need to be given the respect they deserve. This is not only important in the protection of the participant, but also in the protection of the researcher and research field with regard to maintaining a reputation of trustworthiness.

2. To Protect the Researcher from Harm

Another justification for ethical scrutiny is the protection of those undertaking the research. Whilst planning research, it can be easy to think that (a) everything is possible and (b) you are prepared for anything. It can be tempting to think that personal risks are worth taking for the end result of the research data – ethical scrutiny helps to temper such risks, particularly when ethics processes include a health and safety risk analysis. In the majority of instances, however, the researcher is not prioritised in ethics processes to the same degree that participants are. Putting to one side important feminist and/or constructivist ontological debates regarding researchers being co-producers (and thus fellow participants) of knowledge in many forms of sociological research (see Harding, 2020), the physical, mental, and emotional wellbeing of prison researchers is something that arguably needs greater priority within the discipline, and not just at doctoral level. Indeed, one of the most prolific and highly respected prison researchers in the English context has published some reflections on the stresses she and her team experienced: 'It was tempting to drink and smoke more than usual, listen to extra loud music, drive too fast and resort to other stress-related behaviours, to let off steam' (Liebling, 1999: 150).

Anyone who knows me in a research context knows how much emphasis I place upon researcher wellbeing, particularly in a prison research context. Serena Wright's and my chapter on 'Going In Green' (Sloan and Wright, 2015) was prompted by discussions we had with each other about the need to protect and prepare future generations of prison researchers regarding some of the intense stresses and strains that come with undertaking research on prisons, and I have been thrilled to read the growing literature on the topic of researcher wellbeing in the prison context. Although such honesty is improving, it still has some way to go, and it can take serious guts to talk about it openly when such conversations are still not normalised.

Emotional labour and the negative experiences of prison researchers should not be a huge surprise, nor should it be something we leave out of our accounts of research – indeed Reiter suggests that one of the key reasons for a dearth of contemporary prison research in the USA is 'the micro-level personal challenges prison researchers experience in navigating the emotional burdens of "bearing witness" to the pains inherent in modern imprisonment (Farmer, 2003: 28)' (Reiter, 2014: 419). Simply taking a psychological approach, there is evidence that exposure to emotional pictures, words, and other negative stimuli can have unconscious repercussions to the individual and result in negativity bias (Rozin and Royzman, 2001; Schimmack, 2005). Even if we don't go into a prison to focus on the negative, prisons have inherently negative elements to them (that is, to a degree, the point of prison, if we view deterrence as having any real weight in penal processes), and there is an argument that negative entities are given greater weight than positive within animals and humans, with the suggestion that 'one feature of negative events that make them dominant is that negative entities are more contagious than positive entities' (Rozin and Royzman, 2001: 296). As such, it is unsurprising that being in prisons as researchers is emotionally draining and can leave you with negative feelings (see also Schlosser, 2020).

Yet, the majority of ethics review processes tend not to engage with researcher wellbeing – or at least only focus on physical wellbeing. The terrible murder of Cambridge University Ph.D. student Giulio Regeni in Egypt on a research trip in 2016 brought the potential physical risks to researchers more into focus (and has had knock-on effects across HE institutions regarding supervision and health and safety during research). Mental and emotional wellbeing (as in the wider world) are still lacking in attention and support in the research context, often devolved to the supervisor (who is generally not trained in counselling or other forms of therapeutic care) or to generic institutional wellbeing services (which are already heavily used by the rest of the student population, and are rarely specialised) or occupational health and employee support provisions. In the main, the issue of seeking support is problematised and medicalised, and support is given because things are not going well or have had a negative impact on one's work or studies. Wellbeing, support, and debriefing are not prioritised in a more standard formal capacity.

What a difference it would make if we had a formal source of debriefing and peer support in the prison research community as standard from day one of the research process (not having to wait until things start to get overwhelming or too much before help may become available). Lessons could be drawn from others working in the field of 'listening to difficult stories,' such as counsellors and therapists (not that I am claiming prison research to be either of these things!), where peer supervision and debriefing enable individuals to reflect regularly on their own wellbeing and resilience in difficult environments. Although this may be factored into a student–supervisor relationship (unfortunately, it is not always the case), it is rare for such relationships to continue later into prison research careers, especially for those individuals who may not be part of a prison research community within their own institution – the lone researcher needs to keep this in mind.

In Chapter Four, other prison researchers have suggested some tips for the preservation of self in the prison research process. It is important to note that, although ethics processes may suggest they are looking to protect the researcher as well as the participant, sometimes this needs to be given more serious (and honest) thought and reflection. It is not a weakness to express negative emotions – far from it. Indeed expressing negative emotions to others has been found to be associated with positive relationship outcomes 'including elicitation of support, building of new close relationships, and heightening of intimacy in the closest of those relationships' (Graham, Huang, Clark and Helgeson, 2008: 394).

3. To Protect the Institution from Harm

The role of the ethics committee is not just to protect individuals from harm – it is also to protect the institutions researching and being researched.

(a) Higher Education Institutions

The majority of prison researchers are situated within higher education institutions, either as students or as research-active staff. When working within such institutions, there is a multitude of policies, procedures, and protocols that must be followed in order to comply with the risk-management processes that accompany such large-scale institutions, and to protect such bodies from 'harms.' As a result, when it comes to research, it is standard for universities to make use of the 'ethics committee' body. Such bodies review any research to be undertaken under the remit of the university institution, and make judgments on the researcher's acknowledgment of, engagement with, and limiting of, problematic ethical issues.

The ethics committee is often viewed as a hindrance by active researchers – it is fairly normal to hear the 'harrumphs' of academics waiting for ethical approval from committees and reviewers – in the main due to the fact that it imposes restrictions and limitations on what an individual is allowed to do, and can take time in making such decisions. Yet, ultimately, the ethics committee plays an important role in protecting the institution from certain harms that may befall the institution if something were to go 'wrong,' as well as trying to stop that 'going wrong' from happening in the first place. This places a substantial amount of pressure on the committee.

A key 'harm' that institutions need to protect themselves against, and one growing in power, is that of litigation. Increasingly, the role of the ethics review process is to look out for issues that might result in individuals breaching legal requirements, or going beyond the remit of the institution's insurance cover. For instance, there are important considerations that must be given to aspects of data protection when dealing with 'personal data,' certainly in the UK context. Another function of the ethics committee and ethical scrutiny is to ensure the reputation of the institution remains positive. There are certain areas of research that have the potential to bring the institution into disrepute (according to some) and thus may not be seen as something that the university wishes to be associated with. Whilst universities are often able to push the boundaries and undertake research into extremes, there are limitations (and these will depend on the institution in question, the people on the ethics committee, the country, the time, and so on).

(b) Prison Institutions

The other key institution that looks to protect itself is that of the prison – although in England and Wales, we must take a step further back to the organisation that governs it: His Majesty's Prison and Probation Service (HMPPS). As was seen in Chapter Three, HMPPS has its own research committee process which scrutinises potential research projects. Similarly to HE institutions, HMPPS looks to protect the institution of the prison, as well as the greater prison estate and the organisation of HMPPS itself, from a number of key potential issues.

HMPPS carries a duty of care to protect those it works with, and those working for it: Prison Service Instruction (PSI) 16/2015 creates the 'Adult Safeguarding in Prison' policy, which aims 'to ensure that all adult prisoners (aged 18 or older) are protected from abuse and neglect. It describes the processes that prisons must put in place to ensure that prisoners receive a level of protection that is equivalent to that provided to adults in the community with care and support needs who are at risk of abuse or neglect' (NOMS, 2016: 1). Feminist research principles state that there should be reciprocity within the research relationship (see Powell and Takayoshi, 2003; Morris and Morris, 1963), that we should practise 'locating the researcher in the same critical plane as the overt subject matter' (Harding, 1987: 8), and that we should see research participants as more than mere 'resources' within the research process. From the perspective of the prison, there is an ethical duty to protect those within the prison from research that could cause harm. Indeed, there is a history of problematic research being undertaken upon incarcerated individuals (Schwenzer, 2008: 1347).

Another function of ethics review that ties in with the protection of the inhabitants of the prison, is that of preventing over-researching from occurring. Whilst increasing the amount of research occurring within the prison estate may produce a host of interesting conclusions, it does use up resources, and it does also run the risk of over-researching individuals, and 'using' prison inhabitants (prisoners and staff together) as resources rather than human beings. Ethical scrutiny of the proposed research allows such considerations of the placement of the research participant to be taken into account.

The reputation of prisons is also a complex matter. Prisons start from a somewhat negative position – they are rarely seen in a positive light, and the addition of moral panics (Cohen, 1972), negative media portrayals, stories of escapes, violence, poor conditions, and negative inspection reports adds to the negative reputation held by them. Although some prisons function highly effectively, public perceptions and stereotypes are that prisons are unpleasant spaces – indeed, the very function of deterrence depends upon it. As such HMPPS may be cautious regarding research into its estate that has the potential to damage its reputation further.

Researching in prisons does use resources – it requires staff (and prisoner) time, security checks, potentially room resources, etc., and such resources are becoming more and more precious as austerity measures impinge upon public resources across the globe. Reviewing research from an ethical perspective allows someone to look at whether the research will be worth the resource implications (although this judgment of 'worth' is fraught with values and positionality influences).

4. To Protect Others not Directly Involved in the Research Process, but Who Might Be Impacted by the Research

When researching issues such as crime, punishment, and harm, it must be considered that there will be potential implications for others not directly involved in the research project, who need to be given consideration. Victims, for instance, need to be thought about if undertaking research that looks at individuals' crimes in a lot of qualitative detail. They may, one day, read the research – if writing for publication, you just don't know who will read it! – so this needs to be considered as a potential ethical implication. Yet this also creates a potential rabbit hole to go down – who knows who will be distressed or affected by what your research findings say? I have read many studies that have made me feel sad, angry or worried, but I am glad I read them, and I made the choice to do that. Prison research can be highly unsettling – that should not be shied away from. But consideration should be given to the inclusion of particular (especially potentially identifying) details before considered for inclusion in disseminated publications. As an example, I have recently been reading *Ted Bundy: The Only Living Witness* (Michaud and Aynesworth, 1999), based on numerous interviews with Bundy whilst incarcerated. Whilst it gives a fascinating insight into the mind of a man convicted of serial murder in the United States of America, some of the details will, undoubtedly, have been distressing for some of the victims' friends and families to read. As I say, this should not be an impediment to undertaking research, but should be an ethical consideration.

5. To Protect the Discipline from Harm

Finally, the discipline too needs a form of protection. Similarly to the issue of over-researching, the impact of the research process upon research participants can have severe implications for those who may come next into the field. When we have our time wasted, our views misrepresented, when we are lied to, and when we are treated badly, it leaves a 'bad taste,' and makes individuals less likely to engage in similar experiences in the future. Although this is unlikely to be at the forefront of any ethics committee or research committee's mind when judging the ethicality of a proposed piece of research within the prison estate, many of the considerations that *are* their priority indirectly address the protection of the prison research discipline.

What Happens if You Don't Follow the Rules?

Primarily, breaching ethical codes of conduct and failing to engage with established ethical review processes is a 'wrong' in and of itself, but there are some more tangible, less moralistic, implications for failure to engage.

Reputation

Failure to engage with expected protocols and procedures can have reputational implications – both for the individual researcher, and potentially for the institution they work within. If someone is known not to follow the rules, chances are other organisations may not wish to take risks in working with them, or may have doubts about the professionalism of the researcher. The prison research community is not enormous, and prisons and their staff talk to each other. In addition, ethical processes within higher education institutions are some of the most rigorous in existence, and are often held in high regard by other organisations and institutions who lack such formal policies and practices. In many instances, failure to adhere to ethical processes in this context can result in potential disciplinary outcomes.

Publishing Implications

Increasingly, publishers are requiring some form of guarantee of ethical review processes before they will publish any research findings. Graf et al. (2007) discuss publisher's perspectives on publication ethics, and note that:

> Editors should seek assurances that studies have been approved by relevant bodies (for example, institutional review board, research ethics committee, data and safety monitoring board, regulatory authorities including those overseeing animal experiments).
>
> *(2007: 5)*

As such, failure to engage with ethics processes runs the risk of research being unpublishable in the future – thereby reducing its academic value and promise drastically, as well as having been an immense waste of time and resources. The example of Andersson (2022) and the social media, press, and institutional responses to the publication of a piece with arguably questionable ethical principles (as well as no clear engagement with ethical obligations within the written piece itself – an issue that one would hope would be considered by a researcher, editor, and peer reviewers) shows how wide-ranging and negative the implications of a lack of clarity on the matter can be.

The Ethical Issues of Prison Research

As with all research, there are key ethical issues that need to be negotiated in the research process, such as confidentiality, informed consent, data protection, security, etc. Within the prison setting, these issues can take on additional complexities, due in part to the institutional setting and its closed and controlled nature, and due to the potential vulnerabilities of the participants. These issues will now be considered from a prison-specific perspective.

The 'Vulnerability' of Participants

> Vulnerability is one of the least examined concepts in research ethics [...] Regulations and policy documents regarding the ethical conduct of research have focused on vulnerability in terms of limitations of the capacity to provide informed consent. Other interpretations of vulnerability have emphasized unequal power relationships between politically and economically disadvantaged groups and investigators or sponsors. So many groups are now considered to be vulnerable in the context of research, particularly international research, that the concept has lost force. In addition, classifying groups as vulnerable not only stereotypes them, but also may not reliably protect many individuals from harm.
>
> *(Levine et al., 2004: 44)*

As Levine et al. note, the concept of vulnerability is somewhat complex (hence my use of quotation marks in the subheading). Traditionally in research, people in prison have been defined as 'vulnerable' populations (see Schwenzer, 2008). This is in part due to the abuses they may have suffered in the past which have led them to their current incarcerated predicament, as well as the potential for their being (or feeling) forced into research processes due to the coercive control of the prison institution. In a space where order and power are key, it may be difficult for a potential participant to divorce what they 'have' to do from what they don't 'have' to do. Indeed, prisoners are more likely to experience additional vulnerabilities which may undermine their autonomy and capacity to consent freely to being involved in research (see Pont, 2008). This requires a substantial amount of caution on the part of the recruiting researcher, and can justify defining that population in the realms of vulnerability. Yet, as Sykes (1958) noted, the deprivation of autonomy is seen to be one of the major 'pains of imprisonment.' Although it is vital to note the potential vulnerabilities of the population within the prison, it is also important not to make assumptions about the prison population that disregards their abilities to make decisions about engaging in research for themselves and further disempowers them as autonomous individuals. Such choices – when freely decided upon – allow the prisoner to take control over their lives to a small degree: assumptions that all people in prison are vulnerable and unable to make autonomous choices for themselves further infantilises a group who are already often subject to 'parent-like' controls.

Prison staff are not generally included within the notion of vulnerability, despite certain experiences and daily life processes that may actually demonstrate vulnerable traits. Just as it is important not to assume that all prisoners are inherently vulnerable, so it is important to recognise that staff working within the prison might be experiencing certain vulnerabilities themselves. Research on French prison employees found high levels of post-traumatic stress disorder symptoms, burnout, and stress (Boudoukha, Altintas, Rusinek, Fantini-Hauwel and Hautekeete, 2013), issues that are seen across the globe (Byrd, Cochran, Silverman and Blount, 2000; Cullen, Link, Wolfe and Frank, 1985). Similarly, the immense emotional labour experienced by prison staff has been recognised worldwide (Humblet, 2020; Nylander, Lindberg and Bruhn, 2011; Burke, Millings, Taylor and Ragonese, 2020). Vulnerability, or its lack of, should never be taken for granted in prison research.

Confidentiality

Within the prison setting there are many issues that inflate the seriousness of confidentiality. The stigma associated with incarceration, and its potential implications with regard to a prisoner's reintegration and desistance after release (Moran, 2012), mean that preserving their confidentiality has substantial importance. On the other hand, if an individual within the prison discloses problematic behaviour, there may be instances where that individual requires some protection which may require confidentiality to be undermined – there may be distinct limitations to the confidentiality that can be offered within the research relationship. When undertaking my doctoral research, the prison required a caveat to the confidentiality offered, that being the inclusion of the following statement in the information sheet: 'If you tell me anything that could result in serious harm I may have to ask for guidance from my supervisors at the University, or inform the relevant authorities within the Prison Service.' I remember sitting in an interview with a participant and noticing a lot of scars on his wrists – he clearly had a long (and current) history of self-harming. As this was one of the potential limitations to confidentiality, it was important that the institution was aware of the individual's issues. At the same time, however, I wished to maintain the autonomy and privacy of the individual as much as possible. As such, I tried to change the subject of the interview to the participant's relationship with the institution and whether he felt supported. Fortunately, at this point he started discussing his interactions with mental health services and his own experiences of self-harm. Although it seems like a little thing, the feelings of responsibility to both institution and participant can be difficult and emotionally draining to manage in practice. The limits of confidentiality within the prison setting add complex layers to the research relationship – it is important that such limitations of confidentiality are made clear at the outset of any piece of research, as the researcher has distinct responsibilities placed upon them, often as a condition of being able to research within the prison setting.

Another element of confidentiality that requires serious consideration is whether or not to name the prison in which you are researching in any subsequent publications. King argues that the prison discipline is sufficiently small that most fellow researchers can easily guess the research setting on the meagre contextual information that is discussed: 'I have never quite understood why some reports of prison studies go to great lengths to disguise the identities of prisons [...] When I come across such accounts I cannot resist the challenge of identifying the prisons from the contextual data thus supplied' (King, 2000: 307). At the same time, there are implications for individual confidentiality of participants, as distinct stories from a named prison can lead to an individual being potentially identifiable, particularly if they are a long term prisoner. This kind of matter should be agreed with the prison governor in advance – just to make sure there are no implications at a later date.

Informed Consent

The principle of informed consent is well acknowledged within ethical standards – we know that potential research participants need to be informed about their potential role within the research before they are asked to agree to participate (and that such consent is completely voluntary). This is generally done through the use of information sheets and consent forms, which require a degree of engagement by the participant (i.e. signing a consent form, ticking a box, etc.). When in the prison context, however, this takes on additional complexities. Acknowledgement needs to be made of the potential limitations of language, reading, and writing skills held by people in prisons (see Creese, 2015 – although it is vital not to make any assumptions either way on this matter), and the question of 'how informed?' should be considered carefully. I remember explaining to my participants that I was doing the research for a Ph.D. It still makes me uncomfortable thinking about how much I assumed people knew about higher education – so many just looked at me blankly and said 'What's that?' or waited until the end of the research to ask 'So what is this actually for?' It has taught me never to assume levels of knowledge in others.

Personal Security

When undertaking prison research, access to the institution is likely to involve some form of security briefing. It is important to remember that the role of prison security is to attempt to prevent any breach of security from occurring within a complex and challenging institution – thinking about the worst case scenario is key to risk management in such eventualities. If spending a sustained period of time within the prison, you might be given your own set of keys (and have the associated security briefing for this). As already noted in Chapter Three, holding a set of keys as a prison researcher has had a degree of critical academic discussion (King and Liebling, 2008; Sloan and Wright, 2015; Sloan, 2016). From an ethics point of view, it is important for the researcher to consider questions of power, influence, and hierarchy that come with having a set of keys. On the one hand, the researcher gains a degree of freedom and access to the prison that allows them to see beyond what they are 'shown' (Zhang, 2019). On the other hand, keys take the researcher a step towards being 'of' the institution – having the power to lock up your own participants, for example, places a different dimension upon the researcher–participant relationship.

The Right to Withdraw

The right to withdraw from a research project is often seen as an important ethical right which should be included wherever possible in the research process. If an individual undertakes an interview with you and, on reflection, changes their mind about it being used for research, where possible that view should be respected. The information, the story, the knowledge, belongs to that individual, and how it is used is valuable to them. Clearly there are times when this right cannot be given – in particular, when an individual's responses are anonymous, such as in an anonymous survey – there is no way for that individual's responses to be identified, so the right to withdraw is lost (but the chances of being identified are also reduced, and thus also the potential risks to that individual's reputation). The key is that the participant knows about the position regarding the right to withdraw before they undertake the research, allowing them to make an informed and autonomous decisions about how to use their knowledge and information.

But what about when the right to withdraw is available and the participant wishes to make use of it? I have often scrutinised student information sheets where they offer the right to withdraw, but either do not state how long an individual has to express this wish,[2] or how to go about withdrawing – or they give an email address or phone number. For an incarcerated respondent, this is not an effective means by which to make contact – not having access to email, and phone calls being expensive. Where the researcher is remaining in the prison of research for some time as an ethnographic endeavour, this is less of an issue, as there are ways for the prisoner to get a message to the researcher via internal prison communications (albeit problematic in terms of confidentiality). Where the researcher is not readily available, the means of expressing the wish to withdraw at a later date become even more complex, and essentially give the prisoner participant even less control and ability to change their mind – such eventualities need careful consideration in the context of the work being done.

Beneficence

Whilst we all go into a research project in the hope that we might make some 'difference' for the better, it is important not to over-estimate what positive benefit your work may bring on the wider scale. In a lot of instances, the policy impact comes down to the dissemination process (i.e. getting the 'right' people to read your work, understand and process it, and actually work towards implementing any suggestions you may make). For projects commissioned by organisations or government bodies, the 'right' people are much easier to access in theory than for those undertaking work on a more academic basis. In all cases, dissemination is key – and the format of such dissemination matters. Just remember, policy makers tend to be power-rich, but time-poor.

RESEARCH AND THE HOWARD LEAGUE FOR PENAL REFORM

Anita Dockley

Research underpins the work of the Howard League for Penal Reform. As its name states, the charity works to change, or reform, the penal system. An obvious statement but this emphasis supports an approach that will always seek out research that has the potential to be impactful. The evidence base for seeking reform must be both robust and credible. However, the impact, or change, that is sought is rarely straightforward or linear in criminal justice and more frequently serendipitous or attritional.

As the Howard League's research director, I have been heartened by the research community's focus on impact both with funders and in research assessment. Nonetheless, there is a residual unease. The importance, value, and centrality of practitioners and opinion formers to academic research through co-production, shared agendas, dissemination strategies, and in embedding research findings, is regularly repeated. And, while I sit on panels with colleagues from outside academia to assess grant applications, and on the REF to assess the quality of research impact, I still feel there is something of a reality gap.

I am regularly approached and convinced of the value of research proposals by academic colleagues; sought out for access to samples or institutions; relationships with policy makers, practitioners, and parliamentarians as well as the media. There is no problem with this and to a greater extent it is a two-way relationship. It is possible to develop ideas and issues with academic colleagues based on our experience. Ideas, approaches, and dialogue are not the problem. The problem is the next steps in making the research, and the partnerships, a reality.

I don't think I am being jaded – as conversations with colleagues reveal similar issues. Organisations like the Howard League have routinely given their time, their voice, their energy – and to an extent will continue to do so because of our belief in the need for good solid research as the driver of change – but we need to be valued. All too often I have agreed to take time out to participate in numerous research advisory groups only to have minimal or no contact after an initial meeting and then have to chase research findings and outputs. Or the only real contact is in the dissemination phase with an impact case study in mind.

Securing research funding is difficult as an academic or a charity. Many funders that charities look to often prefer to fund service delivery. In the current funding environment, which places a high value on impact outside academia, these relationships are even more valuable. I think this means the balance of these partnerships needs to be re-thought: funders enabling time and inputs to be appropriately costed; researchers not just including service users and providers on advisory groups. All too often we feel, whatever the researcher may think, that they have no real input into the research and that we are ticking institutional boxes. Academics are encouraged by their universities to work alongside charities like the Howard League to maximise their funding potential.

I understand pressures on academics, universities, and research funders. So, while I am fully behind the drive to ensure that research should make a difference and be the driver for change, I would like a reassessment of the research relationships between funders, academics, and those of us outside the academy who are often pivotal to a proposal but often feel peripheral once support has been secured.

It is vital to remember, however, that 'making a difference' does not necessarily have to be at the policy level. If you are interacting with other human beings, you will be making a difference – to them. Whether you see or speak in person or via letter, you have the potential to be an important part of their day, and are a way in which their often hidden voices can subsequently potentially be heard. This matters. For those subject to incarceration, seeing someone different and not 'of the institution' has the potential to be very beneficial to them – as does just being out of one's regular space in a day (be that space physical or mental).

In addition, researching and writing about these groups in and of itself can be highly beneficial in terms of raising general and/or academic awareness, or stimulating further research – as long as the research that you do is ethical and high quality research in the first place. I regularly have discussions in my methodology classes with students who incorrectly assume that secondary research using the data generated by others is automatically free from ethical problems and can be relied upon, which raises an important question: should we undertake research founded upon data that has been collected in a problematic manner, albeit by others so we are not the primary 'offenders'? I would argue that we should not, although sometimes it can be difficult to ascertain the level of ethical consideration given in a piece of research, particularly given the tendencies of many to avoid long discussions of methodological challenges in the past. Harm can travel and expand like ripples in a pond (just take, for example, Iganski's model of waves of harm with regard to hate crime as a theoretical starting point (Iganski, 2001), and we need to show an ethical awareness at each level of the ripple where we join the research journey. Indeed, we have a responsibility as researchers to generate research that others can ethically and methodologically rely upon, and to leave the research setting and participants in a state that is not damaging to those who come after (British Society of Criminology, 2015).

Ethical Responsibilities

As a prison researcher, one may be granted access to highly closed off places, and see things that generally go unseen. In addition to the responsibilities entailed in doing 'good' research, following ethical guidelines and notions of non-malfeasance and beneficence, what other potential responsibilities does the researcher hold? What if they see problematic practices, abuse, harm, or something else of the like? It can be challenging when your research hinges on access being granted by gatekeepers who, in theory, you may have to challenge if harm is observed. This is one of the reasons why it is important to have constructive and positive relationships with gatekeepers, and hopefully to have someone that you trust within the institution that you can talk to, *and* why it is important that final control over the publishable content remains with *you*. If nothing else, being able to discuss problematic practices through publication and dissemination of your research may lead to change in and of itself, and certainly raises awareness in the long term.

There is a risk that all of these ethical considerations can sometimes feel overwhelming and off-putting (see Dalen and Jones, 2010). Yet, as some seasoned prison researchers note:

The imposition of safeguards is not always antithetical to expressing trust and facilitating authenticity, whereas pre-ordained risk management strategies can over-regulate the research process, curtail spontaneity (through encouraging researchers to avoid situations involving ethical compromise) and consequently numb researchers' ethical sensibilities.

Taming the research process through legalistic adherence to ethical protocols could have damaging consequences for both ethical practice and research outcomes: it could result in researcher withdrawal from difficult and hidden areas of social life or encourage dishonesty about the realities of this work.

(Armstrong, Gelsthorpe and Crewe, 2014: 213–214)

Such dangers are extreme: prison research *needs* to be done, and prison researchers *must* be honest about the realities of the findings, methodologies, and experiences. Arguably, the key to overcoming many of the potential ethical barriers discussed is for the researcher to acknowledge their own positionality, and also to attempt to place themselves regularly in the position of the potential participant. Such reflection and (auto)ethnographic positioning can allow much greater honesty, integrity, and understanding in the research process.

BREAKING OUT OF THE 'SUFFERING SLOT': THE VALUE OF CONDUCTING ETHNOGRAPHIC RESEARCH WITH MEN CONVICTED OF SEXUAL OFFENCES

Alice Ievins

'As a woman, why do you want to study the imprisonment of men convicted of sex offences?' This question, which was asked by a senior academic early in the development of my Ph.D., has haunted my work to date, but I have always heard it as interrogating my feminism rather than my femininity. The question implies that there might be physical but also a moral, intellectual, and political danger in conducting research with this stigmatised group. Certainly, this field of study exposes researchers to 'narrative risk' (Waldram, 2007: 966), and there are many legitimate reasons for wishing to avoid hearing the disturbing and distressing stories which might be shared. But asking this question also implies a fear that such research relies on and promotes misplaced empathy with men who have sexually offended ('himpathy,' as Manne (2017) calls it), and that it ignores the stories and needs of women who have been hurt. These critics bolster their case by arguing that people convicted of sex offences are particularly likely to tell distorted and dishonest stories about their offending, and perhaps about their experiences in custody (Digard, 2014), and thus that research conducted with this group might serve the interests of neither justice nor truth.

The question grows out of the instinctive belief that our research can and should mirror our politics – which, for sociologists, are normally progressive and left-leaning (Becker, 1967; Klein and Stern, 2005) – and that the subjects of our research should be those with whom we most deeply sympathise. The goal of such research should be to validate and amplify the voices and humanity of people who have suffered, to show how the world has mistreated them, and perhaps to feed into policies which might help them. In the anthropological context, Joel Robbins (2013) has called such research 'suffering slot ethnography' – that is, research which makes sense of the world through its identification of trauma and the resulting establishment of an emotional connection – and there is little room in such ethnography for research on those who perpetrate suffering (Waldram, 2007).

The quest to identify the suffering slot provides an incomplete framework for research, and one which relies on and perpetuates a constraining binary between perpetrator and sufferer (Christie, 1986). As Robbins (2013: 456) argues, suffering slot ethnography is 'secure in its knowledge of good and evil and works toward achieving progress in the direction of already accepted models of the good.' But just as one goal of our research is to 'look beneath official definitions of reality' (Liebling, 2001: 475) made by power-holders, another goal should also be to question interpretations of the social world as a morality play (Becker, 1967: 245) in which it is easy to identify victim and offender, and in which those moral statuses provide irrefutable information about social reality. At its best, appreciative ethnographic research with men convicted of sex offences can help us to look beyond the assumptions which we make when confronted with people assigned with the stereotyped social identity of 'sex offender' (Moolman, 2015). Such research does not require us to minimise the very serious harms caused by sexual violence, and minimisation should not be its goal. But there is both an academic and a political benefit in recognising that 'sex offenders' are not an easily distinguishable group, that sexual violence is also perpetrated by those who do not easily fall into this stereotyped category, and that our responses to sexual violence might cause their own harms. By undertaking ethnographies which do not take social and moral categories for granted, we can conduct research which doesn't straightforwardly mirror our politics, but which may be a better way to further its underlying values.

The Supervision and Support of Prison Researchers

There is (another) UK 'Concordat to Support the Career Development of Researchers' (Vitae, 2011). This is 'an agreement between funders and employers of research staff to improve the employment and support for researchers and research careers in UK higher education' (Vitae, 2011), and imposes certain ethical responsibilities upon HE institutions to look after their researchers, and adds an important degree of institutional supervision requirement. When read alongside the prison as the research setting, it is clear that such principles could be extremely useful in the provision of support for prison researchers, which is somewhat lacking at present.

As noted, one of the central aspects of ethics in research is to 'do no harm.' In reality, most of us think of the potential harm that could befall participants in our studies – we rarely foreground ourselves as prison researchers as potentially 'harmed' individuals. Yet, as has already been discussed, in reality, prison research can be intense with regard to the emotional labour involved (Drake and Harvey, 2014). Emotional labours can be particularly pertinent for those 'green' to the prison research process (Sloan and Wright, 2015) – especially doctoral researchers (Waters, Westaby,

Fowler and Phillips, 2020). Undertaking a Ph.D./doctorate can be extremely lonely and emotionally draining at the best of times; add to this the prison as a research setting, and it becomes apparent that there is an important need to support doctoral prison researchers in an extended manner to the normal supervisory process. Many doctoral prison researchers may not be being supervised by staff who have prison research experience, which adds a new dimension of strain on the supervision relationship – the challenges of researching in a prison setting are often difficult to explain and articulate to those who have not gone through that process themselves (hence the reason for this book to try to help!).

In addition, supervisors should provide students with space to talk about ethical challenges (see Armstrong, Gelsthorpe and Crewe, 2014), and what they may have seen or heard – not necessarily in any academic capacity. Graduate student mental and emotional well-being generally is known to be problematic (Hyun, Quinn, Madon and Lustig, 2006). More specific research into doctoral students researching prison is lacking, but anecdotal evidence suggests the pressures of researching within a confined environment, hearing stories of serious personal harm and trauma, and seeing such negative cases of personal well-being, can have serious implications for student well-being. In addition to processes of self care and space creation advocated by Waters et al. (2020), students' supervisors should consider looking for services for their students to support them on their research paths. Given that most institutions have such support services (universities *and* the HMPPS, for example, both have services recognising the potential support needs of those working within them), this may be more a case of signposting and recognition of need, although more specialist services might be useful for some. That said, this is not the case across the globe – indeed Gariglio highlights that in the Italian prison he was in, 'officers do not receive psychological counselling and that they often hide their problems and managers turn a blind eye to them, because for any particular officer, declaring psychological issues could produce great problems and result in unemployment' (2016: 372). The stigma of mental health has a lot of pain to answer for.

In addition, it is vital that doctoral prison researchers network with others who are, or who have been, there already. I often speak to doctoral students at conferences about prison research, and see a weight lifted when talking about challenges they have experienced but cannot seem to explain to others – what to wear, how to act as a woman in a men's institution, how to manage the researcher identity presentation, whilst avoiding being seen as prison management, etc. Talking to those who have gone before helps. Jewkes notes from her experiences as a doctoral supervisor that 'many Ph.D. students [...] frequently ask questions, not only about how they should dress, act, respond to prisoners and staff, and so on, but also about what they should expect to feel, what they should do if they become anxious, and so on' (2012: 72–73), and that 'many not only want to "know" and "understand" but also want to anticipate how they will "feel" when they experience a prison environment for the first time' (2012: 64).

Of course, it is important not to forget the supervision process that comes with supervising undergraduate and master's dissertations in the field of prisons. Just because access to prisons is restricted for those groups, does not mean that they cannot still undertake prison research which will still potentially have value and impact. Critical literature reviews are often the main tool available to the undergraduate prison researcher, and in these cases it is important for the supervisor to acknowledge the issues associated with such research. A critical literature review is not to be seen as the 'easier option' that many students think when compared to primary data collection. One might be able to do the entire project in pyjamas from the comfort of your sofa (although not necessarily a good choice for lumbar support), but therein the 'ease' of the literature review often ends. Finding, sampling, and interpreting valid and reliable literature is *not* always an easy task. As well as the potential challenges with regard to accessing relevant research (particularly bodies of research written from a non-Western prison perspective), the supervision of document-based studies still requires emotional support and advice due to the content being read about, and the particular proclivities of prison research literature. It is partly as a result of the lack of consistent engagement with details of methodological process within prison research writing that *this* book is even being written, and students who have never 'been there' or are new to research in general may easily miss the subtleties of the prison research process that can frame findings and recommendations, in the lack of detail within the word-restricted write-ups that they regularly face.

It can also be challenging for students to understand and make sense of the enormous differences between interpretations of different prisons in the same legal jurisdiction, let alone those in locations with alternative approaches to imprisonment and punishment more generally. In my own experience, having completed a mediocre critical literature-review master's dissertation looking at prison rape in South Africa, England and Wales, and the USA, I only really started to appreciate how little I knew and understood about prisons once I was well into my empirical doctoral research in a category C prison in England. Looking back on it now, I'm amused at my naïve assumption that I might be able to scratch the surface of the literature of such a topic in one jurisdiction, let alone comparing across three! As a supervisor, particularly one with prison research experience, your understanding, experiences, and reflections can prove an invaluable source of knowledge for budding students.

The Ethicality of Prison Research

The other question that we need to ask ourselves as prison researchers – a challenging question at its heart – is, ultimately, should we be researching prisons at all? Arguably, whenever we undertake research where there is no tangible benefit to the participant, yet there may be to ourselves (i.e. career progression, educational qualifications, academic reputation), we must ultimately question why we are doing it, and whether we really should. At the same time, however, it is difficult to know whether our research will actually have a tangible impact in reality – the 'impact' of social science research is remarkably hard to gauge, despite being one of the ultimate measuring tools of research excellence. In the UK, the Research Excellence Framework (REF) process has, since 2014, placed considerable stock upon notions of impact 'beyond academia' (REF, 2021: 2). In comparison to the physical sciences, social science research is much less obvious in its impact, and even where a piece of research may have real impactful implications, it is rare that the influencing research is clearly referenced in policy or practice documents!

Another key question is that of who is doing this research. As noted, the majority of published prison research is undertaken by those in the global North, situated within Western democracies, and often English speaking. Prison research from the global South is increasing (see Chapter Eight), but is still seen to be unusual – as such, the voices that are being heard within the global prison population are often highly Western in origin. Such imbalances stem from global dimensions of power, knowledge, and control within academia, as well as wider notions of ethnocentrism (Wiarda, 1981) and questions regarding the politics of knowledge production and representation (Jazeel and McFarlane, 2009). Yet these are ethical issues that result in imbalances of power and influence, and potentially allow conditions of inequality and inequity to continue. As such, questioning the origin of the voices being heard – and those that are not heard – is another ethical dimension that needs consideration when looking at (a) existing literature, (b) methodologies, (c) research designs, and (d) the conclusions we draw from our findings as researchers.

Conclusion

This chapter has attempted to map the myriad ethical dimensions of prison research, including consideration of the reasons for following ethical processes and guidelines (and what might happen if you don't); and looking in particular at some of the specific challenges posed in prisons when it comes to matters such as confidentiality, informed consent, personal security, the right to withdraw, and so on. Ethical processes, particularly when looking at prison contexts, can be challenging, frustrating, and time consuming, but they are important with regard to notions of protection (both of individuals and institutions). What is key, when considering notions of ethical restrictions, is the need to consider the well-being of everyone involved in the research process, both now and in a potential future.

Notes

1 Not that ethical issues are as easy as 'right and wrong' in many instances – but their consequences can have differing levels of potential harm.
2 It is important to give a deadline for withdrawal – otherwise you may have already begun analysis/writing/dissemination when that request comes in (albeit unlikely, giving a deadline to withdraw by is essential).

References

Andersson, K. (2022) I am not alone – we are all alone: Using masturbation as an ethnographic method in research on shota subculture in Japan. *Qualitative Research*, 14687941221096600.

Armstrong, R., Gelsthorpe, L., & Crewe, B. (2014) From paper ethics to real-world research: Supervising ethical reflexivity when taking risks in research with 'the risky'. In *Reflexivity in Criminological Research*, pp. 207–219. London: Palgrave Macmillan.

Beauchamp, T. L., & Childress, J. F. (2001) *Principles of Biomedical Ethics*, 5th edn. Oxford University Press.

Becker, H. (1967) Whose side are we on? *Social Problems*, *14*(3), 239–247.

Boudoukha, A. H., Altintas, E., Rusinek, S., Fantini-Hauwel, C., & Hautekeete, M. (2013) Inmates-to-staff assaults, PTSD and burnout: Profiles of risk and vulnerability. *Journal of Interpersonal Violence*, *28*(11), 2332–2350.

British Society of Criminology (BSC) (2015) British Society of Criminology Statement of Ethics, available at: www.britsoccrim.org/documents/BSCEthics2015.pdf

Burke, L., Millings, M., Taylor, S., & Ragonese, E. (2020) Transforming rehabilitation, emotional labour and contract delivery: A case study of a voluntary sector provider in an English resettlement prison. *International Journal of Law, Crime and Justice*, *61*, 100387.

Byrd, T. G., Cochran, J. K., Silverman, I. J., & Blount, W. R. (2000) Behind bars: An assessment of the effects of job satisfaction, job-related stress, and anxiety on jail employees' inclinations to quit. *Journal of Crime and Justice*, *23*(2), 69–93.

Christie, N. (1986) The ideal victim. In Fattah, E. A. (ed.) *From Crime Policy to Victim Policy*, pp. 17–30. Basingstoke: Palgrave Macmillan.

Cohen, S. (1972) *Folk Devils and Moral Panics*. London: MacGibbon and Kee.

Cullen, F. T., Link, B. G., Wolfe, N. T., & Frank, J. (1985) The social dimensions of correctional officer stress. *Justice Quarterly*, *2*(4), 505–533.

Dalen, K., & Jones, L. Ø. (2010) Ethical monitoring: Conducting research in a prison setting. *Research Ethics*, 6(1), 10–16.

Digard, L. (2014) Encoding risk: Probation work and sex offenders' narrative identities. *Punishment & Society*, 16(4), 428–447.

Farmer, P. (2003) *Pathologies of Power*. Berkeley: University of California Press.

Drake, D. H., & Harvey, J. (2014) Performing the role of ethnographer: Processing and managing the emotional dimensions of prison research. *International Journal of Social Research Methodology*, 17(5), 489–501.

Gariglio, L. (2016) Photo-elicitation in prison ethnography: Breaking the ice in the field and unpacking prison officers' use of force. *Crime, Media, Culture*, 12(3), 367–379.

Graf, C., Wager, E., Bowman, A., Fiack, S., Scott-Lichter, D., & Robinson, A. (2007) Best practice guidelines on publication ethics: A publisher's perspective. *International Journal of Clinical Practice*, 61(s. 152), 1–26.

Graham, S. M., Huang, J. Y., Clark, M. S., & Helgeson, V. S. (2008) The positives of negative emotions: Willingness to express negative emotions promotes relationships. *Personality and Social Psychology Bulletin*, 34(3), 394–406.

Harding, N. A. (2020). Co-constructing feminist research: Ensuring meaningful participation while researching the experiences of criminalised women. *Methodological innovations*, 13(2), 2059799120925262.

Harding, S. (1987) Introduction: Is there a feminist method? In Harding, S. (ed.) *Feminism and Methodology*. Bloomington and Indianapolis: Indiana University Press; Milton Keynes: Open University Press.

Humblet, D. (2020) Locking out emotions in locking up older prisoners? Emotional labour of Belgian prison officers and prison nurses. *International Journal of Law, Crime and Justice*, 61, 100376.

Hyun, J. K., Quinn, B. C., Madon, T., & Lustig, S. (2006) Graduate student mental health: Needs assessment and utilization of counseling services. *Journal of College Student Development*, 47(3), 247–266.

Iganski, P. (2001) Hate crimes hurt more. *American Behavioral Scientist*, 45(4), 626–638.

Jazeel, T., & McFarlane, C. (2010) The limits of responsibility: A postcolonial politics of academic knowledge production. *Transactions of the Institute of British Geographers*, 35(1), 109–124.

Jewkes, Y. (2012) Autoethnography and emotion as intellectual resources: Doing prison research differently. *Qualitative Inquiry*, 18(1), 63–75.

Justice Committee (2016) Prison safety. 16 May 2016, HC625 2015–16.

King, R. D. (2000) Doing research in prisons' in King, R. D. & Wincup, E. (eds) *Doing Research on Crime and Justice*, 1st edn. Oxford University Press.

King, R. D., & Liebling, A. (2008) Doing research in prisons. In King, R. D. & Wincup, E. (eds) *Doing Research on Crime and Justice*, 2nd edn. Oxford and New York: Oxford University Press.

Klein, D. B., & Stern, C. (2005) Professors and their politics: The policy views of social scientists. *Critical Review*, 17(3–4), 257–303.

Levine, C., Faden, R., Grady, C., Hammerschmidt, D., Eckenwiler, L., & Sugarman, J. (2004) The limitations of 'vulnerability' as a protection for human research participants. *American Journal of Bioethics*, 4(3), 44–49. Doi:10.1080/15265160490497083

Liebling, A. (1999) Doing research in prison: Breaking the silence? *Theoretical Criminology*, 3(2), 147–173.

Liebling, A. (2001) Whose side are we on? Theory, practice and allegiances in prisons research. *British Journal of Criminology*, 41(3), 472–484.

Manne, K. (2017) *Down Girl: The Logic of Misogyny*. London and New York: Penguin Books.

Michaud, S. G., & Aynesworth, H. (1999) *The Only Living Witness: The True Story of Serial Sex Killer Ted Bundy*. Texas: Authorlink.

Moolman, B. (2015) Ethnography: Exploring methodological nuances in feminist research with men incarcerated for sexual offences. In Drake, D. H., Earle, R. & Sloan, J. (eds) *The Palgrave Handbook of Prison Ethnography*, pp. 199–213. Basingstoke: Palgrave Macmillan.

Moran, D. (2012) Prisoner reintegration and the stigma of prison time inscribed on the body. *Punishment & Society*, 14(5), 564–583.

Morris, T., & Morris, P. (1963) *Pentonville: A Sociological Study of an English Prison*. London: Routledge & Kegan Paul.

National Audit Office (NAO) (2017) *Mental Health in Prisons*. Report by the Comptroller and Auditor General, HC 42, Session 2017–2019.

National Offender Management Service (NOMS) (2016) *Adult Safeguarding in Prison*. PSI 16/2015.

Nylander, P. Å., Lindberg, O., & Bruhn, A. (2011) Emotional labour and emotional strain among Swedish prison officers. *European Journal of Criminology*, 8(6), 469–483.

Oakley, A. (1981) Interviewing women: A contradiction in terms. In Roberts, H. (ed.) *Doing Feminist Research*. London: Routledge and Kegan Paul.

Pont, J. (2008) Ethics in research involving prisoners. *International Journal of Prisoner Health*, 4(4), 184–197.

Powell, K. M., & Takayoshi, P. (2003) Accepting roles created for us: The ethics of reciprocity. *College Composition and Communication*, 54(3), 394–422.

REF (Research Excellence Framework) (2021) Key facts. Available at https://www.ref.ac.uk/media/1848/ref2021_key_facts.pdf

Reiter, K. (2014) Making windows in walls: Strategies for prison research. *Qualitative Inquiry*, *20*(4), 417–428.

Robbins, J. (2013) Beyond the suffering subject: Toward an anthropology of the good. *Journal of the Royal Anthropological Institute*, *19*, 447–462.

Rozin, P., & Royzman, E. B. (2001) Negativity bias, negativity dominance, and contagion. *Personality and Social Psychology Review*, *5*(4), 296–320.

Schimmack, U. (2005) Attentional interference effects of emotional pictures: Threat, negativity, or arousal?' *Emotion*, *5*(1), 55–66.

Schlosser, J. A. (2008) Issues in interviewing inmates: Navigating the methodological landmines of prison research. *Qualitative Inquiry*, *14*(8), 1500–1525.

Schlosser, J. A. (2020) *Prison Stories: Women Scholars' Experiences Doing Research behind Bars*. Lanham, MD: Lexington Books.

Schwenzer, K. J. (2008) Protecting vulnerable subjects in clinical research: Children, pregnant women, prisoners, and employees. *Respiratory care*, *53*(10), 1342–1349.

Sloan, J. (2016) *Masculinities and the Adult Male Prison Experience*. London: Palgrave Macmillan.

Sloan, J., & Wright, S. (2015) Going in green: Reflections on the challenges of 'getting in, getting on, and getting out' for doctoral prisons researchers. In Drake, D. H., Earle, R. & Sloan, J. (eds) *The Palgrave Handbook of Prison Ethnography*, pp. 143–163. Basingstoke: Palgrave Macmillan.

Sykes, G. M. (1958) *The Society of Captives: A Study of a Maximum Security Prison*. Princeton, NJ: Princeton University Press.

Universities UK (2012) *The Concordat to Support Research Integrity*. London: Universities UK.

Vitae (2011) *Concordat to Support the Career Development of Researchers*. Available at https://www.vitae.ac.uk/policy/concordat-to-support-the-career-development-of-researchers

Waldram, J. B. (2007) Everybody has a story: Listening to imprisoned sexual offenders. *Qualitative Health Research*, *17*(7), 963–970.

Waters, J., Westaby, C., Fowler, A., & Phillips, J. (2020) The emotional labour of doctoral criminological researchers. *Methodological Innovations*, May–August.

Wiarda, H. J. (1981) The ethnocentrism of the social science implications for research and policy. *The Review of Politics*, *43*(2), 163–197.

Zhang, S. (2019) Unresolvable tensions and ethical dilemmas: Reflecting on the experience of doing 'prison research' in China: A research note. *The Prison Journal*, *99*(6), 662–682.

Six

CHOOSING METHODS

There are some key choices that one must make when undertaking a research project within the prison setting – in particular, what methods do I use and who do I apply them to? On the face of it, these questions may seem straightforward to anyone with a basic sociological methods training that tends to come with undergraduate and/or postgraduate study. Yet often research methods take on a different dimension when operating within the prison setting: interviews and focus groups have problems of security and interpersonal politics attached which are magnified by incarceration; surveys are problematic when considering literacy and linguistic problems experienced by prisoners; and ethnographic routes require additional security, the potential need to carry keys, and associated risks and responsibilities. Not all methods may be viable, but it is important to remember that 'All methodologies contribute to our knowledge, and, when put together like pieces of a puzzle, they offer a clearer picture' (Caprioli, 2004: 257). In this chapter, we examine these extra dimensions which prison adds to standard research methods, as well as the importance of reflection and introspection on the researcher identity when undertaking such a task.

The Literature-Based Approach to Prison Research

Whilst the majority of discussions around prison research methods focus on the practicalities and problems of being within a prison setting, in reality, many scholars undertake desk-based research

DOI: 10.4324/9781315297217-6

prior to (as part of a literature review) – or instead of – entering the prison estate. The literature-based approach is not easy or without its own emotional labour: there is only so long that you can read about things before they start to affect your moods and subconscious. Indeed, the cumulative effect of reading multiple traumatic reports has been noted to have serious impacts on well-being (Guerzoni, 2020; Moran and Asquith, 2020). In practice, literature-based prison research can often have its own challenges as a result of the penal context, given the potentially secretive and security-conscious nature of the topic, and the lack of discussion about some of the more 'hidden' elements of prisons and prison research processes. That said, there is a wealth of information out there in terms of prison policy documents and annual reports which can be an invaluable view into the functioning of the prison.

PRISON POLICY DOCUMENTS: MINES, CULTURAL OBJECTS AND AGENTS

Louise Brangan

What sorts of insight can be yielded from a prison report? How can it help us understand the nature of prisons and penal power? Annual reports should also be read as instruments that frame and reframe a government's penal power. However, my research – a comparative and historical study of imprisonment regimes in Ireland and Scotland from 1970 – pushed me to reconsider how I was analysing and using the annual prison report as evidence, and the lessons I took from this are certainly relevant to people interested in penal policy more generally. Ireland and Scotland are close historical, cultural, and geographical neighbours, yet how they imprisoned people changed over time and significantly differed from each other. In explaining these divergences and transformations I came to rely on the annual prison report as a window into the internal logic of government, seeing it as a reflection of (1) socio-cultural sensibilities of the policymaking worlds that manage, change, and order prisons, and (2) as a governing tool which is a material expression of penal power.

We rightly dig through the annual report for statistics. But the annual report is not merely a neutral representation of hard facts. Entwined with the stats and metrics, the annual report presents a narrative of who prison is for and why it is justified. Reading annual prison reports comparatively I was confronted by starkly different social and cultural narratives. I began to ask: how were prisoners represented, what sorts of metaphors and taken for granted social conventions were embedded in seemingly straightforward prisoner categories? For example, in Scotland in the 1970s long-term was an objective prisoner category, but this category was also understood as containing those prisoners felt to be the most recalcitrant and vexatious members of Scotland's perceived underclass, with regular dismissive references made to their likely communities of origins. A full social narrative of their dangerousness and its sources became visible, and often justified the extreme uses of segregative control that characterised Scottish prison regimes. Thus the annual reports affirmed a narrative of prisoners' criminality that legitimised and/or denied certain kinds of penal interventions for certain kinds of prisoners. It was these conventions of socio-cultural order, regularised in annual reports, that were drawn on to justify divergent conventions of prison practice in Ireland and Scotland.

In addition to enforcing the social and cultural narratives that shape prison regimes, an annual report should also be read as an instrument that frames and reframes a government's penal power. One way of examining this is to read the report as a material representation of state power. The prison report may be a relatively standard feature of modern governments, but how it looks and the order it takes has not been static across the twentieth century. For example, I found that the most dramatic moments of prison transformation in Ireland and Scotland could be literally seen in the changing physical format of prison reports. The sometimes home-printed look and irregular reporting style of previous publications were replaced by sleek, glossy A4 documents. Without having to literally read their content or narrative framing, these documents sent viscerally attainable signals demonstrating new practices of penal administration. Moreover, and critically, these newly polished reports helped reinforce and standardise an extension of penal power in both jurisdictions, which in turn changed how prisons were presented, perceived, and internally ordered.

Therefore, the annual report constructs as much as it reveals and should not merely be mined for numbers. The annual prison report represents the making and implementation of penal taxonomies, codified beliefs, the construction of facts, clusters of moral codes, and the strengthening of penal authority. Viewed materially and culturally, penal policy reports can help us explain why we incarcerate in the way we do, and why that differs between places and changes over time.

In addition to current policy and practice, there is also a wealth of information about sites of confinement to be found within historical documents. Prisons and punishment have a rich history, and this temporal dimension to the penal estate is, by its very nature, seated within the literature and/or archival data. It is unlikely that anyone undertaking research on the early processes of punishment and incarceration will set foot within an active prison as part of the project (although they may well visit sites of historical interest which were formerly used as sites of incarceration as part of the penal tourism estate [see Chapter Two]). Yet it is vital that we recognise the importance of these methods for understanding the here and now of prisons.

As Godfrey notes, 'Crime historians tend not to publish books about methodology' (2012: 159) (although this has recently been remedied somewhat by the work of penal historian Ashley Rubin, particularly her outstanding 2021 book *Rocking Qualitative Social Science: An Irreverent, Practical Guide to Rigorous Research* – an utterly brilliant addition to the research methods literature which I would strongly recommend). Yet there is a growing collection of penal historians who are increasingly finding historical and archival data which is of great use in understanding today's prisons and prisoners. Godfrey highlights some of the key developments in crime history methodologies to be the huge growth in sources available; the 'overlapping of current historical enquiries into the late twentieth century' (2012: 170); the plentiful amount of comparative research across places, times and cultures; the emerging notion of the importance of ethical practice in crime history methods; and 'the coming together of crime history and criminology into a form where each can be understood by the other and a common methodological foundation can be built between historical and social science research' (2012: 171). Such developments indicate a healthy growth of research and discourse on prison history, and make it extremely important to recognise some of the challenges and practices of undertaking such a project.

Rubin's Qualitative Social Science book is original in the way that it is inclusive in the integration of archival processes within more general fieldwork discussions. As Rubin notes, 'people don't *usually* call archival work fieldwork' (2021: 251), yet including such an approach in discussions of research processes more generally does help one to see the importance in thinking logically about research proposals, and asking the right questions of the data, regardless of where it originates. Sampling questions (2021: 136–137), the impact of the Hawthorne effect and need to test results (2021: 154–156), and the importance of fieldnotes (2021: 262–264) are all practically the same in archival and non-archival field research. Indeed, the emotional side of fieldwork is equally applicable to the archival research method – Rubin describes the chain of chance events that had to occur in order for one book to sit before her within an archive to be 'humbling' (2021: 234), and it is impossible to disconnect the fact that real human beings created these documents and told these stories.

PRISONS FROM HISTORICAL PERSPECTIVES

Ashley Rubin

I study prisons, but mostly from historical perspectives. While I would love to be able to study people who are currently living and working in prisons, I've never been able to get access to prisons for research purposes. Although a lot of my scholar friends have been more successful at this, I've mostly stopped trying to get access. Instead, I've built up my research agenda around my main interest, prison history.

I love recreating things that happened in the past and trying to understand what life was like for reformers, prison administrators, and prisoners, especially in the nineteenth century. I am also interested in understanding why different styles or modes of punishment were popular at different times and how their popularity can be traced to large-scale developments in society, like the Enlightenment or the American Revolution, or to smaller-scale happenings like personality conflicts among prison administrators or between prison administrators and reformers.

While I am enamoured by history, I do not really have formal training in history, beyond my undergraduate history major and a few seminars during grad school. When I first went on a research trip to an archive in Philadelphia, I received very little advice other than "Bring a knit hat; archives get cold." At the time, there was also little advice online. So I approached the archive with the only qualitative methods training I had at the time – in ethnography. It turned out to be great, and not too different from how real historians approach the archives. It's also how I had been analysing my other data – archival documents that were available online.

My main ethnographic strategy was taking fieldnotes in a Word document. My fieldnotes document always included the date (so I could see the progress of my thoughts), a note about what documents I planned to and did request from the archivists, and then my notes and/or transcriptions of these documents. I didn't transcribe whole documents usually, just the parts that were really relevant. My thoughts on these documents ranged from my own surprise or glee at a particular find, to puzzlement, to speculation, to actual analysis. In the morning before going into the archive, I'd re-read my notes from the day before and pull out particularly noteworthy developments or themes and write short memos about them.

> Back from the archive, I continued to use this fieldnote strategy while I also used atlas.ti (content analysis software) to systematically code other documents. These were documents I had collected online – annual reports of the prison I studied that had been scanned and made available by Google – or that I had requested from other archives as microfilm that I scanned. This systematic analysis let me see trends over time, and across different prison administrators, and catalogue concrete events. The more I researched, the better my memos became, piecing together insights by triangulating across types of documents (e.g., the wardens' private diaries, a reform organisation's meeting minutes, the annual reports).
>
> While I know there are holes in the historical record, in the end, I am pretty confident in what I was able to assemble from these different resources and with the ethnographer's toolbox.

The human dimension to archival and documentary work raises an issue around processes of ethics, which is another area where there has been a perceived disconnection between historical and non-archival research processes. Richardson and Godfrey (2003) raise the point that the use of transcribed interviews in archives has implications around notions of informed consent, confidentiality, and the implications of the 'more distant and more tenuous' (2003: 348) responsibilities and relationships between the reader and the research participant, compared to those ties between the interviewer and participant at the time of data collection.

Ethics and ethicality have been discussed already in Chapter Five, but it is important to revisit the need to think ethically in the processes of choosing methods and participants for a research study on prisons: indeed, just because one's research choices do not involve directly talking to individuals, does not mean that the voices and stories told to others are 'fair game' and any less worthy of ethical protection. If anything, the fact that an individual's voice is being used for a purpose other than that originally intended, and they don't have the option to rebut contentions, or say no to the use of their data, adds an additional layer of vulnerability and fragility to the individual which is worthy of the highest respect and consideration.

HISTORICAL PRISON RESEARCH

Tony Murphy[1]

The nature of research on prisons/imprisonment varies according to the time period of interest. Contemporary work, or that focused on the recent decades, normally affords the ability to directly engage with serving or former prisoners (through interview work for example), and the record-keeping associated with prisons is now clearly very dense. This means that it is possible to capture crucial aspects of imprisonment and experiences of it in a way not directly available for previous eras. This is despite there being issues relating to modern prison research, including 'access,' the sheer amount of data out there and the decision-making this dictates for a researcher, the closure rules, and so on. Historical prison research presents several additional challenges because the subject matter (prisoners), are no longer able to engage with your research (depending on how far back you want to go), and processes of record-keeping and administrative bureaucracy were less robust in the past. It was not until the nineteenth century that record-keeping became somewhat standardised and inclusive of the sorts of aspects of prisoners' lives that we now take for granted within our record-keeping.

The development of the penitentiary in that period, and indeed Australian convictism, helped to forge the proliferation and use of information: arguably, the Australian convict records were in the vanguard of this, according to Maxwell-Stewart (2016). Indeed, the transportation system was closely linked to the development of the modern prison system in Britain (see Murphy, 2021). The proliferation of record-keeping in this period coincided with a wider movement towards the creation of nominal and institutional records, and wider bureaucracy. However, prisons served several functions in the past; prior to the late eighteenth and early nineteenth centuries when prisons became primarily a means of punishment for crime, imprisonment was commonly used, for example, as a means of holding people awaiting trial, and for holding debtors. Thus, different types of prison existed, including gaols, bridewells, and debtors' prisons. Therefore, researching prisons of the past does not always entail studying convicted criminals.

A series of sources exist which enable a researcher to grapple with the nature of imprisonment in the past. Historical records on prisons became denser and more consistent over time, and there was a significant shift forward from the beginning of the nineteenth century. Of course, the early modern prisons generated records, but these were limited in scope, and they have poor survival rates. Records can tell us something about the numbers sent to prison, the sentences they faced, the broad nature of the penal regimes experienced, and so on. Plus, records can also offer insight into the ways in which prisoners experienced their sentence (at group or individual levels), the conduct of prisoners during sentence, the routines and disciplinary practices they lived, and even the early life and post-sentence life of a convict. The latter is linked to the research strategy of record-linkage. Biographical or autobiographical accounts of individual prisoner lives are also an important route to 'getting at' prison lives of the past. For example, Priestley's seminal text on the subject (1999) explores many features and aspects of prison life during the Victorian era, primarily based on the writings of prisoners themselves.

Crone's *Guide to the Criminal Prisons of Nineteenth-Century England* offers a detailed statistical and archival overview of those prisons, on a level hitherto not offered (Crone, 2018). Historical prison research can be facilitated by the court and prison records; parliamentary papers; diaries, letters, and autobiography; newspapers or periodicals which circulated information on offending and court cases; and in the case of life-course analysis, sources relating to employment, marriage, birth, and death. The National Archives is important within much of this (it has physical and digital resources to explore), so too are bespoke criminal justice related digitised resources, such as the *Digital Panopticon* and the *Old Bailey Online*. Genealogy sites are also useful, including *Ancestry and Findmypast*. There can be some problems with digital sources, for example, the *Digital Panopticon* and the *Old Bailey Online* perpetuate a London-focus of criminal justice research owing to the data they hold, when in fact there is a wider wealth of records on local prisons for researchers to use. In the context of this, Crone (2018) offers a call to arms of sorts for more regional work.

In addition to archival and policy data, there is also a wide variety of quantitative data sets available for use in research. Official data may be publicly available or subject to certain restrictions on access, and researchers should be wary and consider the methodologies used and ethical principles followed in the generation of that data. The definition of different concepts needs careful consideration, especially if the use of this quantitative data is being combined with other methodologies through triangulation or the use of mixed methods approaches. Another method of desk-based data collection is the use of online resources. Indeed, Novisky, Narvey and Semenza undertook a study to assess correctional responses to Covid-19 in the USA, using 'a manual web-based data scraping methodology' (2020: 1248), generating both qualitative and quantitative data. Whilst they collected a huge amount of fascinating data, they were subject to the deficiencies of individual state data provision: information that they needed was often missing from websites and thus beyond their control.

In-Prison Methods and the Incarceration Dimension

There are numerous methodological issues encountered by virtue of entering the prison setting that add to the complexity of already challenging methods. In this section, I consider each potential method and the associated prison-centric complexities. It should be noted that there are many generic methodology texts that can give in-depth details about the challenges and advantages of each methodological approach: Bryman's *Social Research Methods* (2016) is one of my favourites, along with Crow and Semmens' *Researching Criminology* (2007), and, of course, Rubin's *Rocking Qualitative Social Science* (2021). In addition, for those wishing to combine more than one approach, there are extremely useful texts about how to triangulate (Denzin, 1970) and how to undertake mixed methods in a systematic manner in the criminological context (Heap and Waters, 2019).

Interviews

Jennifer Schlosser makes the point that 'from beginning to end, the process of interviewing inmates is a powerful one' (2008: 1522). Indeed, the one-on-one basis of the individual interview provides an excellent opportunity for the individual prisoner to get to know the researcher, and vice versa. When speaking to those in prisons, this can bring some key challenges with regard to power and security within the prison. Oakley (1981), with regard to the feminist approach to interviewing, advocates reciprocity in the interview context; that there should not be a power imbalance between respondent and researcher, which is inherent in the traditional interview process where the researcher 'takes' from the researched with little to no benefit. Whilst this approach makes assumptions about notions of power in interview relationships, it does raise the issue that, in prisons, reciprocity is problematic to say the least.

Another key issue when undertaking interviews is the challenge of finding a location that is private, secure, and suitable for undertaking an interview. A balance must be maintained between personal safety within contexts of confinement (depending on the prison type and risk level), and the privacy that all researchers strive for when trying to maintain levels of confidentiality and protection. When I was doing my doctoral research in prison, the roll call became a well-known part of the daily routine – tracking where prisoners are, and who they are with is a foregone conclusion: the prison will know that an individual is talking to you (albeit not what they are saying). Such a limitation of perfect privacy needs some form of engagement – even if just an acknowledgment of the limitations of privacy that can move from the carceral context into the research relationship.

That said, interviews within prison are common – individuals will often meet with their offender managers, or psychologists, etc., to discuss their personal progress. There are likely to be facilities that can be used for interviews – although the researcher may have to give priority to the arguably more important meetings that are going on between prison staff and prisoners. If you can get access to such facilities, it is important to remember the context of the room that you are in – your research participant is likely to have encountered it in the context of their sentence planning, or another form of carceral control imposed upon them by the institution. Even if not, remember that almost every prisoner will have undergone an interview in the past – with the police. I was reminded of this when one of my participants noted the similarities between our research interview and the police interview that led to them going to prison, when I asked if I could record their interview.

Time can also be an issue – commonly, there are few practical time constraints on the interview process – if it is going well, and everyone is happy, the interview can go on for a longer than anticipated period of time. Yet in the prison, this is much more difficult to achieve – roll calls, routines and the tight control of prison time means that interviews often have to stick within constricted time frames, after which an individual must go on to what is dictated by the regime. Although this can be flexible sometimes, it is something that needs to be considered within the practicalities of interviewing in prisons.

Interviews can generate enormous amounts of data and knowledge, depending on what you ask, how you ask it, what order you ask the questions in, and, vitally important, how comfortable the participant is with you as a researcher *and* how comfortable you are with the participant. Do what you can to be comfortable and confident going into the interview situation – make sure you are organized, but be open to things taking a turn in a direction you don't expect, and be aware that you may need to rethink your questions and how/when you ask them on the spot: terminology may need explanation or definition, the question may need explanation, and you might be taken down a route that you weren't expecting.[2] Make sure you are aware of the interview beyond the words: consider the body language, eye contact and other non-verbal cues that might also be inherent in the interaction. Whilst feminist scholars argue for reciprocity, this is something you may want to think through before entering the interview: how much of yourself are you willing and able to share? As Schlosser notes, 'as active participants in the narrative construction process, researchers [...] will need to think critically about the roles we play and our influences on the final product' (2008: 1522). And remember to be respectful and interested in what your participant tells you: they are telling you their story, giving you their information and data – it is their gift to give.

Focus Groups

Contrary to the one-to-one interview, the focus group allows the researcher to discuss research questions with a number of participants all at once, getting the benefit of interpersonal dynamics and social discussions. In the non-prison setting, this is a challenging research tool to use effectively. Within prison, there are substantial associated issues, including interpersonal dynamics between people in prison – as Dresler-Hawke and Vaccarino note, 'it is unlikely that an outside researcher will know the dynamics within the prison, and also the specific dynamics which exist between and within groups throughout a particular prison' (2010: 172–173). There are numerous other ethical implications that follow from undertaking focus groups within prisons – not least the fact that one's personal data and views cannot be fully retracted after the event: other people will have heard any disclosures, and although they may not be used as data for the research, they are still 'out there' (Dresler-Hawke and Vaccarino, 2010).

There are also security dimensions – focus groups can be resource-intensive for the institution if staff are needed to maintain a security presence due to the numbers of prisoners in one room. There are also aspects of prison politics and interpersonal dynamics that can wreak havoc with a focus group (and potentially have serious security implications). What if one of your participants is officially classed as a 'vulnerable' prisoner who is currently being segregated from the general prison population for safety reasons? Or if you wish to speak to a group of staff who are working on different shift patterns? Arguably the dynamics of conversations will depend hugely on who is in the group and their associated identities. This also raises the issue of confidentiality being limited within such groups – whilst it is commonly understood that confidentiality cannot easily be maintained within a focus group setting amongst participants, this potentially takes on new dimensions of seriousness when discussing more sensitive topics within prison focus groups. That said, focus groups are not actually that alien to the prison setting – many offending behaviour courses involve group work and discussion which functions very similarly to a research focus group. In addition, it is common to establish ground rules within the focus group around matters of confidentiality and care (Buck, Tomczak and Quinn, 2022). As such, despite the challenges that appear to be imposed on focus groups, their use within prisons is not uncommon and has actually yielded some rich data through group dialogue in numerous contexts (see Pollack, 2003; Walter, 2017; Nurse, Woodcock and Ormsby, 2003; Woodall, Dixey and South, 2013; Woodall and Tattersfield, 2017).

FOCUS GROUPS IN PRISONS

James Woodall

Focus groups are frequently used in prison research studies and a useful way of encouraging participation and accessing rich and insightful data (Maycock, Meek and Woodall, 2020). They are also used during prison inspection processes as a way of ascertaining the lived perspective of prison life (Woodall, Freeman and Warwick-Booth, 2021). Focus groups are particularly appropriate when the research intends to explore phenomena using a series of open-ended questions. It enables research participants to explore the issues of importance to them, in their own vocabulary, generating their own questions and pursuing their own priorities (Kitzinger, 1995). Studies have shown the usefulness of focus group discussions with all constituents of the prison, including: prisoners, prison staff, and prisoners' families (Dixey and Woodall, 2012). My own research has been enriched through focus groups, through hearing shared concerns of prison life and highlighting where there are inconsistencies in experiences. Although not designed in this way, focus groups have also offered, albeit for a short time period, the opportunity for mutual support and the sharing of solutions to overcome challenges. Tangible examples included a focus group with a group of prisoners' families who openly discussed their approaches to managing anxiety prior to a prison visit. Such strategies were of benefit to those families who were new to prison visiting.

Hollander (2004) describes the concepts of 'problematic silences' and 'problematic speech' during focus group discussions which resonates in prison research. Problematic silences occur when participants do not share their experiences or viewpoints within the group and instead withhold their own point of view and perspective. In my own experiences this has been rare – people in prison do want to share their story and generally want to create a 'better' system for others. That said, people in prison may be reticent to share personal information, especially when the levels of trust are low in the group and where people in prison can be wary and concerned with the presentation they give of themselves. In contrast, problematic speech occurs when participants offer opinions that do not represent their true beliefs. Problematic speech often arises when there are pressures to conform, thereby leading participants to adjust their contributions to match others or when participants feel an expectation to offer information that they think the researcher wants to hear (Hollander, 2004). This has occurred in my own research with young people in prison. It has been a feature of prison research for some time, as noted in Sykes' (1958: 135) seminal work:

> the observer is constantly in peril of being 'conned' by highly articulate, glib prisoners ... Such inmates are quite ready to

talk – in fact, they are far too ready – and the observer must make a great effort to shake loose and to get at their more reticent, inarticulate fellow captives.

The skill of the focus group facilitator is paramount in any situation, but perhaps most of all in prison environments. This includes both the skills in facilitating open discussion and dialogue and embracing areas of tension or disagreement, plus the skills and abilities it is necessary to employ before the focus group discussion to secure appropriate access and ethical permissions. On both of these points, focus group size and composition is an important factor when designing research studies. In order to ensure people in prison can participate fully in the dialogue and discussion and feel fully heard, it is sometimes helpful to have fewer (e.g. 6–8 participants) people involved. Moreover, and depending on the topic being discussed, prison life can be an emotive subject and so ensuring there is clear guidance on confidentiality, and ensuring appropriate support is in place should any issues arise as a result of the discussion, is paramount.

Similarly to interviews, it is vital that you are organised, and aware of both the verbal and non-verbal elements within the focus group: indeed, body language can tell you a lot about how individuals within the focus group see and relate to each other. With a focus group, however, this is even more complex, so you may wish to include more than one observer/researcher to undertake these groups (if resources allow). Filming said groups has huge advantages in terms of returning to recordings in order to see who is saying what and to see those non verbal cues, but the practical, legal, security, and ethical dimensions to taking a video camera into a prison setting may well prevent this from being a viable option – so another pair of eyes and ears can be invaluable. Due to there being more than one individual in the room, security might be more hands-on, and you may have a prison officer in the room with you: these are things that need to be discussed and negotiated at an early stage in the research discussion with the prison so that you know what to expect and what are potential limits to confidentiality, and so that the prison also knows the potential resource implications of the focus groups.

Questionnaires/Surveys

Surveys or questionnaires are an extremely common form of prison research – indeed, His Majesty's Chief Inspector of Prisons (HMCIP) runs an annual 'Stakeholder Survey' (https://www.justiceinspectorates.gov.uk/hmiprisons/about-hmi-prisons/stakeholder-survey/). Surveys enable a potentially large number of individuals to be accessed at the same time in a quick and easy (and relatively low cost) manner, and do not require high levels of resource to administer, complete or collect: in theory they can be completed in the 'privacy' of an individual's cell or office space. Yet there are some caveats to this seemingly straightforward method, not least the fact that one cannot take for granted levels of language, literacy, and comprehension within participant populations. If your participants are Foreign Nationals, this may require additional translation processes (which in turn is tricky when trying to achieve equivalence in meaning across different languages); and if there are disabilities or reading impairments, these also need consideration.

The nature of surveys has also changed substantially over the past few years, with a general movement to online which makes for fast dissemination and easier data processing into data sets. Such digital processes cannot be assumed in the prison context, where access to technology is limited and restricted – chances are, if you are surveying prisoners, you may well need to do it on paper. And provide a pen. In such instances, you also need to consider how you plan to tell potential participants about, and disseminate these surveys, and how you plan to collect them when completed. A box for individuals to return surveys at their own convenience may not be the most secure option, and asking staff to collect them for you is resource intensive and potentially undermines principles of confidentiality if not managed effectively.

In some contexts, however, computer-assisted self-administered interviews (CASI) have been used – these are particularly useful when asking sensitive questions: it is a key method used in the USA to understand sex in prisons (see, for example, Struckman-Johnson, C., Struckman-Johnson, D., Rucker, Bumby and Donaldson, 1996; Wolff, Blitz, Shi, Bachman and Siegel, 2006). Tourangeau and Smith found that such computer-assisted self administration tools enhanced participant willingness to admit potentially embarrassing information (1996: 299 – see also Weinrott and Saylor, 1991), and others have reported benefits from the removal of interviewer effects and social desirability bias with enhanced confidentiality and accessibility for low literacy populations through the use of colour coding and audio (Kauffman and Kauffman, 2011). Similarly, Newman et al. (2002) found enhanced reporting of 'stigmatized behaviours' with computerised mechanisms, but that there were issues when discussing certain topics:

> It appears that the process of collecting information regarding depression is facilitated by the face-to-face interview process. It is possible that 'impersonality' bias for particular types of question does, in fact, exist. Respondents may underreport to the computer because the impersonal nature of a computer interview is incongruent with the personal nature of questions regarding one's emotional or mental health.
>
> *(2002: 296)*

As such, the particular aspect of research topic must be balanced carefully against the choice to use computerised methods of interaction (as well as choice of method – surveys or interviews, for instance). Sometimes there is nothing better than face-to-face interaction – indeed, in one Chinese study looking at suicidal ideation in prisons, while a self-report questionnaire was used for the majority of participants, 'for those who were illiterate or had trouble comprehending the content of the questionnaire (approximately 6%), research personnel collected the data by interviewing them' (Zhang, Liang, Zhou and Brame, 2010: 966).

It is important to remember that, as surveys are relatively quick and easy, they are used fairly frequently within prisons, which does run the risk of their over-use and research fatigue. Prisoners in particular are constantly subject to questions and form filling, and thus may not be excited at the chance to fill out yet another survey that seemingly has no immediate benefit to them. Prison staff too have many other priorities and pieces of paperwork to complete, and visitors have other priorities. As such, making yourself more than simply a name on a sheet can be extremely valuable, as can making yourself known to gatekeepers and participants (which also adds to the level of information available when making the decision to participate or not).

Arguably one of the most well known and impactful surveys developed in England is that of Alison Liebling with Helen Arnold on *Prisons and Their Moral Performance* (Liebling, 2004). This project aimed to look at the measurement of the quality of life in prisons, and used appreciative inquiry (using interviews and workgroups as a starting point), followed by:

> the development and administration of a detailed quality of life survey [...] We worked closely with groups of staff and prisoners in the identification of themes for the survey, trying to 'imagine' each prison at its best, drawing on experiences of 'appropriate treatment' and agreeing a set of dimensions each group would wish to see reflected in any attempt to measure it.
>
> *(2004: 133)*

The generation of questions from those who have a stake in the potential findings and who live with the experiences being measured on a day-to-day basis is rather beautiful and insightful – an example of the way that appreciative inquiry can really help the researcher to work 'with' the researched.

As with all surveys, it is important to think carefully about the practicalities: How many questions? How will they be phrased and defined? What order should they go in? Do they make sense? Are there too many questions/long answers? Do any scales used make sense? Do you want to generate quantitative data, qualitative data, or both? You may want to pilot the survey to get some feedback on how it works in practice before using it on your valuable participants! Indeed, you may also want to consider if the very process of undertaking a survey in prison is a subject for academic consideration in its own right – Azbel et al. (2016) undertook the first bio-behavioural survey in prisons in the Former Soviet Union – in

Ukraine – and in addition, also undertook interviews to assess 'the barriers and facilitators' to doing such research, talking to 'research coordinators, research assistants, and prison administrators before the start of research, mid-way through the study, and upon its completion' (2016: 79). They found methodological challenges at the respondent level, staff level, and institutional level, but found that one key element of successful research for them was 'dialogue and culturally sensitive planning. This requires a delicate balance between honouring the stringent rules of these institutions and upholding scientific ethics in an environment that breeds significant challenges to providing healthcare' (2016: 85).

Observations

Observations in prison settings are often occurring without our even realising it as researchers. The very act of entering a prison environment stimulates our senses to see, hear, smell and feel the prison. Even if it is not a noted methodological choice, our observations of the prison that we experience in the process of entering the prison site can inform how we interpret and understand other forms of data that are collected. Keeping a research diary is invaluable in such cases.

Prisons are sites of surveillance: observation lies at their very heart. Prisoners are used to being the subject of observation by staff, other prisoners, and visitors, and often police their behaviour accordingly within public spaces. Crewe, Warr, Bennett and Smith (2014) note the fact that 'prisons have a distinctive kind of emotional geography, with zones in which certain kinds of emotional feelings and displays are more or less acceptable' (2014: 56): this is important to recognise when undertaking observations within the prison, as where you are in the prison can completely change the way an individual behaves.

Although prisons are sites of observation and surveillance, this does not necessarily mean that your research observations will be normalised – far from it. The fact that everyone watches everyone else so much means that a new observer will also be fairly quickly observed (at which point, the value of insider research can come into its own!). The value ascribed to a particular audience viewing an individual can be huge and extremely influential on the behaviours manifested: the 'audience that matters' (Sloan, 2016: 168) can strongly influence masculine behaviours, for instance. The other issue is the inherent secrecy within sites of confinement – even if you can get access into this 'social "black site": physically located outside of our communities, invisible to the public and the researcher alike' (Reiter, 2014: 417), the very door of a cell can shut out (or in) the observer from the reality of what is going on behind those doors.[3]

When undertaking observation, there are a number of practicalities that need to be considered. How and when will you take field notes? Will you do this in front of people, or slip away and record your observations in private? Are there potential implications of this choice (will it look a bit weird if you keep disappearing to the loo – if that is even possible in the area of the prison you may be observing?) Will you remember everything if you don't write it down straight away? Will your notebook and note taking change the situation (even sitting in the office spaces away from prisoners, staff commented on the fact that my note taking made me look like I was paparazzi). Also, what are you observing? And don't forget to go beyond just what you see – think too about what you can hear, smell, feel, and taste!

Mixed Methods Prison Research

Many will want to use more than one methodological approach to maximise the time available in such a hard to access setting. Indeed, as Webb notes, 'every data-gathering class – interviews, questionnaires, observation, performance records, physical evidence – is potentially biased and has specific to it certain validity threats' (Webb, 1970: 451). Indeed, mixed methods research theory is becoming more and more important within contemporary methodological fora, as people are beginning to acknowledge that mixed methods is more complex than merely designing a research project that contains multiple methods and bringing them together. I'm afraid I don't have the space to go into this theory in detail, but would strongly recommend Heap and Waters (2019) again for those looking for more detail.

In simple terms, triangulation is an important aspect to undertaking research using more than one method, theory or data set – as Lokdam, Stavseth and Bukten found, undertaking triangulation allowed 'tangible inputs on the strengths and limitations of a study sample and can be a feasible method to investigate the external validity of survey data' (2021: 140; see also Hancock and Raeside, 2009). The interesting thing about triangulation in prison research is that it is often not directly acknowledged despite its prevalence – even when a single formal method is in use, it is often supplemented by additional informal data, such as from personal reflection on the prison setting, be that due to prisons being sites of difference for those to whom the environment is 'alien'; or due to researchers being 'insiders' and/or part of the 'convict criminology' community. We regularly use our own reflections on the research setting and/or process to add depth to our interpretations of the data we have generated, and similarly use our data to attempt to make some kind of sense of our own reflections upon our experiences, especially within the field of prison ethnography, where a degree of immersion in the prison is necessitated methodologically. Triangulation is almost always there, albeit often implemented holistically rather than formally, which might lead purists to question the methodological rigour of such triangulation processes. Like many aspects of prison methodological practice, it is often another detail left under-examined in publications, in favour of the juicy data we really want to know about.

A Collection of Methods: Ethnography

Ethnography is the most basic form of social research – and resembles the way in which people ordinarily make sense of their world. Sometimes this is regarded as its major strength and sometimes this has been regarded as its major weakness. It can include observation, participation, interviewing, and almost any other form of interaction between ourselves, the researchers, and the social world. The critique of ethnography is that it is messy.

(Liebling, 2001: 471)

PRISON ETHNOGRAPHY

Ben Crewe

In their 1988 article, 'Mind Games,' Kathleen McDermott and Roy King note that 'Although staff and prisoners felt that we would not fully appreciate it, they were agreed that life in prison is essentially life on the landings' (1988: 359). For the novice prison researcher, this statement needs some clarification. In my first major research project – an ethnography of a medium-security prison – I spent much of my time worrying that the action was happening some-where else. Life on the wings was typically dull and eventless, with almost no action of the kind that I had expected to characterise prison life, though really I knew so little about prisons at that point that I am not sure what action I was expecting: fights, perhaps, or outbursts of emotion, exuberant social interactions or flurries of trading activity. Such things happen of course, but very irregularly. Imprisonment is characterised more by inaction than by the sharp punctuations that the term 'action' suggests. But being present on the landings is invaluable because so much of what matters in prisons takes place in and through the apparently banal interac-tions between and among prisoners and staff. With experience, it becomes much easier to recognise the significance of minor pleas-antries, an arm around a shoulder, or the widespread wearing of flip flops, all of which reveal something about institutional culture, staff–prisoner relationships, and the flow of power.

At the same time, much of what is important to prisoners oc-curs elsewhere. Many of the most fruitful research encounters take place beyond the wings and landings, in visits rooms or educa-tion corridors, which provide alternative zones for the expression of selfhood and emotion. Other spaces of significance – such as cells – are almost impossible to observe, yet widespread cell-sharing in England & Wales means that it is within these semi-private do-mains that the experience of imprisonment is determined. One reason, then, why in-depth interviews are such a key method within prison research is that they enable a form of access to these otherwise impenetrable places and dynamics, as well as to the internal deliberations – about how to navigate the prison environment, about external relationships, and about the offence itself – that take up so much headspace. Prisoners' public narratives and conversations represent only the sharp tip: so much of their identities and preoccupations is beneath the surface.

Within the interview room, what matters most is to be affectively present: fully focussed on the interviewee, in a way that communicates a sincere interest in their experience. Good interviewers find a way to combine courage with sensitivity, so that they are willing to wade into emotional complexity and ask probing questions (or live with silences), but do so with an ethical sensibility that recognises the limit points of these practices. Little of this can be taught, and, in any case, I am not a great fan of 'technique-ing' the interview, because it is so inconsistent with the kind of authentic engagement which is at the heart of person-centred research. For me, a key part of this engagement is also treating my research participants as collaborators in the process of working things out, able to reflect on and refine the hunches and emerging theories that I often raise within these exchanges.

For those of us who have not lived or worked in prisons, ethnography, a method Ben Crewe is well known for (Crewe, 2012), is one way to attempt to get a flavour of what it is like to be in that world for a sustained period of time, and has arguably started to dominate the field of prison research in the British context at least (see Drake, Earle and Sloan, 2015). Getting access to undertake a degree of immersion in the prison context is a real privilege, and the methodological challenges can be complex: you have all the challenges of the individual methods (as considered above – and these then need to be interpreted together[4]) in combination with the fact that you are spending a sustained period of time in the prison, which is emotionally laborious and can require additional considerations, such as researcher identity: if you are to become a part of the institution (albeit temporary and transitory), what identity are you going to embody? What security considerations do you need to take into account? Will you need keys? Will you need constant supervision/escort from area to area? How do you want to be seen by your participants? These matters are not to be taken for granted: ethnographic experiences range from insider ethnographers who are a formal part of the institution in some form (Bennett, 2015; Carr; 2015; Harvey, 2015; Davies, 2015) to those who enter the prison setting intending to experience life as close to those incarcerated as possible:

> I have accompanied public defenders, human rights advocates and senior government officials to prison, slept in prison, taught in prison, run a focus group in prison, participated in therapeutic activities in prison, had my hair cut and beard trimmed in prison, sat on cell bunks talking about philosophy and religion in prison, and more generally spent many hours hanging out with prison inmates, guards, governors and administrators.
>
> *(Darke, 2018: 32)*

Even if one may hope to achieve such levels of unfettered access, it is not a given that the institution will allow (or want) you to undertake such work: the level of access you may be afforded will depend on a variety of different factors including the location of the prison; security level of those incarcerated; legal and policy provisions; and potentially your identity, such as age and sex. That said, ethnography is being used extremely effectively across the world to understand prison life – in Bangladesh (Mehta, 2014), Brazil (Darke, 2018), India (Bandyopadhyay, 2010), Iran (Anaraki, 2021), Myanmar, (Gaborit, 2020), Nicaragua (Weegels, 2020), Norway (Ugelvik, 2014), Portugal (Cunha, 2020), Peru (Bracco Bruce, 2020), Sierra Leone (Schneider, 2020), Uganda (Max Martin, 2015), and Tunisia (Jefferson and Schmidt, 2019) amongst many others.

When deciding which specific methods you plan to use as part of your ethnography, it is vital that you are organized and prepared to observe, record and acknowledge all the different types of data that may come your way: which ones will you want to record? What you see? Smell? Hear? What people tell you (which people?)? What you are shown or what you observe? You may not exactly know before you start[5] – the key is to be open to the experience of the environment around you, and be open to all the data available. Often ethnographies combine immersion and 'hanging out' with more formal interviews, documentary analysis, focus groups, and/or surveys – brought together these different data forms can give a much deeper view of the prison experience than one alone, and the 'hanging out' is often particularly valuable to give context to what you learn in the more formal data collection methods. You may read about a policy, but until you see how it is implemented, you are unlikely to appreciate the reality. Conversely, you may learn much more about individuals in a 1:1 interview than in the 'hanging out' process with can often be framed by group dynamics. I remember one pertinent interview with an individual who would show off and be loud, brash and a bit silly when on the wing of the prison in front of others, but when in a 1:1 interview, was able to talk much more emotionally, intelligently, and thoughtfully. For me, researching masculine identities within the prison, this was invaluable in understanding the importance of the particular audience for an individual's gendered performance (Sloan, 2016).

Personally, I would strongly advocate the use of a reflective journal as a means to record your observations and reflections: I found my reflective journal during my doctoral research an invaluable tool for recording things I saw, heard, smelled, and felt; as well as being a vital means of debriefing myself at the end of a hard day in the prison. I would sit in my car and write out my reflections before I then went home, and this gave me a place to 'put' everything, so that I could return to 'normal' and not carry as much of the prison around with me as I might otherwise.

Research Diaries

Research diaries can be a vital element of the reflective process, as well as a fundamental addition to the research as a means of data collection and recording physical, emotional, and sensory observations. The importance of talking about difficult subjects is becoming more and more recognised in society, with talking therapies and support groups playing vital roles within the field of mental health support. Yet this can face issues when one is under rules of confidentiality unless in a formal medical or research environment, and sometimes we don't actually want to talk about the things we have seen or heard in the course of our research.

Enter the research diary

This can be as structured as you want it to be, can be included in the research, or never see the light of day (be warned though, you will still need to keep it secure as data). As one example of an available tool (but there are many more out there), Eaton (2019) has developed *The Reflective Journal for Practitioners Working in Abuse and Trauma*, which sets reflective tasks over a range of areas, including discrimination, barriers, frustrations, beliefs, and self-care, amongst others, which can be a good starting point for those looking for a more structured approach to the process of reflection. Personally, I just picked up a notebook and started writing all manner of notes, observations, and reflections – initially this was just as a form of debrief for my own personal use – to get the events of the day out of my head and onto paper. I had not actually considered, when I began by doctoral work, that the prison would change or shape me, yet my research diary as a method of 'emotional attentiveness' (Piacentini, 2007: 153) and a record was of great importance – indeed,

> Field notes are vital: they are an informal diary of events and personal impressions which should be kept up to date and can act as a powerful memory aid. They also form part of reflexivity whereby the researcher can reflect upon the research process and his or her effect upon it and its outcomes.
>
> *(Martin, 2000: 225)*

Similarly, as Warr notes, 'it is possible to have an empathetic understanding of other people's experiences through research' (2004: 578), which may even be 'a significant guide to or even source of valuable data' (Liebling, 1999: 147).

It is OK – no, it can be a *good* thing, to acknowledge one's emotions and distress where it arises. It is not 'self indulgent' (Cunliffe, 2003: 990), it is important. As Liebling notes,

> The absence of 'pain' or emotion from quantitative (and indeed, most qualitative) research accounts of prison life has always baffled me. Research in any human environment without subjective feeling is almost impossible (particularly, I would argue, in a prison). These feelings – belonging to staff, prisoners and researchers – can be a significant guide to or even source of valuable data.
>
> *(1999: 149)*

A Collection of Methods: Evaluation Research

Many researchers may undertake research to evaluate a particular project, intervention or programme within the prison. Most prison research that is put out to tender by government agencies or charitable organisations or NGOs is evaluation research, whereby an intervention is already in use, and its effectiveness needs to be established (especially in terms of value for money and the need to justify further funding of said programme). As such, a combination of methods will be used in order to try to demonstrate the effectiveness of such interventions in achieving their aims. Such research would do well to give consideration to the work of Sherman et al. (1998) and their creation of the 'Maryland Scale of Scientific Methods,' which created a scale on the strength of internal validity in a sample of crime prevention project evaluations. The authors determined the 'gold standard' of evaluation research (with regard to the reduction of intervening variables) to be those works that measured before and after the intervention; contained multiple units to measure; used randomisation processes; and used control groups. This aligns with the high credibility assigned to randomised control trials in the experimental world, yet creates standards that place emphasis on evaluations that are often highly resource intensive with regard to time and money.

In reality, this is extremely difficult to achieve in the prison setting – the intervention may well already be in use (in which case there's unlikely to be any chance for 'before and after' measurements), and the use of randomised control trials also becomes quite tricky, especially if the intervention is being administered by the prison, a charity or an NGO, who may well be targeting it at those for whom it may be most suitable. It should also be noted that, depending on who has commissioned that evaluation, the researcher's ownership of data collected may be negligible, and therefore the right to use such data in future publications may be restricted, or even prevented altogether.

Evaluations are not 'a method' – they are a collection of methods used together to determine an intervention's effectiveness. As such, they may involve interviews, observations, focus groups, policy analysis, or any other host of methods, generating qualitative and/or quantitative data, and drawing from a wide range of samples and research designs. Of particular importance is how to combine those different data sets collected, and how to bring them together to paint the picture of effectiveness of that intervention – the ordering of different methodological approaches, in addition to the significance afforded to the different methods when combined, are design decisions that must be given careful consideration as an ongoing process.

Evaluations are often somewhat political in nature – they involve a judgment being made on the effectiveness of an intervention that has taken time, money and often institutional support. Where such evaluations are invited by formal bodies, they raise important considerations, noted by Liebling: 'Should we accept invitations to carry out research on policies we disapprove of?' (2001: 480). Such reflections and careful thinking need to be undertaken, not least because, as Professor Liebling so aptly states, 'It is impossible to be neutral. Personal and political sympathies contaminate (or less judgmentally, inform) our research. But do they distort it?' (2001: 472).

An Approach to Methodology: Appreciative Inquiry

Arguably one of the most uplifting approaches to research for change within institutions is that of Appreciative Inquiry, described as 'a "family" of techniques and processes which share the same positively framed values-based principles' (Lavis, Elliott and Cowburn, 2017: 188). As with evaluation, it is not, in itself, a 'method.' Rather, Appreciative Inquiry is an ideological approach based on identifying 'energy for change' (Elliott, 1999: 2) within organisations and institutions; it is a way of using different research methods in order to elicit information for positive change from within. As such, it is not appropriate for all research – indeed, by its very nature it is designed to facilitate change through inclusion of the views of stakeholders. It has been used within prison research in England for a number of decades (see, for example, Cowburn and Lavis, 2013; Liebling, Price and Elliott, 1999; Liebling, Elliott and Arnold, 2001; Lavis, Elliott and Cowburn, 2017); as well as in Australia (Leeson, Smith and Rynne, 2016), Belgium (Croux, Vandevelde, Claes, Broesens and De Donder, 2021) and Israel (Geiger and Fischer, 2018), amongst other places.

Appreciative Inquiry follows a four stage process of *Discovery, Dreaming, Designing* and *Destiny* (with some arguing there is a fifth stage of *Defining* – see Stavros and Hinrichs, 2009). This section is not intended to provide a comprehensive instructional approach to undertaking Appreciative Inquiry – there are far better sources written by people who have spend many hours working in the Appreciative Inquiry mindset (see, for example, Elliott, 1999; Lavis, Elliott and Cowburn, 2017). Those undertaking Appreciative Inquiry will still be making use of some of the methods discussed already as a foundation – be that focus groups, interviews, documentary analysis. The key feature of Appreciative Inquiry is, however, the fact that it is an approach being used for transformative impact rather than simply knowledge generation. As such, the involvement and buy-in from the institution itself is essential, and the work is likely to have real world impact in some way: that is, essentially, the point of it. Appreciative Inquiry challenges the problem-focused approach that is inherent within prisons (and often in prison research which is looking to 'solve' or investigate a problem), and instead is about using appreciation, positivity, and reflection to find out about the working of a policy, practice, or process.

Sensory Methods

Anyone who has been into a functioning prison will have no doubt noticed the wide range of senses that are awoken upon entry – the sights, smells, sounds, even tastes, all combine to produce a much broader experience than simply 'seeing.' Indeed, this fascinating area of criminological research has started to become recognised, such as in the Sensory Criminology website (https://sensorycriminology.com/home/) and the brilliant edited collection *Sensory Penalties* (Herrity, Schmidt and Warr, 2021). This can pose new challenges to the prison researcher in terms of data collection and recording, but is an extremely exciting development in the methodological field, and really helps to bring the reality of prison to life.

One prominent sensory penologist is Dr Kate Herrity – referred to by some of the men in the prison she was researching as 'the sound lady under the stairs,' due to her focus on the significance of sound through aural ethnography (i.e. listening).

THE SOUND LADY UNDER THE STAIRS: LESSONS FROM AN AURAL ETHNOGRAPHY

Kate Herrity

I first experienced the prison soundscape a number of years before I went back to school, and more before I was able to explore the research questions evoked by this experience. What significance did this dizzying cacophony have for those living and working within it? And what might examining this tell us about the prison social world? How to proceed without a well-trod map was a daunting task. The chasm between textbook teachings and practical experience is never wider than those first few steps, though I had spent some time in prisons by this point. I drew on what I had learned in other prison spaces, and time working in pubs and bars. I used 'The reality and potency of carnal know how, the visceral, bottom-up grasp of the social world – in the double sense of intellectual understanding and dexterous handling – that we acquire by acting in and upon it' (Wacquant, 2015: 3). Only past a certain point in the nearly eight months I spent at HMP Midtown (a local men's prison) did the research process become clear.

I had devised 'listening' schedules alongside interview guides and various paraphernalia of ethical practice, but it was not until I was sufficiently familiar with the environment to make sense of it that I became confident of the project's direction. 'Sensemaking' is a term used in organisational theory; I use it here to refer to that gradual familiarisation with and adaptation to the rules and rhythms of a particular social context (Herrity, 2020). Gradually the muddled din of prison daily life unfolded its secrets and I could begin to discern individual contributions to the concerto of the everyday tune. More time and concerted listening still, and I could start interpreting and deciphering its meanings; I had attuned to the ebb and flow of daily life at HMP Midtown.

Sensemaking and attunement were the product of more than observation, constituting a social enterprise between me and much of the prison community. I sought to privilege my ears, rather than my eyes. I was often the subject of bemused inquiry – what was I doing? What was I writing? Why was I sat on a wall everyone else passed by, or squidged in a corner? I cautiously introduced myself to the overwhelming sensescape and its inhabitants by tentative degree. A ready explanation would have been useful, but in retrospect what I was doing was of far less concern than why. Some confusion remained, but I became the sound lady under the stairs; my endless questions greeted with unfailing good humour. "Listening" is a loaded term in a place where many feel unheard. In contrast to the tight, inflexible daily regime my curious, sympathetic ear had endless time for all who wished to bend it. Listening to the community opened my mind to a broader field of understanding than would have been possible otherwise. I left with a different sense of order and survival in this most particular of spaces, by listening to its rhythms and routines.

Another sensory approach is through the further use of bodies in the process of 'body mapping.'

BODY MAPS AND MEMORY WALKS: MATCHING METHODS TO THEORY AND ETHICS

Ben Nevis Barron

I have spent much of the last two years reading and thinking about my doctoral dissertation's proposed topic: a qualitative study with the participants of the State Wildland Inmate Fire Team (SWIFT) in Colorado, USA. SWIFT is a program that trains and deploys incarcerated men as wildland firefighters. There is so much I am eager to learn about the program. How does each participant's sense of self, both embodied and articulated, change through his involvement in SWIFT? How are risk and power dynamics racialized and classed through the political economy of this particular form of labour? How would an analysis of the program change if the wildfire were considered as an actor with more-than-human agency?

Beginning to answer these questions requires a broad array of methods, and I will briefly detail two that I intend to use here: body maps and memory walks. Both methods are meant to tap into the haptic, affective realm of felt experience, a line of inquiry informed by a feminist conviction that the body is a primary medium through which we engage with and develop knowledge about the world. I hope to explore the embodied ways participants experience the radically different spaces of the SWIFT program – from the prison cell to the fireline.

In body mapping, participants detail a life-size outline of their body using drawing, painting, annotation, scrapbooking, or other creative means to convey the embodied experience of a given moment. Participant's bodies will change during the SWIFT program as they gain new physical skills and strength through intensive training, and experience collaborative action on the fireline. Body maps will provide insight into these changes that might not be gleaned from articulated accounts. While body maps can include words, articulated knowledges serve to complement embodied knowledges, not to represent them entirely. Body maps can then be used to prompt further interview questions and discussion.

I also intend to invite SWIFT participants whose incarceration has ended to participate in memory walks in a burn scar, ideally from a fire on which the participant served. Mnemonic methods can reveal the intricacies of space-time, as certain stories and feelings return to the interviewee when they are physically in the space where those stories and feelings initially took place that might not occur to them in a conventional interview.

Before commencing research, it is important to develop a robust methodology grounded in theory (in my case, theories of feminism, racial capitalism, and more-than-human geography) and ethics (a steadfast commitment to respecting each participant's expertise of their own lived experience). Such commitments require methods that can generate rich and useful data and also resonate with the tenets of the theoretical and ethical stance assumed by the scholar. Of course, my study may evolve in directions that might not include these specific methods, and flexibility is part of the toolkit – but I believe that marshalling an array of promising methods is an important preparatory practice, regardless of the outcome.

Arts-Based Methodologies

Arts, crafts and expressive work are used a lot in prison settings as a means of therapy and relaxation for those incarcerated – but these are also increasingly being used as creative research tools. Such 'different' and creative methods and tools can be invaluable in creating sites of conversation and expression, as well as being spaces that are symbolically somewhat removed from the harshness of the prison itself. Gariglio (2016) discusses the use of photo-elicitation in prison ethnography, whereby images are used to stimulate discussions in a freer way than standard semi-structured interviews. The method is claimed to help to overcome barriers, challenge power imbalances between participants and researchers, and 'often empowered the interviewees and gave them more freedom both to take turns and to freely express their experiences' (2016: 369). It is not often that research can be claimed to be 'empowering' or 'enriching,' and such developments are fantastic ways with which to address some of the fundamental power imbalances that are inherent in the researcher–researched relationship.

The interesting thing about most arts-based methodologies is the pre-existence and pre-acceptance of the arts within the prison sphere prior to it becoming a research endeavour – this may well explain the general successes of such methodological approaches in terms of connecting with people in prison.

CREATIVITY AND ENRICHMENT ACTIVITIES IN PRISON

Charlotte Bilby

My research is about the impact of taking part in creative or enrichment activities with sentenced men and women in prisons and community settings. The work has always been a form of participant observation, with the balance of participation shifting over the years.

Initially, I went to art and craft classes and talked with people while they were making. Their own work was used as a form of elicitation. Alan talked about art classes helping him to share paints and cooperate with the other men on his wing. Bert shared that if he could not choose what to include on his collage, then he knew it was not a good day to make other decisions. When talking and making, participants go quiet, processing what they have just said, bound up in the actions of making a stitch or a brush stroke. The silence is not uncomfortable as it might be in a more traditional semi-structured interview. It allows for reflection, empowering participants to feel less pressure to disclose.

After talking to Chris about how his work had progressed from monochrome pictures of screaming, zombie-like heads, slashed horizontally which were, in his words 'me telling you to F off,' to panels of found objects sent to national art exhibitions and then mounted outside of the health care unit, he took me to his cell, showed me the model car he had been working on and told me how he had saved for the vinyl to make the seats. Then we went round the wing while considering how art works were used as gifts and currency. I understood that a shared interest in making was a way to get conversations flowing.

During a week-long music course in an open prison, I found it hard to get the men to talk to me about what they were creating. This was probably because I had not taken part; I was observing a process that was allowing people to try things out and make mistakes, and had not had the courage to dive in too. Acknowledging this would have helped to chip away at the power play that exists in prison research.

More recently, I hoped to get women inside and outside prison, who had been groomed, abused and trafficked by groups of men, to talk to me about support they had received in coping with their experiences. Because of the multi-site nature of the project, I needed a way to see if the women would note their experiences in between my visits. Drawing on ideas of cultural probes, a design led co-creation research technique, I developed individual packs of craft resources and prompts. I wanted the women, some still teenagers, to respond to innocuous questions, adding to a small journal using postcards, pens, stickers, ribbons and fancy papers. Rather than just leaving the packs and expecting them to buy into the process, I set up a session where we made things together and talked. It was about getting to know and trust each other. I took the packs and my knitting, an easy, stocking stitch hat in a bright colour, something that I could either concentrate on, or knit while looking at the women in the room and actively listening.

Just as knitting in public provokes people to ask what on earth you are doing, knitting in a space normally used to confront difficult and criminal behaviour can encourage remembrance. Participants, who you really want to tell you about how they are managing, often will tell stories of a favourite older woman who could knit while watching the telly and made cardigans they hated, but now wished they had kept. They will tell you about gifts given to children who are not seen any more, having been removed from their care. They will tell you that they had never been good at anything at school, but in prison discovered they could paint, draw or make emotive poetry. They will tell you how the skills they have learnt will help them maintain positive relationships when they are released.

Stories of people's lives and the things they hope to change are shared when you make a connection. For me, connections come through making, talking about the processes, and the pride or lessons learnt in the outcome. I do not just want 'to talk about painting' as one man said to a new member of the art group I was visiting, but it is a good place to start.

These 'different' methods which draw on creativity and expression are growing in popularity, but sometimes the shadow of 'tradition' and methodological hegemony can cause problems in terms of the seriousness and value ascribed to such research choices. Charlotte went on to tell me more about her experiences of this:

I was used to my prison textile-making interests lying outside of the usual realms of mainstream criminology, but it also felt it was not a serious part of cultural criminology, with its connections to traditional, conservative ideas of femininity. I was once greeted by a former colleague who said, with a barely disguised sneer, 'how's the knitting going?' Another professor, when I returned from a book binding session at a local prison, exclaimed 'we pay you to do this?!' I was used to being put into the session the morning after the conference dinner, with other pot-luck papers that seemed have no relationship to one another or to the narrow conference theme. When I first started to teach about creative activities taking place in the criminal justice system, a student, with arms crossed and a look of disgust, blurted in the middle of a seminar 'this really is all a bit shit, isn't it?' to much giggling from the rest of the group. I have always assumed she was talking about the topic and not my teaching style.

Such experiences as this are, I think, exceptionally sad, and also remind me of the inherent tensions that tend to be posed between 'traditional' and feminist methodologies more generally within research spheres, as well as the ultimate quantitative/qualitative question tension[6] (I vividly remember attending the American Society of Criminology conference in 2007. After sitting through a fabulous presentation about qualitative prison research, one audience member said how interesting it was, and what a shame that there was no quantitative work to give it more weight). The thing about prison research is that it can be so difficult to get people to agree to your proposal, allow you access, and interact with you at all, that any and all (ethical) methods should be welcomed and encouraged.

Correspondence Methodology, Participatory Action Research (PAR), Peer Researchers, and Convict Criminology

In traditional prison research, the researcher–researched division is often stark. Those seminal penal texts considered earlier in Chapter Two were, more often than not, the product of an outsider entering the prison to report back to the reader sitting in the comfort of their office. As prison research has developed, however, the voices of those actually experiencing prison have been empowered much more, and given greater and greater value and credibility, not least due to the move towards participatory action research, peer researchers, and the growth of convict criminology. Cooperation is vital when attempting to instigate any form of positive change.

RESEARCHING PRISONER RADIO

Heather Anderson

Prisoner radio is a growing field, described as audio and radio that involves prisoners and their communities, either produced inside or outside of incarceration (Anderson and Bedford, 2017a). Sometimes broadcasts are limited to, and targeted towards, a prison-based population; other iterations of the genre can be heard by the general public, often via community radio or podcasting. Examples include Beyond the Bars (annual live broadcasts from inside prisons in Victoria, Australia; see Anderson, 2013), Ear Hustle (pre-produced podcast series produced both inside and outside, from California, USA) and National Prison Radio (pre-produced content produced mostly inside, exclusively for prison audiences via in-cell TVs, across England and Wales; see Bedford, 2018).

As a community radio, and prisoner radio, practitioner and scholar, I've experienced the privilege of working alongside prisoners and their communities in a number of locations. From a research perspective, primarily working alongside Dr Charlotte Bedford, my aim is to investigate how audio production can support prisoner communities, both during and post-incarceration, by applying an action research methodology. Our action research projects (Anderson and Bedford, 2017b; 2017c; 2019) have produced induction materials in both men's and women's prisons, and led to a community radio program presented by a grassroots organisation led by, and for, women of lived prison experience.

Action research involves testing ideas in practice as a means of increasing knowledge and improving social conditions (Hearn et al., 2009). It is a valuable tool that aligns with feminist-oriented approaches to social justice to bring researchers and participants together as partners (Pickering, 2014). Our research can also be situated within an arts-led research model, grounded in the understanding that radio (as an art-form) can 'engage in research as a participatory act that allows those involved to more directly express their voices' (Walsh, Rutherford and Crough, 2013: 121).

While action research and arts-based research methods have been identified and employed as effective and appropriate for working with prisoners, and the formerly imprisoned (see, for example, Jarldorn, 2016), there has been little other work that specifically addresses the outcomes of projects involving radio.

As we work through the stages of action research, it is important to apply the principles of critical autoethnography – the 'study and critique of culture through the lens of the self' (Holman Jones, 2018: 4). Self-reflexivity is a key component of the process, as an iterative and cyclical practice of self-awareness that makes visible the construction of knowledge within research (Pillow, 2003). We gather data through a number of distinct approaches; observations and reflection notes taken during and after workshops, analysis of official documents produced during the project (e.g. project proposal, grant application), content analysis of the audio produced, and any other relevant audio recorded but not used for broadcast.

In applying a critical autoethnographic approach to action research, in a prisoner radio context, we take the direction of Holman Jones (2018: 5), and aim to encourage two key actions, in ourselves and the readers of our work; that is, to scrutinise institutions, discourses and systems that privilege some and marginalise others, and, as a result, to put theory into action. This is not an 'anti-intellectual position … (r)ather, it means thinking and writing unapologetically to contribute to the toolboxes and fuel supplies of actual struggles against racism, imperialism and colonialism' (Choudry, 2020: 29).

TAPPING INTO CREATIVITY AND IMAGINATION IN PRISON RESEARCH

Katherine Albertson

Critical sociologists have long embraced participatory research and co-operative inquiry. Yet it has largely not ocurred to practitioners of mainstream prison research that what we 'do' as researchers across the criminal justice system can positively benefit our research participants in the real world. I assert, however, that part of our role in facilitating genuine engagement in research and evaluation in prison means introducing the art of imagination to all stakeholders; in prison particularly it is as important an element as the study's contribution to knowledge and policy development.

Participatory research study designs are by their very nature adaptive and interactive. Acknowledging that the full range of research participants involved are all experts in their own experience of the custodial setting is key to participatory research approaches. That is not to ignore inherent power imbalances, rather encourage our respondents to think through them critically. Likewise for the prison researcher, being able to think quickly and creativity in response to an unpredictable environment dynamic is a key skill required when attempting to facilitate compassionate collaboration and further understanding between very different stakeholder groups in the prison environment.

Over the last 20 years I have endeavoured to work in this way across the criminal justice system including those compelled to reside in the prison, alongside: policymakers; prison management; prison officers; and third sector staff. This has involved having quickly to adapt methods to meet establishment regime requirements (which are often not explicit until you arrive), be it at a dangerous serious personality disorder unit, high security and all the categories in between. On reflection, it seems to me that engaging the imagination of all stakeholder groups has proved the most challenging aspect of my position.

Engaging the imagination makes it possible for human beings to invent (if not enact) their own alternative possibilities, behaviours, and strategies. Therefore, supporting all research participants to think through from 'what is' to 'what could be' is key to the genuine engagement of all voices in the research process. The ability to 'see' or 'imagine' something that does not exist, whilst challenging, means enabling participants not only to focus on what they already know, which is only part of our research task. We cannot just leave them there, as this can limit their ability to imagine the same situation from another person's perspective, and impede innovative thinking.

I have found that short, indeterminate, and life-sentence prisoners respond temporally differently to research and evaluation activities, depending on their sentence length and the stage they have reached in their sentence. For example, workshop participants from a 'People Convicted of a Sexual Offence' wing were erudite and engaged enthusiastically with the participatory evaluation activities. Yet, participants from a Mainstream (people convicted of non-sexual offences) wing, in contrast responded despondently to the very same activities. Whilst this could be said to reflect the challenges of evaluation with prison residents with more or less cultural capital or previous experience of being asked for and expressing opinions, it is also an issue of successfully engaging imagination for the research tool designer, and also relates to the experience and skills base of the fieldwork researcher.

Similarly, during my career I have also experienced challenges when attempting to motivate delivery staff across the criminal justice sector to think more strategically about their practice and also more strategic staff to be more operational-impact wise about their strategy. By drawing out every stakeholder's imagination by utilising participatory research, action, and co-operative inquiry, as researchers we can encourage abstract thinking that boosts the creativity of all the people we work with from a strength-based approach. Imagination is deeply connected with not just describing everyday reality, but combined with the knowledge researchers seek, this is the dynamic duo. A dynamic duo lending everyone greater perspective, increasing cognitive, creative, and social skills, and enhancing creative problem solving.

During the Covid-19 pandemic, Participatory Action Research was a particularly effective way of continuing to reach prisoners and hear their voices when institutions were closed off to outside visitors – one such project was 'Coping with Covid in Prison: The Impact of the Prisoner Lockdown' (User Voice and Queen's University Belfast, 2022).

PARTICIPATORY ACTION RESEARCH (PAR) IN PRISON

Shadd Maruna

I have made a career out of doing research, most of it qualitative, with people in prison and those who have been released from prison. Most of this research utilises extremely primitive methodological tools: I speak to people basically; I ask them questions, I get them to reflect, and I then aggregate and interpret what they tell me. I make no apology for this research. I am proud of the things the work has achieved, and I know I have been ethical in the way I have carried out the work, seeking always not to exploit or harm those who agree to participate in the studies.

That said, I admit that I have (from the first time I 'entered the field' to do this work) felt pangs of discomfort about the research dynamic, and, over the past decade or so, these pangs have taken the form of explicit doubts about the traditional dynamic of the 'researcher' and the 'researched.' Who am I, after all, to 'give voice' to the experiences of prisoners and ex-prisoners, when so many people with actual lived experience of incarceration or reintegration are fully capable of telling their own stories?

This growing discomfort with the image of the colonial anthropologist swanning into the prison or the 'hood to meet the 'natives' and bring back their stories motivated me (and many of my colleagues) to explore the possibility of Participatory Action Research or PAR. PAR seeks to 'flip' the top-down power dynamic of the research relationship by empowering the 'subjects' of the research project to become co-researchers.

Although PAR studies often involve fairly small-scale projects, rather stupidly, my first real foray into the method (which I did with the help of the User Voice organisation) was the opposite: a 10-prison study involving 99 people in prison, trained in research methods, and surveying over 1,600 of their peers. The reason for jumping into the deep end like this was because the research was conducted in the dark days of the Covid crisis. Virtually the only way we were going to be able to survey such a large number of prisons was to get those inside prisons to carry about the work themselves. Did this design involve enormous ethical issues? Absolutely. When peers interview peers, the risks of breaking confidentiality and other harms are plentiful. In addition, the research ran a real risk of exploiting the labour of some of the most marginalised people in society: the imprisoned.

However, we managed to mitigate these potential risks, and the research ended up being among the most impactful of any work I have done in my career. The reasons for this, without question, is that we were able to involve prisoners and former prisoners in leadership roles at every stage of the research project from design to analysis, and even dissemination. This co-production made the research process much more difficult but also far more rewarding, producing insights we never would have reached on our own. Moreover, the research ironically restored my faith in my own value as a traditional researcher. Neither group (the peer researchers or the academics) could have completed this important study without the other, and much of the power of the analysis came from the interactions between our different perspectives.

PAR and the associated correspondence methodology were vital during the Covid-19 lockdowns (see Maycock, 2022; Maycock and Dickson, 2021). Maycock (2021) highlights some of the key challenges of this approach, including the fact that letters can (and do) go missing (see also Bosworth, Campbell, Demby, Ferranti and Santos, 2005); the time lag between letters which can have implications if a participant demonstrates a need for support; small sample sizes; and the problems of low literacy levels within the prison estate. Similarly, Bosworth et al. (2005) note that there are challenges with doing research by post, including the fact that 'it may be difficult, once time has elapsed between the sending and receiving of mail, to remember the precise tone and wording of the original question' (2005: 252). In addition, the 'ambivalent nature'; blurring of public/private boundaries; and the fact that 'letters destabilize some of the usual parameters of social science research' (2005: 253) mean that particular care needs to be taken when planning out such a research project and its implications. That said, Bosworth et al. (2005) note the value of letters as familiar methods of communication to people in prison and the fact that an individual is not able to be interrupted can make this approach very useful in engaging those who are often difficult to reach face-to-face, as well as enabling academics to work '*with* prisoners directly, rather than writing *about* them' (2005: 261).

In 1988, Davidson wrote that

> while the direction of research has changed, the profile of people doing it has not. The production of knowledge on crime, justice, and punishment continues to be as closed off from the people who are the objects of that research as ever before.
>
> *(Davidson, 1988: 2–3)*

Nearly 40 years later, in many jurisdictions, this statement no longer holds completely true – some of those voices (albeit not all) are being heard. There is now a growing field of 'convict criminology,' where those who have direct personal experience of the prison setting return to the field as researchers (see Earle, 2016; also www.convictcriminology.org/). Indeed, the University of Ottawa Press has been publishing the *Journal of Prisoners on Prisons* since 1988, and 'convict criminology' was initially established by Jeffrey Ian Ross and Stephen C. Richards in 1997 as 'an intellectual enterprise as well as a means for mentorship and activism' (Ross, Darke, Aresti, Newbold and Earle, 2014: 123). In the first edition, Howard S. Davidson explains that the function of the journal is

> dedicated to encouraging prisoners and former prisoners, educators and students, political activists, prison and community workers, and policy-makers to question their theoretical assumptions by reading and responding to the analysis of men and women for whom imprisonment is not a word but an immediate experience.
>
> *(1988: 4)*

Although not the 'traditional' research process, this is exceptionally important in the production of knowledge from the inside and bringing the resources to engage with academic dissemination to those who are not readily given standard access (Davidson, 1988: 2–3).

Convict criminology is not only seen in the global North – it is also beginning to develop in other regions beyond Western neoliberal educational contexts, such as in South America (Ross and Darke, 2019). It is a vital area of research, integrating the lived experiences of prison with theoretical constructs often written by 'outsiders' and those who have never really 'been there' or seen the reality beyond the veneer presented on infrequent visits. The perspectives that those contributing to the field of convict criminology bring to the discipline fill many of the gaps that even the most immersed non-prisoner ethnographer could never truly appreciate: not least the emotional and mental implications of the threat and experience of incarceration and its accompanying stigmatisation and marginalisation (see Bozkurt with Aresti, 2018).

PRISON CONVICTIONS, BIOGRAPHIES, RACISM AND PRISON RESEARCH

Rod Earle

In 2006 I was recruited by Coretta Phillips to work on her ESRC funded study of men's social relations in prison, focussing on questions of race, racism, ethnicity and identity (Phillips, 2012). The research design involved sustained periods of immersion in two prisons in southeast England. It wasn't my first research position, but it was my first time in prison since I served a sentence in HMP Norwich in 1982. It was also my first time working on race and ethnicity, and with a black/mixed race research lead. Both have proved formative, propelling me into reflexive considerations of my own positionality and identity. Two small episodes illustrate a process that is still unfolding in my work.

The first occurred about halfway way through the fieldwork in the first prison. I had been visiting the prison and getting myself known on its various wings. I'd struck up a reasonably friendly rapport with a talkative young white man. He had opinions on a lot of things and was keen to share them with me. On the subject of prison research, he commented 'what I can't understand is why you don't get someone like me, someone who's been in prison, to do your research. If you haven't been in prison there's stuff you're never gonna know.' Anyone who's done prison research has probably heard something similar. I had to pause, sensing how awkwardly I would stumble through a disclosure that I had served a prison sentence with all its ambiguous, troubling connotations of authentic experience versus research artifice, insider expert versus outsider idiot. There were nearly 30 years between me and that prison sentence, and the same between me and the guy telling me how I could do my job better. A master's degree and six years working in criminology hadn't equipped me with many ideas on how to do it better along the lines being suggested. At the end of the research I discovered something called Convict Criminology, and have invested in working out its possibilities and potentials (Earle 2016).

The second occurred as Coretta and I made one of our first visits to a wing during the evening association period, to explain what we were doing in the prison. An hour or so later we compared notes. I had spoken to barely a handful of men, most of them white. No one seemed very interested in me or the research. Coretta had been mobbed. Stories of racism and racial dynamics in the prison had been freely shared by the men, mainly black, who had quickly gathered around her, eager to find out more. Prison staff in the prison were nearly always white. Prison researchers were nearly always white. Coretta stood out. Inside I felt like an outsider.

The more I worked with Coretta, the more it became obvious to both of us how our respective biographies, our life stories, were tangled in the research questions. We searched vainly for methods and antecedents in criminological literature for examples of how to proceed, and produced an article for the *British Journal of Criminology* (Phillips and Earle, 2010). 'Reading difference differently' was based on the frequency with which aspects of my 'whiteness' aligned with class and gender to refract experiences at odds with Coretta's. We worked with those odds, and that work continues in the conviction that while race is the structuring regime of the modern world, it will shape prison orders as it shapes our research lives.

Indeed, increasingly individuals still serving prison sentences are engaging with prison research:

RESEARCH FROM PRISON BY A SERVING PRISONER

Carl Gordon

I am currently 15 years into my sentence, which is quite complicated to explain. In 2005 I began a life sentence with a minimum tariff of 16 years for murder, along with a 14-year sentence to run concurrently for attempted murder. However, in 2014 I was sentenced to a further 14 years for supplying firearms and ammunition in 2011 from HMP Swaleside. This sentence was recorded as running concurrent to my life sentence, however in 2019 after being transferred to open conditions, it was discovered that this sentence was consecutive to my life sentence. I am now back in a C-cat HMP Coldingley where I am studying for my Ph.D. in Criminology with the University of Westminster.

There are many advantages and obvious disadvantages to conducting research as a serving prisoner. The disadvantages have recently been further highlighted by the restrictions imposed due to Covid-19.

The main advantage I would say is having lived experience, what is more powerful is that I am still 'living it' as a serving prisoner?

Once released, you are relying on memories, so the research is not as raw. This can often have a negative impact on you as an individual, depending on the subject matter and how you process your current experiences. My study is on how Private Family Visits (PFV) (which is a scheme in Canadian prisons) could impact us here in the UK. Given this particular subject, you begin to analyse the negative impact that the UK prison system and their policies have had on you, your family, other prisoners and these relationships.

Another advantage of this lived experience is that you will have a much better level of understanding and capability to interpret other prisoners' experiences. I also feel there is less of a 'researcher/subject' boundary when conducting research on other prisoners. For this reason I feel the interviews could flow more smoothly as there are already mutual understandings. These are less instances where the subject would need to elaborate on things that someone who is not familiar with prison life wouldn't understand. There are possibly higher levels of trust and openness too. The combination of lived experience/living experience and a decent level of academia to interpret them is quite powerful.

The major disadvantage of carrying out research from prison is all the restrictions. There is no internet access for prisoners, so any online research must be carried out by people on the outside. I have had to write lists to my family, friends and tutor. Having books sent in is also not an easy process, especially after Chris Grayling thought it was a good idea to ban this. I had to get permission from the Number 1 Governor here, which was also hard due to Covid-19. All mail is photocopied here to try and stop drugs, so readings sent in also take a lot longer to arrive.

I was given permission by the Number 1 to have a laptop in my cell over a year ago. We are still in the process of sorting that out. Due to Covid we have been locked down a lot more than usual, and movement is also restricted. I have not been able to have access to a computer to type, hence this is actually being written by hand.

Alongside having ethics approved by the university, it must also get approval from MOJ and the prison staff who are generally uncooperative.

Such 'insider' perspectives are essential to understand the reality of life behind bars and the challenges experienced, and do the most wonderful job of moving prison research away from its ivory tower – after all, if you've been there, you have a much better insight into the experience of incarceration than I do, and those voices and perspectives are vital. Ph.D. student Rachel Fayter, a former female prisoner, is currently researching resilience in prison as a result of her experiences in prison in Canada.

RISKS AND CHALLENGES OF CONDUCTING CRITICAL PRISON RESEARCH AS A PRISONER

Rachel Fayter

The prison system is not conducive to critical prison research studies, especially when the researcher is a prisoner. The penal environment and the stigma of prison creates unique challenges for the incarcerated scholar. There is a huge amount of emotional labour that goes into this work, while our inmate status presents significant risks for both researcher and participants. Surviving the trauma of incarceration takes incredible strength and resiliency. Many prisoners stand in solidarity to resist systemic injustice and are committed to emancipatory research and action. Our commitment to social justice outweighs the risks and challenges of engaging in this work.

Prisoners have absolutely no privacy. Research ethics concerning anonymity and confidentiality are essential. Staff frequently go through our personal belongings, reading any documents they find. When I decided to write a Ph.D. thesis on my lived experience of incarceration, I maintained a personal journal for one year. I never included any names or identifying information because I knew I was vulnerable. Despite my caution, I did not anticipate my journal would be seized when I was sent to segregation for 32 days. After one week staff opened my cell door to pass me personal belongings I had requested, including clothes, books, letter writing materials, and my journal which was unexpectedly included. Staff made a point of handing me the journal separately saying, 'Look what we found' in a confrontational tone. I immediately noticed the first few pages were ripped out. I still have no idea what was written on those pages. When I questioned staff, I was informed that Security Intelligence Officers had seized my documents, placing them in my security file. I was using this journal to record instances of unprofessional staff behaviour towards prisoners and their families including harassment, policy breaking, human rights abuses, and any situation potentially requiring advocacy or support. I was recording these events almost daily.

While imprisoned, I wrote and published two articles. An autoethnographic piece reflecting on the empowering pedagogy of the Walls to Bridges prison education program. The second article was an ethnographic policy paper that included a case study and input from other prisoners. The case example focused on a young mother who had her baby in prison. She provided a critically honest narrative about her experiences with the Mother-Child program, which had not been positive. I was extremely cautious when obtaining and using her story because she was facing severe, punitive consequences and risked loss of visits with her newborn. Because there are so few women prisoners in Canada,[7] with only a handful giving birth inside, the removal of any identifying information was not enough to ensure her anonymity from the administration. I had to be creative in submitting this article. Rather than using the regular inmate mail system, which is closely monitored by staff, I gave the article to a lawyer to submit. Since legal mail is protected, it was the only way to ensure my submission would not be seen by the institution.

The incarcerated scholar faces distinct practical and emotional methodological challenges when conducting critical prison research. The absolute power and control the system exerts over prisoners discourages any dissent, inhibiting free speech and prisoner solidarity. Despite these risks to our safety and freedom, prisoners remain committed to resisting systemic injustice and raising public awareness to promote transparency and accountability.

Convict criminology has not been able to give voices to all 'the people who are the objects of that research' (1988: 2–3), as Davidson would describe them – those who have access to the world of convict criminology still need a certain level of education and privilege to be able to reach those people and programmes that may allow their voices to be heard, and the realm of convict criminology is, as has been noted, very much seated within Western democratic jurisdictions. The very fact an individual has such valuable 'lived experience' can mean that there are inherent challenges and barriers to accessing such sites of confinement, such as through security vetting and checks that can be a condition of entry for research. But the fact that convict criminology exists at all, and that people within the prison are able to act as conduits to the outside world for all those voices they hear inside – it's a start.

Conclusion

In this chapter, I have attempted to consider the methodological choices available to those wishing to research prisons – from the desk-based and historical, to the more traditional interviews, observations, focus groups, and surveys, and then considering some of the more recent developments in terms of sensory and arts-based methods. The importance of the involvement of those being researched, through Participatory Action Research, correspondence, and through Convict Criminology, has also been discussed. What I hope this chapter has done, is shown you that there are myriad different types of method available, all of which can bring very different perspectives of the prison to light. The key is to make sure the methods you choose are suitable, achievable, and respectful.

Notes

1 Special thanks to Dr Ros Crone (The Open University) for her input and guidance on this piece.
2 I vividly remember one interview as part of my Ph.D.: it was one of my first few interviews, and the participant went in a lot of different directions beyond my standardised interview questions. I came out of the interview downcast, thinking it had not gone well. When I got to

transcription, however, the wealth of information that was revealed in that transcript was immense: things I had not asked about, but which were invaluable. It is also important to remember that, when something like that happens, there is a reason why the participant wants to share this information with you, and that should be given some respect.

3 The prison cell itself is a highly significant embodied space – Turner and Knight's (2020) edited collection gives a fascinating insight into this.

4 The challenges of whether this is triangulation or mixed methods research can be seen interrogated in Denzin, 2012.

5 Although you will need to think fairly broadly when applying for ethical approval and access, as you want to have all your methods broadly covered before you start – retrospective ethical approval is rare in many institutions. At the very least, it is advisable to note that you will be observing, or keeping a reflective journal of your observations, as well as any interviews, focus groups or surveys you may also include. It is far better to be 'over-covered' for ethical and methodological eventualities!

6 Reiter argues that there is a need for mixed-methods approaches to overcome the 'pixelated' issue of prison research and to enable contextualisation of data (2014: 423).

7 Grand Valley Institution in Kitchener, Ontario, is the largest women's federal prison in Canada with just over 200 prisoners.

References

Anaraki, N. R. (2021) *Prison in Iran: A Known Unknown*. Basingstoke: Palgrave Macmillan.

Anderson, H. (2013) Beyond the bars: Prisoners' radio strengthening community. *Media International Australia, 149*, 112–127.

Anderson, H., & Bedford, C. (2017a) Theorising the many faces of prisoner radio: Developing a holistic framework through process and product. *Media International Australia, 164*(1), 92–103.

Anderson, H., & Bedford, C. (2017b) 'What I know now': Radio as a means of empowerment for women of prison experience. *Journal of Alternative and Community Media, 2*, 14–27.

Anderson, H., & Bedford, C. (2017c) *Mobilong Prison Radio Pilot: Final Report*. Adelaide: University of South Australia. https://apo.org.au/node/115686

Anderson, H., & Bedford, C. (2019) On what it means to be free: Radio as a tool of desistance for formerly incarcerated women in Adelaide, Australia. *Radio Journal: International Studies in Broadcast and Audio Media, 17*(1), 7–27.

Azbel, L., Grishaev, Y., Wickersham, J. A., Chernova, O., Dvoryak, S., Polonsky, M., & Altice, F. L. (2016) Trials and tribulations of conducting bio-behavioural surveys in prisons: implementation science and lessons from Ukraine. *International Journal of Prisoner Health*, 12(2), 78–87.

Bandyopadhyay, M. (2010) *Everyday Life in a Prison: Confinement, Surveillance, Resistance*. Hyderabad, India: Orient BlackSwan.

Bedford, C. (2018) *Making Waves Behind Bars: The Prison Radio Association*. Bristol: Bristol University Press.

Bennett, J. (2015) Insider ethnography or the tale of the prison governor's new clothes. In Drake, D. H., Earle, R. & Sloan, J. (eds) *The Palgrave Handbook of Prison Ethnography*. Basingstoke: Palgrave Macmillan.

Bosworth, M., Campbell, D., Demby, B., Ferranti, S. M., & Santos, M. (2005) Doing prison research: Views from inside. *Qualitative Inquiry*, 11(2), 249–264.

Bozkurt, S., with Aresti, A. (2018) Marginalized voices on the criminalization of women: Absent voices: Experiencing prison life from both sides of the fence – a Turkish female's perspective. *Journal of Prisoners on Prisons*, 27(2), 17–36.

Bracco Bruce, L. (2020) Decolonising and de-patriarchalising prison: Governance, social life and gendered subjectivities in a women's prison in Peru. Ph.D. thesis, University of Warwick, http://wrap.warwick. ac.uk/148652

Bryman, A. (2016) *Social Research Methods*. Oxford University Press.

Buck, G., Tomczak, P., & Quinn, K. (2022) This is how it feels: Activating lived experience in the penal voluntary sector. *British Journal of Criminology*, 62(4), 822–839.

Caprioli, M. (2004) Feminist IR theory and quantitative methodology: A critical analysis. *International Studies Review*, 6(2), 253–269.

Carr, L. (2015) Re-entry to prison: Transition from HMP researcher to 'independent' researcher. In Drake, D. H., Earle, R. & Sloan, J. (eds) *The Palgrave Handbook of Prison Ethnography*, pp. 371–389. Basingstoke: Palgrave Macmillan.

Choudry, A. (2020), Reflections on academia, activism, and the politics of knowledge and learning. *The International Journal of Human Rights*, 24(1), 28–45.

Cowburn, M., & Lavis, V. J. (2013) Using a prisoner advisory group to develop diversity research in a maximum-security prison: A means of enhancing prisoner participation or participatory research? *Groupwork*, 23(3), 32–44.

Crewe, B. (2012) *The Prisoner Society: Power, Adaptation and Social Life in an English Prison*. Oxford University Press.

Crewe, B., Warr, J., Bennett, P., & Smith, A. (2014) The emotional geography of prison life. *Theoretical Criminology*, 18(1), 56–74.

Crone, R. (2018) *Guide to the Criminal Prisons of Nineteenth-Century England*. London: London Publishing Partnership.

Croux, F., Vandevelde, S., Claes, B., Brosens, D., & De Donder, L. (2021) An appreciative inquiry into foreign national prisoners' participation in prison activities: The role of language. *European Journal of Criminology*, 14773708211000633.

Crow, I., & Semmens, N. (2007) *Researching Criminology*. Maidenhead: McGraw-Hill Education.

Cunha, M. I. (2020) Inside out: Embodying prison boundaries. *The Cambridge Journal of Anthropology*, 38(1), 123–139.

Cunliffe, A. L. (2003) Reflexive inquiry in organizational research: Questions and possibilities. *Human Relations*, 56(8), 983–1003.

Darke, S. (2018) *Conviviality and Survival: Co-Producing Brazilian Prison Order*. Basingstoke: Palgrave Macmillan.

Davidson, H. (1988) Prisoners on prison abolition. *Journal of Prisoners on Prisons*, 1(1).

Davies, W. (2015) Unique position: Dual identities as prison researcher and ex-prisoner. In Drake, D. H., Earle, R. & Sloan, J. (eds) *The Palgrave Handbook of Prison Ethnography*, pp. 463–478. Basingstoke: Palgrave Macmillan.

Denzin, N. K. (2012) Triangulation 2.0. *Journal of Mixed Methods Research*, 6(2), 80–88.

Dixey, R., & Woodall, J. (2012) The significance of 'the visit' in an English category-B prison: Views from prisoners, prisoners' families and prison staff. *Community, Work & Family*, 15, 29–47.

Drake, D., Earle, R., & Sloan, J. (2015) *The Palgrave Handbook of Prison Ethnography*. Basingstoke: Palgrave Macmillan.

Dresler-Hawke, E., & Vaccarino, F. (2010) The ethics of focus groups in correctional settings. *International Journal of Learning*, 16(12).

Earle, R. (2016) *Convict Criminology: Inside and out*. Bristol: Policy Press.

Eaton, J. (2019) *The Reflective Journal for Practitioners Working in Abuse and Trauma*. Research Triangle, NC: Lulu.com. ISBN: 9780244198343.

Elliott, C. (1999) *Locating the Energy for Change: An Introduction to Appreciative Inquiry*. Winnipeg, Canada: International Institute for Sustainable Development.

Gaborit, L. S. (2020) Visited by spirits – 'Betwixt and between' in meditation and solitary confinement in Myanmar. *Incarceration*, 1(1), 2632666320936431.

Gariglio, L. (2016) Photo-elicitation in prison ethnography: Breaking the ice in the field and unpacking prism officers' use of force. *Crime, Media, Culture*, 12(3), 367–379.

Garrihy, J., & Watters, A. (2020) Emotions and agency in prison research. *Methodological Innovations*, 13(2).

Geiger, B., & Fischer, M. (2018) What works in Israeli prison-based sex offender rehabilitation programs: Program participants' perspective. *International Journal of Offender Therapy and Comparative Criminology*, 62(9), 2601–2623.

Godfrey, B. (2012) Historical and archival research methods. In Gadd, D., Karstedt, S. & Mesner, S. (eds) *The Sage Handbook of Criminological Research Methods*, pp. 159–175. New York: Sage.

Guerzoni, M. A. (2020) Vicarious trauma and emotional labour in researching child sexual abuse and child protection: A postdoctoral reflection. *Methodological Innovations*, 13(2), 1–8.

Hancock, P., & Raeside, R. (2009) Analyzing communication in a complex service process: An application of triangulation in a case study of the Scottish Prison Service. *Journal of Applied Security Research*, 4, 291–308.

Harvey, J. (2015) The ethnographic practitioner. In Drake, D. H., Earle, R. & Sloan, J. (eds) *The Palgrave Handbook of Prison Ethnography*, pp. 390–402. Basingstoke: Palgrave Macmillan.

Heap, V., & Waters, J. (2019) *Mixed Methods in Criminology*. Abingdon: Routledge.

Hearn, G., Tacchi, J., Foth, M., & Lennie, J. (2009) *Action Research and New Media*. Cresskill, NJ: Hampton Press.

Herrity, K. (2020) Hearing order in flesh and blood: Sensemaking and attunement in the pub and the prison. In Herrity, K., Schmidt, B. E. & Warr, J. (eds) *Sensory Penalities: Exploring the Senses in Places of Punishment and Social Control*. Bingley: Emerald.

Herrity, K., Schmidt, B. E., & Warr, J. (eds) (2021) *Sensory Penalities: Exploring the Senses in Places of Punishment and Social Control*. Bingley: Emerald Group Publishing.

Higgins, P. (1980) *Outsiders in a Hearing World: A Sociology of Deafness*. London: Sage.

Hollander, J. A. (2004) The social contexts of focus groups. *Journal of Contemporary Ethnography*, 33, 602–637.

Holman Jones, S. (2018) Creative selves/creative cultures: Critical autoethnography, performance, and pedagogy. In Holman Jones, S. H. & Pruyn, M. (eds) *Creative Selves/Creative Cultures: Critical Autoethnography, Performance, and Pedagogy*, pp. 3–20. Cham, Switzerland: Palgrave Macmillan.

Jarldon, M. (2016) What can Ruby do with a camera? Ex-prisoners use Photovoice to reverse the rules of surveillance. *Qualitative Social Work*, 15(2), 209–230.

Jefferson, A. M., & Schmidt, B. E. (2019) Concealment and revelation as bureaucratic and ethnographic practice: Lessons from Tunisian prisons. *Critique of Anthropology*, 39(2), 155–171.

Johnson, P., Duberley, J., Close, P., & Cassell, C. (1999) Negotiating field roles in manufacturing management research: The need for reflexivity. *International Journal of Operations & Production Management*, *19*(12), 1234–1253.

Kauffman, R. M., & Kauffman, R. D. (2011) Color-coded audio computer-assisted self-interview for low-literacy populations. *Epidemiology*, *22*(1), 132–133.

Kitzinger, J. (1995) Qualitative research: Introducing focus groups. *British Medical Journal*, *311*, 299–302.

Lavis, V. J., Elliott, C., & Cowburn, M. (2017) Exploring the response to diversity and equality in English prisons. In Books, J. & King, N. (eds) *Applied Qualitative Research in Psychology*. London: Palgrave.

Leeson, S., Smith, C., & Rynne, J. (2016) Yarning and appreciative inquiry: The use of culturally appropriate and respectful research methods when working with Aboriginal and Torres Strait Islander women in Australian prisons. *Methodological Innovations*, *9*, 2059799116630660.

Liebling, A. (1999) Doing research in prison: Breaking the silence. *Theoretical Criminology*, *3*(2), 147–173.

Liebling, A. (2001) Whose side are we on? Theory, practice and allegiances in prisons research. *British Journal of Criminology*, *41*(3), 472–484.

Liebling A. (2004) *Prisons and Their Moral Performance: A Study of Values, Quality, and Prison Life*. New York: Oxford University Press.

Liebling, A., Elliott, C., & Arnold, H. (2001). Transforming the prison: Romantic optimism or appreciative realism? *Criminal Justice*, *1*(2), 161–180.

Liebling, A., Price, D., & Elliott, C. (1999) Appreciative inquiry and relationships in prison. *Punishment & Society*, *1*(1), 71–98.

Lokdam, N, T., Stavseth, M. R., & Bukten, A. (2021).Exploring the external validity of survey data with triangulation: A case study from the Norwegian Offender Mental Health and Addiction (NorMA) Study. *Research Methods in Medicine & Health Sciences*, *2*(4) 140–147.

Martin, C. (2000) Doing research in a prison setting. In Jupp, V. & Davies, P. (eds) *Doing Criminological Research*, pp. 215–233. London: Sage.

Max Martin, T. (2015) Accessing and witnessing prison practice in Uganda. In Drake, D. H., Earle, R. & Sloan, J. (eds) *The Palgrave Handbook of Prison Ethnography*, pp. 424–441. Basingstoke: Palgrave Macmillan.

Maxwell-Stewart, H. (2016) Big data and Australian history. *Australian Historical Studies*, *47*(3), 359–364, at 359–360.

Maycock, M. (2021) 'I do not appear to have had previous letters.' The potential and pitfalls of using a qualitative correspondence method to facilitate insights into life in prison during the Covid-19 pandemic. *International Journal of Qualitative Methods*, *20*, 16094069211047129.

Maycock, M. (2022) 'Covid-19 has caused a dramatic change to prison life.' Analysing the impacts of the Covid-19 pandemic on the pains of imprisonment in the Scottish Prison Estate. *The British Journal of Criminology*, 62(1), 218–233.

Maycock, M., & Dickson, G. (2021) Analysing the views of people in custody about the management of the COVID-19 pandemic in the Scottish Prison Estate. *International Journal of Prisoner Health*, 17(3), 320–334.

Maycock, M., Meek, R., & Woodall, J. (2020) *Issues and Innovations in Prison Health Research*. London: Palgrave.

McDermott, K., & King, R. D. (1988) Mind games: Where the action is in prisons. *The British Journal of Criminology*, 28(3), 357–375.

Mehta, R. (2014) The mango tree: Exploring the prison space for research. *Reflexivity in Criminological Research: Experiences with the Powerful and the Powerless*, pp. 47–57. Basingstoke: Palgrave Macmillan.

Moran, R. J., & Asquith, N. L. (2020) Understanding the vicarious trauma and emotional labour of criminological research. *Methodological Innovations*, 13(2), 1–11.

Murphy, T. (2021) Penal transportation from Britain to Australia, 1788 to 1868: Four phases of penal administration and experimentation. *Journal on European History of Law*, 12(2), 70–78.

Nadin, S., & Cassell, C. (2006) The use of a research diary as a tool for reflexive practice: Some reflections from management research. *Qualitative Research in Accounting & Management*, 3(3), 208–217.

Newman, J. C., Des Jarlais, D. C., Turner, C. F., Gribble, J., Cooley, P., & Paone, D. (2002) The differential effects of face-to-face and computer interview modes. *American Journal of Public Health*, 92(2), 294–297.

Novisky, M. A., Narvey, C. S., & Semenza, D. C. (2020) Institutional responses to the COVID-19 pandemic in American prisons. *Victims & Offenders*, 15(7–8), 1244–1261.

Nurse, J., Woodcock, P., & Ormsby, J. (2003) Influence of environmental factors on mental health within prisons: Focus group study. *British Medical Journal*, 327(7413), 480.

Oakley, A. (1981) Interviewing women: A contradiction in terms. In Roberts, H. (ed.) *Doing Feminist Research*. London: Routledge and Kegan Paul.

Phillips, C. (2012) *The Multicultural Prison: Ethnicity, Masculinity and Social Relations among Prisoners*. Oxford University Press.

Phillips, C., & Earle, R. (2010) Reading difference differently? Identity, epistemology and prison ethnography. *British Journal of Criminology*, 50(2), 360–378.

Piacentini, L. (2007) Researching Russian prisons: A consideration of new and established methodologies in prison research. In Jewkes, Y. (ed.) *Handbook on Prisons*. Cullompton: Willan.

Pickering, B. J. (2014) 'Picture me different': Challenging community ideas about women released from prison. *Canadian Journal of Counselling and Psychotherapy*, 48(3), 270–283.

Pillow, W. (2003) Confession, catharsis, or cure? Rethinking the uses of reflexivity as methodological power in qualitative research. *International Journal of Qualitative Studies in Education*, 16(2), 175–196.

Pollack, S. (2003) Focus-group methodology in research with incarcerated women: Race, power, and collective experience. *Affilia*, 18(4), 461–472.

Priestley, P. (1999) *Victorian Prison Lives: English Prison Biography, 1830–1914*. London: Pimlico.

Reiter, K. (2014) Making windows in walls: Strategies for prison research. *Qualitative Inquiry*, 20(4), 417–428.

Richardson, J. C., & Godfrey, B. (2003) Towards ethical practice in the use of archived transcripted interviews. *International Journal of Social Research Methodology*, 6(4), 347–355.

Ross, J. I., Darke, S., Aresti, A., Newbold, G., & Earle, R. (2014) Developing convict criminology beyond North America. *International Criminal Justice Review*, 24(2), 121–133.

Ross, J. I., & Darke, S. (2019) Interpreting the development and growth of convict criminology in South America. *Journal of Prisoners on Prisons*, 27(2), 108–117.

Rubin, A. (2021) *Rocking Qualitative Social Science: An Irreverent, Practical Guide to Rigorous Research*. Stanford, CA: Stanford University Press.

Schlosser, J. (2008) Issues in interviewing inmates: Navigating the methodological landmines of prison research. *Qualitative Inquiry*, 14(8), 1500–1525.

Schneider, L. T. (2020) Degrees of permeability: Confinement, power and resistance in Freetown's Central Prison. *Cambridge Journal of Anthropology*, 38(1), 88–104.

Sherman, L. W., Gottfredson, D. C., MacKenzie, D. L., Eck, J., Reuter, P., & Bushway, S. D. (1998) *Preventing Crime: What Works, What Doesn't, What's Promising. Research in Brief*. Report to the United States Congress. National Institute of Justice. NCJ Number 165366.

Sloan, J. (2016) *Masculinities and the Adult Male Prison Experience*. Basingstoke: Palgrave Macmillan.

Struckman-Johnson, C., Struckman-Johnson, D., Rucker, L., Bumby, K., & Donaldson, S. (1996) Sexual coercion reported by men and women in prison. *Journal of Sex Research*, 33(1), 67–76.

Sykes, G. M. (1958) *The Society of Captives: A Study of a Maximum Security Prison*. Princeton, NJ: Princeton University Press.

Tourangeau, R., & Smith, T. W. (1996) Asking sensitive questions: The impact of data collection mode, question format, and question context. *Public Opinion Quarterly*, 60(2), 275–304.

Turner, J., & Knight, V. (eds) (2020) *The Prison Cell: Embodied and Everyday Spaces of Incarceration*. Basingstoke: Palgrave Macmillan.

Ugelvik, T. (2014) *Power and Resistance in Prison: Doing Time, Doing Freedom*. New York: Springer.

User Voice and Queen's University Belfast (QUB) (2022) *Coping with Covid in Prison: The Impact of the Prisoner Lockdown*. London: User Voice.

Wacquant, L. (2015) For a sociology of flesh and blood. *Qualitative Sociology*, *38*(1), 1–11.

Walsh, C.A., Rutherford, G., & Crough, M. (2013) Arts-based research: Creating social change for incarcerated women. *Creative Approaches to Research*, 6(1), 119–139.

Walter, S. (2017) Focus groups in prison practice. *New Zealand Corrections Journal*, *5*(2), https://www.corrections.govt.nz/resources/research/journal/volume_5_issue_2_november_2017/focus_groups_in_prison

Warr, D. J. (2004) Stories in the flesh and voices in the head: Reflections on the context and impact of research with disadvantaged populations. *Qualitative Health Research*, *14*(4), 578–587.

Webb, E. J. (1970) Unconventionality, triangulation, and inference. In Denzin, N. K. (ed.) *Sociological Methods: A Sourcebook*. New Brunswick, NJ: Transaction.

Weegels, J. (2020) Freedom in the face of Nicaragua's hybrid carceral system. *Cambridge Journal of Anthropology*, *38*(1), 52–69.

Weinrott, M. R., & Saylor, M. (1991) Self-report of crimes committed by sex offenders. *Journal of Interpersonal Violence*, 6(3), 286–300.

Wolff, N., Blitz, C. L., Shi, J., Bachman, R., & Siegel, J. A. (2006) Sexual violence inside prisons: Rates of victimization. *Journal of Urban Health*, *83*(5), 835–848.

Woodall, J., & Tattersfield, A. (2017) Perspectives on implementing smoke-free prison policies in England and Wales. *Health Promotion International*, *33*(6), 1066–1073.

Woodall, J., Dixey, R., & South, J. (2013) Prisoners' perspectives on the transition from the prison to the community: Implications for settings-based health promotion. *Critical Public Health*, *23*, 188–200.

Woodall, J., Freeman, C., & Warwick-Booth, L. (2021) Health-promoting prisons in the female estate: An analysis of prison inspection data. *BMC Public Health*, *21*, 1–8.

Zhang, J., Liang, B., Zhou, Y., & Brame, W. (2010) Prison inmates' suicidal ideation in China: A study of gender differences and their impact. *International Journal of Offender Therapy and Comparative Criminology*, *54*(6), 959–983.

Seven

CHOOSING PARTICIPANTS

One of the central aspects of prison research is the people: the prisoners, the staff, the families. It is these identities and personalities that fascinate and challenge us – and that make us, as prison researchers, see the prison in a very different way to the majority of the public. Researching any sociological dimension arguably requires a serious acknowledgment of the notions of identity and intersectionality, particularly when investigating settings submerged in power and inequality, such as prisons. The term 'intersectionality' was used by Crenshaw in 1989 to deal with the issues faced when there was a failure to realise the 'multidimensionality of Black women's experience with the single-axis analysis that distorts these experiences' (1989: 139), and the theory has subsequently expanded and developed by 'interrogating the inter-locking ways in which social structures produce and entrench power and marginalization, and by drawing attention to the ways that existing paradigms that produce knowledge and politics often function to normalize these dynamics' (Carbado, Crenshaw, Mays and Tomlinson, 2013: 312).

Bizarrely, some have problematised the notion of intersectionality within academic discourse (see Eddo-Lodge, 2017: 160 for a discussion of this in the context of feminist discourse), but I would argue that such an analysis and acknowledgment of the varying strands of identity difference and the implications and impacts of prison upon those differences is a vital consideration to make. There are numerous strands that have serious implications for prison research methodology and how individuals experience prisons. Age, gender, sex, sexuality, race, religion, disability are

DOI: 10.4324/9781315297217-7

some of the more prominently acknowledged and discussed, but it would be remiss of me to say that notions of intersectionality can be limited to a simple checklist of identity politics. At the same time, breaking down each individual into every feasible strand of identity runs the risk of, at best, fracturing results beyond the point of clarity and usefulness, and at worst, disappearing down the rabbit hole never to appear again. What is important is a recognition of difference and identities within the research population, and never to assume that everyone experiences prison equally.

To see the true picture, at the very least we need to take an open approach when analysing the meaning of our results for individuals experiencing the prison, as such experiences – be that by prisoners, staff, visitors, victims or even researchers – will have implications for the outcomes of our work, the conclusions we can draw and the potential changes such conclusions can make. The more stakeholders involved, the more interpersonal and 'management skills' may be required of the researcher, as Nichola Cadet explains with regard to doing needs assessment research in prisons.

UNDERTAKING NEEDS ASSESSMENTS

Nichola Cadet

Undertaking research in an environment with multiple stakeholders requires stakeholder management skills in addition to research skills. To inform commissioning intentions in prison healthcare, I was invited to undertake a health needs assessment by the prison healthcare board, formed of local health representatives, prison governors and service providers (primary care, substance misuse, and mental health). Having buy-in from managers was vital to ensuring access to data, including clinical data, staff and service users. There was some cynicism whether the needs assessment would 'tell them anything new'; however, at that time, information was based on hunches rather than evidence. At the very least, receiving quantifiable information about met and unmet need would aid service development. Staff were also fearful of the potential for prisoner 'wants' to take precedence over 'needs.' Despite management buy-in, the research was constrained by staffing issues, meaning that a planned focus group had to be re-arranged. Additionally, high levels of staff vacancies meant that staff were often covering for more than one area of speciality. Furthermore, some concerns about the commissioning environment meant that some staff were reluctant to share ideas for best practice, for fear that this would lose them a competitive advantage when services were re-commissioned.

Being able to draw keys did reduce some of the staffing constraints, as the researcher was able to access healthcare and other services without the need for a staff escort. This did lead to some prisoners asking whether they worked for the prison, which may have influenced their responses.

The project adopted the University of Birmingham Toolkit for Health Care Needs Assessment in Prisons Methodology, and comprised three elements:

1. Epidemiological data: demographic data; prevalence of diseases; attendance at clinics.
2. Corporate data: 1:1 interviews with staff and prisoners.
3. Comparative data: comparisons with health needs assessments from similar prison establishments, and with community data where this was available.

Interviews with staff and prisoners were summarised and coded, then presented back to staff and prisoner groups by way of focus groups. This ensured that the lived experience added weight to the clinical data, meaning that decisions were able to be undertaken regarding future service delivery. The resultant needs assessment confirmed the former 'hunches' regarding the numbers of older prisoners, and included projections for future numbers based on current sentence durations. This led to re-designing the healthcare pathway for older prisoners, and also led to a change in prison regime to offer more bespoke sessions for older prisoners. The needs assessment also led to improved processes for tracking the costs of escorts and bedwatches. Over time, this meant that more secondary care clinics were brought into the prison, an investment in telehealth services was made, and prisoners reported increased dignity in having their healthcare needs met.

We must also remember the intersectionality of our own identity strands as researchers. This was touched upon by Rod Earle in his reflection in Chapter Six, highlighting the differences in experience he encountered based on differences in race and sex when compared to his co-researcher Coretta Phillips (see Phillips, 2012; Phillips and Earle, 2010). Our identities as researchers shape our epistemological and ontological approaches, as well as our research designs and approaches, so it is important that we reflect carefully on such matters when trying to understand the researcher's place within the research, and how we may shape the knowledge we are generating.

Arguably, we also need to consider the questions we are asking, and whether perhaps these need reframing. Similarly, we need to challenge ourselves as researchers on the questions we ask. Why dont we talk about X, Y or Z? Agozino argues that criminology is 'an imperialist science for the control of others' (2003: 3), and although such assertions might elicit discomfort, it is still an argument that we need to engage with.

Potential Participants and Their Associated Considerations

Prison research can involve a broad range of potential participants, all with slightly different considerations depending on their position within the prison setting.

Prisoners

The majority of discussions thus far have arguably been focused on researching prisoners in prison. The term 'prisoners' is itself problematic, although arguably the less problematic of the many options (i.e. 'convict' – which misses those not yet convicted; 'offender' – which misses those suffering miscarriages of justice, as well as extending well beyond the prison, and so on). It can also be tempting to see this group of individuals as just that – a group – and one must be wary of missing the important differences that inhabit this population in terms of age, race, ethnicity, gender, sex, sexuality, disability, class, educational background, offence type, nationality, and so on. In many instances, arguably the only connecting feature of a prison population is the fact that they all live under the same institutional roof at the same time. Looking at some of the subgroups within this population can bring forward distinct methodological challenges, as Dr Laura Kelly-Corless found.

DEAF RESEARCH IN PRISON: DOABLE BUT DIFFICULT

Laura Kelly-Corless

My doctoral research took the form of an exploratory qualitative study looking at the experiences of d/Deaf people in prison. The primary method of data collection used was semi-structured interviews, carried out across six adult male prisons in England with d/Deaf prisoners and hearing staff members who had worked with them. I conducted 27 individual interviews and one further group interview with 4 of the culturally and linguistically Deaf participants (for further details about the research design see Kelly-Corless, 2019). Because I am hearing and unable to meaningfully communicate in British Sign Language (BSL), a qualified BSL interpreter was used where necessary.

Doing research with d/Deaf people in a prison setting proved to be complex and fraught with challenges for a multitude of reasons, the first relating to sample location. The Prison Service currently has no legal obligation to record numbers and locations of imprisoned d/Deaf people (Kelly, 2017; 2018), and because of this it was very difficult to find participants to interview. To overcome this, I sent a letter to every prison in England and Wales asking how many d/Deaf people were situated there and whether they would be interested in being interviewed. While I received a lot of responses, many establishments were not able to provide numbers, and of those that were, most did not state how d/Deaf somebody was. This was problematic because levels of d/Deafness range vastly, going from mild hearing loss, to severe medical deafness, to cultural and linguistic Deafness, and where an individual sits on this spectrum is likely to have a significant impact on their needs, identity and experience of prison.[1] This lack of d/Deaf awareness persisted once I began to arrange interviews with staff members, meaning that I was often unclear about how d/Deaf someone would be until I got to the interview, and therefore did not know what resources I would need, i.e. interviews with Deaf participants required the presence of an interpreter who needed to be security checked. This lack of d/Deaf awareness actually ended up changing the focus of the study as well, in that before starting the fieldwork I had intended to concentrate largely on the lives of culturally and linguistically Deaf prisoners; however, because staff members did not know what this meant, medical deafness became central too.

The fact that the language and culture of Deaf people is visual gave way to further complexities because it meant that documentation such as information sheets and consent forms needed to be in BSL in a visual format.[2] To ensure that informed consent was given by the Deaf participants, a visual recording device was used to record a BSL interpreter signing the contents of the documents, while a voice read them out.[3] Although copies of this were sent to each of the participating prisons on DVD, access to them was denied by the prisons, with unspecified security violations being cited as the reason. Consequently, all involved prisons violated the ethical conditions for research outlined by the National Research Committee whereby participants must be given access to documentation one week before the interview. To ensure that the Deaf participants actually wanted to be involved, my interpreter signed the contents of the forms to them when they arrived at their interview.

The recording process was also affected by the need for visual adaptations, in that to ensure the data collected during the interviews with Deaf participants was as authentic as possible, a visual device that could record BSL was required. However, the secure and restrictive nature of the prison environment created issues again here, in that I was only given authorisation to use an audio Dictaphone. Because of this, during the transcription process I only had a copy of the interpreter's verbalised interpretation of the raw data, meaning that the authenticity of my findings hinged significantly on the quality of the interpreting. As such, it was important to ensure that the interpreter used was both sufficiently qualified and clear about the remit of the project and the context of the questions. Creating further problems during recording and transcription was the fact that Deaf individuals commonly verbalise loudly (but not necessarily coherently) whilst signing. This meant that Deaf participants often made a lot of noise whilst the interpreter was translating their responses. Sometimes this made the recordings impossible to decipher, and at other points it was possible but only after listening to them many (many) times.[4] Visual recording would remove this issue as I would have had access to the original responses as well.

Finally, and importantly, my status as a hearing person with little comprehension of BSL inevitably had a significant effect on the interviews with the Deaf participants, in that it was often very hard to build rapport with them. On many occasions interviewees directed their answers towards the interpreter rather than me and in one instance an individual attempted to engage them in discussions about the Deaf Community. While I of course understood why this was happening (they could communicate with and relate to the interpreter more overtly), it created a strange dynamic whereby I almost became an outsider in my own research. Although I had anticipated this and had made the interpreter's role clear beforehand, only through doing the interviews did I realise quite how impactful my hearing status would be.

Because I was the first person in England and Wales to carry out research of this type, I became somewhat of a methodological guinea pig, having to make snap decisions about unexpected challenges as the research progressed. Although the nature of prison research means that this will always be the case to some extent, my journey should help future researchers to navigate away from at least some of the complications that I was met with. With this in mind, I recommend that any such person reads Kelly-Corless (2019), where I discuss my research journey in significantly more depth and provide a set of recommendations that could simplify the process, at least slightly that is.

Staff

The other key group of individuals that tends to be researched within prisons is prison staff (although this term is often used to signify prison officers, rather than including all the other individuals working within the prison, such as teachers, nurses, doctors, and so on). Liebling has noted the subtle tensions that can arise between prisoners and prison staff as separate research populations, with concerns that 'no-one is interested in their views, and that outsiders only care about prisoners' (Liebling, 1999: 155), which is an important element to consider when in the prison setting. Indeed, the consideration of staff and management perspectives in prison research is not always given sufficient attention – and where it is undertaken, there are politics as to who can be afforded degrees of sympathy that can raise their ugly heads, as noted by Liebling:

> why is it less affectable to offer the same degree of appreciative understanding to those who manage prisons. Is it because they wield power? Their voices are already legitimated? [...] Why are we not so curious about the constraints under which the so-called powerful operate?
>
> *(2001: 476)*

For those who do work directly with prison staff for research purposes, sometimes access can be complicated and require a slightly different approach to recruitment, as Dirga found in the Czech Republic context:

> To get participants for my research I used the snowball sampling method (Hendl, 2005), when I tried to get contacts to prison guards from my first respondents that I had found on my own social networks. I chose this method because of difficult access to the prison guards' population, which is only enhanced by the difficult access to the inner area of prisons (it has been prohibited for most studies due to the internal security of prison).
>
> *(Dirga, 2015: 118)*

Prison staff are busy people, who may not have time or space to engage in research, and there can be instances of concern about engaging with researchers. In the British context, I found that staff were often slightly wary of me as a researcher: I was jokingly viewed as an undercover journalist by some, as well as others seeing me somewhat like a 'little rich girl.' The influence of the prison on staff can be deep, traumatic, and long lasting – an issue that is recognised in high staff turnover rates, yet is rarely given sufficient formal or informal attention. When I started doing my Ph.D., I thought I would end up on a graduate scheme in the prison service, working on the wings for a few years and then moving into management. It only took a few days inside the prison for me to see that I definitely didn't have what it took to survive and thrive in that hugely demanding role.

RESEARCHING PRISON STAFF

Colette Barry

As part of my Ph.D. I interviewed prison staff in Ireland about their experiences of dealing with the death of a prisoner. These semi-structured interviews were usually lengthy and covered an array of topics, including staff views on policy and procedure, their experiences of deaths in custody investigations, their emotional reactions and the impact of these incidents in their personal lives, and their engagement with support in the aftermath. I interviewed prison-based staff in a range of grades, including prison officers and governors. Most had dealt with several prisoner deaths in custody during their careers.

While recent decades have seen increased research in many jurisdictions on the working lives and cultures of prison staff, there had been very limited Irish research on prison work at the time of my study. As I was negotiating approval and access with the Irish Prison Service, I was reminded by an officer that prison staff in Ireland were unaccustomed to being asked to participate in research themselves, and may be uncertain or wary about my motives and allegiances. As data collection commenced, I found myself wondering about my status as an 'outsider' in the eyes of prison staff and the possible impact on the interviews and research findings.

Overall, participants were comfortable discussing most topics, including the impact of their experiences of deaths on their mental health and in their relationships in their personal lives. As the interviews progressed however, one topic consistently brought my position as an 'outsider' sharply into focus; humour. Informed by previous studies of the occupational cultures of prison staff, I planned to explore the role of humour in staff communication and coping following the death of a prisoner. Like the prison staff in these other studies, participants described this humour as 'black,' 'dark' or 'dry.' Many acknowledged its function in 'breaking the ice' and coping, but were reticent to speak further or give examples of humorous exchanges, citing my position as a researcher (and therefore, an 'outsider'). Some suggested that I would be 'shocked' and 'horrified' by their humour and view prison staff (including them) as 'callous' and 'disgusting.' Others were more succinct; I was a 'human' and they were not.

Conversations about how 'outsiders' or 'humans' may view their humour evolved into participants reflecting upon their identities as prison officers and governors. They spoke about the ways in which they felt changed by their work (including developing what they described as a 'sicker' sense of humour), and how they saw their position in the world outside the prison walls. In this way, these contributions not only illuminated how Irish staff coped and expressed emotions following the death of prisoner, but also how they grappled with the wider impact of their work in their personal lives. While the researcher's 'outsider' status may sometimes feel like a potential limitation when researching prison staff, these perceived differences can also yield rich, and often unexpected, data.

Visitors, Friends, and Family

Central to the prisoner's prison experience are their connections on the outside who act as a conduit to the world beyond the prison:

visitors, friends, and family. Whilst these individuals often do not get into the 'heart' of the prison building (i.e. the cells and spaces just for prison 'insiders'), they are often the 'heart' of the prison experience themselves, and the spaces they can enter take on a very different feel and dimension (see Crewe, Warr, Bennett and Smith, 2014; Hutton, 2016; Moran, Hutton, Dixon and Disney, 2017). Such individuals are another 'hidden' population within prisons:

> Offenders' relatives often only become visible when they enter a prison or a prison visitors' centre and are rarely studied in their own environments [...] As a population, however, offenders' relatives can be difficult to reach and doing so through a prison visitors' centre or self-help group might be the only realistic option.
>
> *(Condry, 2013: 4)*

When researching these individuals, it is vital to recognise the demands placed upon them which are in addition to their existing lives: the time, expense and emotional costs of visiting someone in prison can be high and extensive, and being part of a research project is unlikely to feature high on their list of priorities. Ensuring that any research does not interfere with the visit process is vital.

Other considerations with this group of participants include attention to the existing vulnerabilities for those individuals living with a loved one/friend in prison (see Condry, 2013), as well as the consideration of how much, if any, of a say should the prisoner themselves have in whether their family or friends talk to you – there is no right or wrong answer to this, but it is something that may need some thought. In addition, finding the 'right' setting within which to speak to visitors will also need thought: confidentiality and privacy must be maintained, and this may or may not be achievable in adjoining visitors' centres (if there are any). Condry undertook her interviews in participants' homes where individuals 'would be more relaxed on their "territory", we could break where necessary for a cup of tea, and they could explain events that had occurred in the house or local area with much more ease' (2013: 9–10) – so such 'prison research' is definitely not confined to the prison institutional space itself.

Victims

One other group of individuals who often go unseen in prison research is victims – they are rarely 'in' the prison, and may seem to be disconnected to this area of research: yet these individuals are at the heart of the prison story. Without victims, there are no prisons or prisoners. As such, this is an area that we as prison researchers arguably need to take into consideration even more, as Dr Lauren Bradford-Clarke argues.

VICTIM-CENTRED PRISON RESEARCH? THE IMPORTANCE OF CONSIDERING THE VICTIM'S PERSPECTIVE WHEN IT COMES TO PRISON RESEARCH

Lauren Bradford-Clarke

In a system that has long been criticised for its bold claims that victims are at its heart, there are – on the surface – inherent methodological difficulties when conducting prison research to design and implement a research strategy that incorporates the victim perspective. Since the Victims Charter in 1990, there has been a shift toward integrating the victim perspective in all aspects of the criminal justice system. Crawford and Enterkin (2001) point to this as signalling 'profound changes' to the focus of the Probation Service; however the continued 'toothless' and non-legally binding entitlements mean that the failures and inconsistencies in implementation persist. This continues with the Victims Code of Practice, which was first introduced in 2006 and replaced the Victims Charter with its most recent revision in 2020, simply providing statutory guidance. One of the 'rights' set out in the Victims Code is that,

> where eligible, victims have the right to be automatically referred to the Victim Contact Scheme, which will provide [them] with information about the offender and their progress in prison, and if/when they become eligible for consideration of parole or release. Where applicable, [victims] also have the

> right to make a new Victim Personal Statement, in which [they] can say how the crime continues to affect [them].
> (Code of Practice for Victims of Crime, in Ministry of Justice, 2020: 2)

Victim Liaison Officers are responsible for contacting victims of crime within eight weeks of the offender being sentenced and victims of have the right to certain information when the sentence is for 12 months or longer. Many victims are anxious to know more about the custodial process the offender will be subject to and when the offender is likely to be released.

When conducting research on homicide-bereaved families as a distinctive group of crime victims, it had been my intention to end my exploration of their criminal justice experiences at the stage of sentencing or acquittal at the Crown Court. My research included participants when the original indictment was for murder, although in some cases the outcome was a conviction of manslaughter. An unanticipated and – dare I say – unwanted area of exploration was the victim perspective when it came to prisons and prisoners. Guided by my participants and what they deemed meaningful when it came CJ experiences, the majority of people initiated discussion about their experiences of Victim Liaison Officers. Those that mentioned it expressed their anger and dissatisfaction about this provision due to the high turnover of staff, inability to get in touch VLOs, insensitive and inadequate treatment, and an overall sense of continued disenfranchisement and infantilisation that characterised their criminal justice experiences.

There seemed to be a particular need and desire for information about the custodial behaviour, parole implications and prison location of the person convicted in the death of their family member. In one instance, one person indicated they felt further victimised on learning that the person convicted in their son's death has seriously injured another inmate. She talked about always being desperate to know why her son had been 'selected' by this person. When she learned of his behaviour in prison, she had a further sense of anger around being told her son was in the 'wrong place at the wrong time,' instead seeing this prison incident as confirmation that he was just 'evil.'

Much of the frustration and dissatisfaction around custodial matters was to do with the perceived inadequate and insensitive treatment they received in the communications regarding prisoners by VLOs. The issues faced here were around a tension between the information that victims wanted and that which could be communicated. For instance, many were denied being informed of which prison the person convicted was in, only to later find out from the media. This led to frustration and questions over the withholding of information from those affected, and further embedded the powerlessness experienced throughout various aspects of the CJS. The perception was they were 'the last to know' throughout the entire process. Another point of contention for homicide-bereaved families was that they would be informed of release, but a specific date would not be given. The explanation given to families was 'we do not want you to turn up with a baseball bat on release.' While some indicated they might indeed do that, there was an incredulity at the suggestion of them doing harm after being the injured party – both at the hands of the person convicted and subsequently through secondary victimisation by the CJS. For two participants in my research, this refusal to share an exact date meant that they encountered the person following release in areas that were not subject to parole and licence conditions.

There is a contentious debate – in scholarship, public discourse and the political arena – over whether victims have any right to information regarding 'offenders,' and it is not my intention to arrive at a conclusion on this. Rather the emphasis here is on the methodological importance of recognising that victims are concerned with and impacted by prisons and prisoners. Victims are often used as pawns to further a punitive agenda in what Bottoms (1995) called 'populist punitiveness' but this often ignores 'real' victims' voices. In fact, such debates often distract and are so complex that victims' entitlements continue to be stifled and even sidelined despite claims of victim centrality and 'rebalancing' the system (Walklate, 2012). Rather, much of victim satisfaction comes down to the importance of recognising the experiences and needs of victims of crime. This came through loudly in my research when it came to custodial and release conditions. This emphasis on recognition has been widely accepted since Shapland et al.'s (1985) research and yet continues to be a struggle that victims of crime encounter throughout the CJS. Therefore, despite the methodological, practical, political and emotional challenges presented by considering the victim perspective when conducting prison research, there are potential profound benefits for victims of crime, whether direct or indirect, in recognising and acknowledging their investment in such research and the potential implications prison research might have on them.

Introspection and Reflection: Consideration of the Researcher Identity

I have already noted the importance of recognising intersectionality within the researcher identity, and, elsewhere, have discussed the complexities and challenges faced by the novel or 'green' prison researcher (Sloan and Wright, 2015). Prison research is (a) not easy, (b) emotionally challenging, and (c) a completely different ball-game to other research environments. Yet the support available to prison researchers is lacking, existing only in the form of formal and/or informal networks with others who have gone through the process, and the standard support offered to academics from within the HE institution. This is in spite of the fact that prison staff are given specialist support services in their working careers, and prisoners are also given support in how to cope with the prison environment (be that in the form of the Listeners programme for those struggling, or through psychological help). Although the practical safety elements of researchers are given consideration at the ethics review stage (see Chapter Five), rarely are the psychological or emotional burdens of prison research considered in the planning or support of researchers. As such, many go into the experience expecting challenges in terms of practicalities, rather than the stresses and strains of the process. I say again – no matter how resilient you are, prison research is complex, draining, and difficult – you *will* get tired and stressed, albeit not always immediately, or not noticing it straight away – as Gariglio found when looking back on his data, 'rereading the quote [...] elicited strong feelings within me; yet these feelings were not as strong when I listened to the statement during the [interview]. This may be because the fieldwork was so overwhelming that I was somehow anaesthetised' (2016: 371).

It has been argued that prison researchers are in a privileged position and should not complain about the experience – we have it better than the prisoners, for a start. What I would argue, however, is that to acknowledge one's painful experiences is not to undermine the 'greater' pain of others in a different position. To recognise the difficulty of the environment is important – it tells the truth of the experience, and adds credence to the 'more' negative experiences of those residing and working within the institution. To neglect to state these experiences is disingenuous and not telling the truth, as well as shirking our responsibilities to those who follow us – as Jewkes states,

> in failing to disclose their autoethnographic roles and their own emotional responses to what are frequently challenging and highly charged emotional environments, prison scholars are doing a disservice to those who follow them (e.g., doctoral students) who frequently approach the field with high levels of anxiety.
>
> *(2011: 64)*

Indeed, Sykes noted one of the major methodological difficulties of prison research to be that: 'in the polarized society of the prison it is extremely difficult not to become partisan, consciously or unconsciously' (1958: 148).

When I began writing this book, although reflection and reflexivity were extremely important to my research process (as noted, my reflective diary became an integral part of both my research and my coping and debriefing from the prison setting during my doctoral fieldwork), I had never really considered how important my identity was. Of course I acknowledged the challenges that being a young white woman doing prison research on men brought

(Schlosser, 2020), but I had not appreciated the intersectionality of my own identities as a prison researcher – and had definitely not foreseen the impact that a fundamental change to my own identity might play – that is, becoming a mother. This has had a huge impact on my identity as a prison researcher – and is not simply that I am always tired, have to consider childcare issues, or that I have very little child-free time any more. Rather, my new identity as a mother has made me look very differently at prisons, punishment, prisoners, and what my role is, or should be, in researching them. I did not expect that to happen! This does *not* mean that becoming a parent is a barrier to doing prison research – far from it: many prison researchers have families, and sometimes this can even be useful in developing rapport and shared identities with participants (Hart, 2014; Willingham, 2014). Indeed, as Rossiter, Power, Fowler, Elliott and Dawson note, 'recognising researchers' feelings, experiences and perspectives on parenthood can enrich research with families affected by the criminal justice and child protection systems' (2020: 56). It is important to recognise that reflection and reflexivity are flexible, ongoing processes – life never remains static, and it is important to remember that when considering your position as a researcher, as well as the positions of others in the research.

There is a growing recognition of the importance of taking time to be reflective and reflexive within the research process,[5] particularly within the prison setting. The development of the field of sensory criminology (see Herrity, Schmidt and Warr, 2021) is a byproduct of this – noticing the impact of prison upon senses other than the visual has led to some fantastic research on the lived experiences of the prison, as has already been discussed in Chapter Six. Yet there is often a feeling of trepidation about the reflexive process, whereby it can be viewed as 'self indulgent navel gazing' (Cunliffe, 2003: 990), and not really the point of the research first and foremost. That said, prison autoethnography as a practice is starting to grow in popularity, not least down to Yvonne Jewkes' highly influential 2011 article, in which she 'critically questions the privileging of a methodological orientation that minimizes the significance of emotional experience and downplays the researcher's internal, psychic realm and external, cultural experiences and biography' (2011: 63).

As Jeff Ferrell – criminological autoethnographer extraordinaire, who I will always remember hurling a laptop to the floor at the British Society of Criminology conference plenary he was giving in 2010 – notes,

> Putting it bluntly, ethnographers unable or unwilling to account for their own presence in the research process would strike me as very poor ethnographers indeed [...] while ethnography can and should be carefully attuned to the dynamics of groups and situations, it cannot be made to be 'objective' – it cannot be honestly divorced from the ethnographer's own reflexive presence in the research process.
>
> *(2012: 2)*

Dr Marie Hutton and Dr Conor Murray both highlight these issues in their own research journeys.

REFLEXIVITY IN PRISON RESEARCH

Marie Hutton

A key aim of my ongoing research has been to deepen understandings of the 'empirical reality of human rights' (Murphy and Whitty 2013: 13) in the prison environment. My Ph.D. was inspired by my love of law but also my extensive experiences as a prison visitor for 22 years as I regularly visited my relative in numerous prisons (from Categories A to D). This transition from 'prisonised' visitor to professional 'outsider' (Comfort, 2007) meant traversing my fieldwork with 'insider knowledge' due to my 'biographical congruence' (Wakeman, 2014: 711) while nevertheless maintaining an 'outsider' status as an official researcher. Whether to disclose this 'insider' status to participants explicitly at the outset of the research was a key challenge.

Although my research was undoubtedly auto-ethnographic, I chose not to disclose in my research 'pitch' to participants for several reasons. I was pragmatic enough to know that defining myself as an ex-visitor could have negative practical ramifications. Derogatory comments about visiting families from prison staff were especially common at one of my research sites (Hutton, 2016). I cannot imagine that staff there would have felt quite so comfortable referring to prisoners' children as 'mini-me ASBOs' in front of me if they had known I had previously been one of those children running around the visitors' hall they were complaining about. That said, denying my previous experience outright, as well as being ethically dubious, was a moral impossibility; I was not ashamed of my own or my relative's history. So, I compromised, albeit not in a wholly satisfactory way adopting a 'don't ask, don't tell' policy. If asked outright (which happened several times, for example when I met a prisoner who had served time with my relative and recognized the surname), I would disclose, otherwise, I would say nothing.

Aside from pragmatic reasons, another reason for this stance was recognising Liebling's assertion that ethnography involves 'attentiveness to the lives of others' (Liebling, 2001: 474). I feared that explicit disclosure could lead to what Contreras (2013: 119) describes as a 'standpoint crisis,' the idea that participants would limit their disclosures to me due to their assumption of prior knowledge on my behalf. However, in the few instances where I did disclose, it had a positive impact on the interview. On reflection therefore, I am conscious I was also influenced by a persistent warning not 'to go native' as part of my research training, an exhortation aimed at ensuring objectivity, that paid little attention to whether one was already 'native.' Notwithstanding the troublingly colonial overtones of such a narrative coupled with the conceit of assuming a lack of previous lived experience equated to objectivity, it was always notable that such a diktat was aimed at those who had either been prisoners or members of prisoners' families, and the objectivity of prison governors and other members of prison officialdom was rarely, if ever, questioned. Hence, in my subsequent work, I am much more upfront and explicit about the role my lived experience has played in my research journey.

PROXIMITY AND DISTANCE: CHALLENGES FACING A YOUNG MALE ETHNOGRAPHER IN A YOUNG MEN'S PRISON

Conor Murray

This vignette is based on my experiences of conducting a nine-month reflexive ethnographic study in Hydebank Wood College, which imprisons Northern Ireland's cohort of young men aged 18–24. Coupling methods of semi-structured interviews and participant observation, the main focus of the research was to explore young men's needs and experiences of prison. I adopted an epistemological position that sought to critique the dominant forms of knowledge surrounding men and male behaviour and attempted to analyse the young men's experiences through the lens of critical masculinities studies.

From this epistemological standpoint, it is important to consider my positionality. I am a white, Catholic, heterosexual male, from a relatively middle-class background. During the fieldwork period I was 26. I was born and raised in Belfast, in an area about four miles from the City Hall (regarded as the centre of the City) and one mile from Hydebank. As an adolescent I associated with individuals who had spent time in Hydebank (two of whom took their own lives, and others are now housed in other prison institutions in NI) and during the fieldwork period knew some of the relatives of those who were imprisoned in Hydebank. In adolescence I experienced interactions with police and spent time in their custody. I was charged with a number of Public Order Offences, which were dealt with via a range of restorative justice measures, including being assigned a Youth Diversion Officer. Fortunately, none of my charges progressed to the stage of conviction. As I matured I became more involved in working with young people in the community and began volunteering as a local youth worker and coaching a local youth football team. While spending time providing support to boys and young men in the community, I continuously queried the decisions I made as a boy and young man. I became more and more interested in the feminist literature surrounding gender and masculinity, which led to my motivations to conduct research on young men and masculinities in prison. I refer to these experiences not to try to appear as some form of 'insider' to the prison setting, but to highlight personal and professional experience working with young and vulnerable individuals from a range of backgrounds.

The distance and proximity of my positionality in relation to the young male prisoners posed a number of challenges to me as a researcher. Warren (1988: 13) suggests that the way a researcher is received by the prisoner society is a 'cultural contextualisation' of the researcher's characteristics. This can be based upon their physical appearance, age, gender, ethnicity and marital status (Warren, 1988). Therefore, as a young, white, straight, unmarried man, it was perhaps unsurprising, and inevitable, that the prisoners – and prison staff – categorised me into a certain age- and gender-specific role, that of a 'young man' (also see Carr, 2015; Rowe, 2015; Whetter, 2015). The significant challenge in this regard was remaining friendly and familiar with the young men who were participating in the research, but who often openly expressed misogynist, homophobic and restrictive notions of masculinity in my presence. At times this left me feeling isolated and distant, I felt it was important not to express my support for the profeminist standpoint during the research out of fear that it might discourage the young men from interacting with me. Additionally, because I was exploring masculinities, I did not want to discourage them from speaking in a way that was natural to them about women or other expressions of masculinity. Bearing these factors in mind, I primarily adopted a situational withdrawal (Goffman, 1970) approach when young men were speaking in this manner, remaining collusively silent (Crewe, 2009). I felt most distant on the occasions when my masculinity was directly and publicly tested. In one instance, in the very early stages of the research, I accompanied the young men to the Lyric Theatre. In front of a larger group of prisoners one of the young men started questioning me about my sexual desires and whether or not I would like to engage in sexual intercourse with a specified theatre staff member. This made me feel extremely uncomfortable, and over time I developed pre-determined responses to most of these situations and attempted to provide non-committal and diplomatic answers to the others.

There were also some inescapable aspects of proximity which posed challenges. Shortly after I conducted an interview with him, one of the research participants committed suicide. I was extremely upset at the time, but upon reflection, it impacted me more than I had realised. It forced me to relive personal experiences of the suicide of family and friends. I constantly replayed the interview in my head and listened to the audio recording of the interview on a daily basis. I could not stop contemplating how his optimism for the future in the interview changed so dramatically during a short two-week time-frame. I felt an unshakeable sense of despair and helplessness; an 'emotional paralysis' (Yuen, 2011: 75).

Conclusion

This chapter has given consideration to the choice of participants in the prison research process – looking at the distinct considerations of researching prisoners, staff, families, victims, and the importance of considering yourself as a researcher within the process. Your choice of participant will affect the methodological choices you make and have available to you, and it is important to remember the importance of considering the individual and their subjectivities, rather than thinking of your participants as a homogeneous group. Whoever you choose as participants, it is vital to be kind (and that includes to yourself), and to remember that the information these people are giving is their gift to give – you have a responsibility to treat that gift with respect.

Notes

1 For the purposes of clarity, definitions of medical and cultural d/Deafness are provided here. Medical deafness is a clinical condition which

sits on a spectrum according to the quietest sound that an individual is able to hear. The extent to which a person is medically deaf varies significantly from those whose hearing is only slightly impaired, to individuals who are hard of hearing (HoH), and finally to those who are severely deaf (Action on Hearing Loss, n.d.). In contrast to this, cultural definitions of d/Deafness focus on identity, and the way in which an individual identifies with their d/Deafness. Thus, individuals who are culturally and linguistically Deaf identify as being part of a culturally distinct minority group, who commonly use BSL to communicate (Padden, 1980). These individuals are seen as being part of the Deaf Community, which is comprised of people who are proud to be Deaf and share the same language, similar cultural values and common life experiences (Leigh, 2009). This contrasts significantly with those who are medically deaf (but not culturally Deaf) who usually view their deafness as a problem, and commonly feel stigmatised by it (Higgins, 1980).

2 Deaf people often do not speak or write meaningfully because their language is visual.

3 The inclusion of the voice was important because without it the Prison Service could have deemed the recording to be a violation of security, given that receiving staff members were unlikely to be able to understand the signed contents.

4 This process was even more difficult during the group interview with four culturally and linguistically Deaf participants, as discussed further in Kelly-Corless (2019).

5 Although autoethnography has also been subject to criticism, especially in the wake of the publication of a particularly controversial paper on the use of masturbation as an ethnographic method (Andersson, 2022) (see Matthews, 2022).

References

Action on Hearing Loss (n.d.) Definitions of deafness. Retrieved from https://www.actiononhearingloss.org.uk/your-hearing/about-deafness-and-hearing-loss/definitions-ofdeafness.aspx

Agozino, B. (2003) *Counter-Colonial Criminology: A Critique of Imperialist Reason*. London and Sterling, VA: Pluto Press.

Andersson, K. (2022) I am not alone – we are all alone: Using masturbation as an ethnographic method in research on shota subculture in Japan. *Qualitative Research*, 14687941221096600.

Bottoms, A. (1995) The philosophy and politics of punishment and sentencing. In Clarkson, C. & Morgan, R. (eds) *The Politics of Sentencing Reform*, pp. 17–50. Oxford: Clarendon Press.

Bradford, L. (2020) Hidden victims: An exploration of the criminal justice experiences of homicide bereaved people in England and Wales. Doctoral thesis, University of Sheffield.

Carbado, D., Crenshaw, K., Mays, V., & Tomlinson, B. (2013) Inter-sectionality: Mapping the movements of a theory. *Du Bois Review: Social Science Research on Race*, 10(2), 303–312. doi:10.1017/S1742058X13000349

Carr, L. (2015) Re-entry to prison: Transition from HMP researcher to 'independent' researcher. In Drake, D. H., Earle, R. & Sloan, J. (eds) *The Palgrave Handbook of Prison Ethnography*, pp. 371–389. Basingstoke: Palgrave Macmillan.

Comfort, M. (2007) *Doing Time Together: Love and Family in the Shadow of the Prison*. University of Chicago Press.

Condry, R. (2013) Families Shamed: The Consequences of Crime for Relatives of Serious Offenders. Abingdon: Routledge.

Contreras, R. (2013) *The Stickup Kids: Race, Drugs, Violence, and the American Dream*. University of California Press.

Crawford, A., & Enterkin, J. (2001) Victim contact work in the probation service: Paradigm shift or Pandora's box? *British Journal of Criminology*, 41(4), 707–725.

Crenshaw, K. (1989) Demarginalizing the intersection of race and sex: A black feminist critique of antidiscrimination doctrine, feminist theory and antiracist politics. *University of Chicago Legal Forum*, 1989(1/8). Available at: http://chicagounbound.uchicago.edu/uclf/vol1989/iss1/8

Crewe, B. (2009) *The Prisoner Society: Power, Adaptation and Social Life in an English Prison*. Oxford University Press.

Crewe, B., Warr, J., Bennett, P., & Smith, A. (2014) The emotional geography of prison life. *Theoretical Criminology*, 18(1), 56–74.

Cunliffe, A. L. (2003) Reflexive inquiry in organizational research: Questions and possibilities. *Human Relations*, 56(8), 983–1003.

Dirga, L. (2015) The possible applications of the guard's world concept in the analysis of the Czech prison system. *Acta Fakulty Filozofické Západočeské Univerzity v Plzni*, 7(3), 115–131.

Eddo-Lodge, R. (2017) *Why I'm No Longer Talking to White People about Race*. London: Bloomsbury.

Ferrell, J. (2012) Autoethnography. In Gadd, D., Karstedt, S. & Messner, S. F. (eds) *The Sage Handbook of Criminological Research Methods*. London and Thousand Oaks, CA: Sage.

Gariglio, L. (2016) Photo-elicitation in prison ethnography: Breaking the ice in the field and unpacking prism officers' use of force. *Crime, Media, Culture*, 12(3), 367–379.

Goffman, E. (1970) *Asylums*. Harmondsworth: Penguin.

Hart, E. L. (2014) Power, pregnancy and prison: The impact of a researcher's pregnancy on qualitative interviews with women prisoners. In Lumsden, K. & Winter, A. (eds) *Reflexivity in Criminological Research*, pp. 102–114. Basingstoke: Palgrave Macmillan.

Hendl, J. (2005) *Kvalitativní výzkum*. Prague: Portál.

Herrity, K., Schmidt, B. E., & Warr, J. (eds) (2021) *Sensory Penalties: Exploring the Senses in Spaces of Punishment and Social Control*. Bingley: Emerald Group Publishing.

Higgins, P. (1980) *Outsiders in a Hearing World: A Sociology of Deafness*. London: Sage.

Hutton, M. (2016) Visiting time: A tale of two prisons. *Probation Journal*, 63(3), 347–361.

Jewkes, Y. (2011) Autoethnography and emotion as intellectual resources: Doing prison research differently. *Qualitative inquiry*, 18(1), 63–75.

Kelly, L. (2017) Suffering in silence: The unmet needs of d/Deaf prisoners. *Prison Service Journal*, November, p. 234.

Kelly, L. (2018) Sounding out d/Deafness: The experiences of d/Deaf prisoners. *Journal of Criminal Psychology*, 8(1), 20–32.

Kelly-Corless, L. (2019) Delving into the unknown: An experience of doing research with d/Deaf prisoners. *Qualitative Inquiry*, 26(3–4), 355–368.

Lammy, D. (2017) The Lammy Review: Final report: An independent review into the treatment of, and outcomes for black, Asian and minority ethnic individuals in the criminal justice system. Available at https://assets.publishing.service.gov.uk/government/uploads/system/uploads/attachment_data/file/643001/lammy-review-final-report.pdf

Leigh, I. W. (2009) *A Lens on Deaf Identities*. New York: Oxford University Press.

Liebling, A. (1999) Doing research in prison: Breaking the silence. *Theoretical Criminology*, 3(2), 147–173.

Liebling, A. (2001) Whose side are we on? Theory, practice and allegiances in prisons research. *British Journal of Criminology*, 41(3), 472–484.

Matthews, W. (2022) Masturbation journal paper exposes deeper problems in research. *Times Higher Education*, 19 August 2022, available at https://www.timeshighereducation.com/news/masturbation-journal-paper-exposes-deeper-problems-research

Ministry of Justice (2020) *Code of Practice for Victims of Crime*. London: Ministry of Justice. Available at: https://www.gov.uk/government/publications/the-code-of-practice-for-victims-of-crime/code-of-practice-for-victims-of-crime-in-england-and-wales-victims-code. Accessed on 3 May 2023.

Moran, D., Hutton, M. A., Dixon, L., & Disney, T. (2017) Daddy is a difficult word for me to hear: Carceral geographies of parenting and the prison visiting room as a contested space of situated fathering. *Children's Geographies*, 15(1), 107–121.

Murphy, T., & Whitty, N. (2013) Making history: Academic criminology and human rights. *British Journal of Criminology*, 53(4), 568–587.

Phillips, C. (2012) *The Multicultural Prison: Ethnicity, Masculinity, and Social Relations among Prisoners*. Oxford University Press.

Phillips, C., & Earle, R. (2010) Reading difference differently? Identity, epistemology and prison ethnography. *British Journal of Criminology*, *50*(2), 360–378.

Padden, C. (1980) The deaf community and the culture of deaf people. In Baker, C. & Battison, R. (eds) *Sign Language and the Deaf Community: Essays in Honour of William Stokoe*, pp. 89–104. Silver Spring, MD: National Association of the Deaf.

Rossiter, C., Power, T., Fowler, C., Elliott, K., & Dawson, A. (2020) Reflexivity in correctional research: Researcher perspectives on parenthood in a study with incarcerated parents. *Qualitative Social Work*, *19*(1), 56–74.

Rowe, A. (2015) Situating the self in prison research: Power, identity and epistemology. In Drake, D. H., Earle, R. & Sloan, J. (eds) *The Palgrave Handbook of Prison Ethnography*, pp. 347–370. Basingstoke: Palgrave Macmillan.

Schlosser, J. (2020) *Prison Stories: Women Scholars' Experiences Doing Research behind Bars*. Lanham, MD: Rowman & Littlefield.

Shapland, J., Willmore, J., & Duff, P. (1985) *Victims in the Criminal Justice System*. Farnham, Surrey: Gower Publishing.

Sloan, J., & Wright, S. (2015) Going in green: Reflections on the challenges of 'getting in, getting on, and getting out' for doctoral prisons researchers. In *The Palgrave Handbook of Prison Ethnography*, pp. 143–163. Basingstoke: Palgrave Macmillan.

Sykes, G. M. (1958) *The Society of Captives: A Study of a Maximum Security Prison*. Princeton, NJ: Princeton University Press.

Wakeman, S. (2014) Fieldwork, biography and emotion: Doing criminological autoethnography. *British Journal of Criminology*, *54*(5), 705–721.

Walklate, S. (2012) Courting compassion: Victims, policy, and the question of justice. *The Howard Journal of of Criminal Justice*, *51*(2), 109–121.

Warren, C. A. B. (1988) *Gender Issues in Field Research*. Newbury Park, CA: Sage.

Whetter, L. (2015) 'To thine own self be true': Having faith in the prison researcher. In Drake, D. H., Earle, R. & Sloan, J. (eds) *The Palgrave Handbook of Prison Ethnography*, pp. 371–389. Basingstoke: Palgrave Macmillan.

Willingham, B. C. (2014) Prison is my family business: Reflections of an African American woman with incarcerated relatives doing research on incarcerated African American fathers. In Lumsden, K. & Winter, A. (eds) *Reflexivity in Criminological Research*, pp. 138–149. Basingstoke: Palgrave Macmillan.

Yuen, F. (2011) Embracing emotionality: Clothing my "naked truths". *Critical Criminology*, *19*, 75–88.

Eight

PRISON RESEARCH ACROSS THE GLOBE

RESEARCHING PRISON LIFE IN BRAZIL

Sacha Darke

Since 2008 I have researched prison life in Brazil. This journey began three years earlier, when in 2005 I visited the ruins of the infamously large and overcrowded Carandiru prison in São Paulo, scene of Latin America's most deadly prison massacre, when in 1992 a specialist police force responded to a relatively minor rebellion by killing 111 male prisoners. Many were shot at point-blank range in their cells. What struck me most about my visit, however, was not the physical conditions of the prison, or even the pile of rubble that had been the cellblock where the massacre took place – although I still keep some of this on display in my office – but the hundreds of murals that adorned the walls of the remaining cellblock yards, corridors and cells. These spoke of camaraderie and survival as much as conflict and suffering. This ultimately became my research focus. I have now visited approximately 40 prisons across the country, several on numerous occasions. Most of these have been half-day visits, although I have also completed two short but intensive ethnographic studies, during one of which I stayed inside the prison walls.

During this research, I have witnessed much human suffering. Most Brazilian prison cells are chronically overcrowded and medical conditions and injuries are often left untreated. In normal times, most prisoners are at least able to spend daylight hours in

---

DOI: 10.4324/9781315297217-8

an exercise yard. But some prisoners are deemed too vulnerable to leave their cells at all. One experience that will always haunt me occurred at a prison unit in the state of Goiás in 2016 when I passed through a corridor where a number of women accused of killing their infant children were being held in isolation cells for their own protection. These women were considered so vulnerable that the windows to their cells were placed three metres above the ground and were no more than a few inches in diameter. The pale faces that stared out at me and bid me good morning remain stitched to my memory. Two years later, I met a group of male prisoners held ten to a single cell on a vulnerable person's wing in the state of Espírito Santo. Some had been convicted for sexual violence but others were locked up in such horrific conditions simply because of their sexuality.

Strange as it may sound, my research is equally punctuated with positive memories. Many of these have arisen due to the nature of my research – I always prompt prisoners to relate stories of individual and especially collective human resilience – but others relate to the depth of welcome I have become accustomed to receiving from prison inmates and prison staff. A re-occurring theme is the confusion I cause when I am invited to stay to eat and say that for more than 30 years I have not eaten anything that used to walk, fly or swim! When I am lucky, this means being taken out for lunch, but when I am with prisoners it more often means being watched with bewilderment while I dig through my rice and beans and pass rancid bits of meat around the table. The final day of my first ethnographic study – at a police holding facility in which prisoners were recruited to work in the place of guards – ended with jokes from the governor that if I got into trouble with the police he would always have a job for me, but that they would first learn to cater better for vegetarians.

In 2012, I was lucky enough to be involved in a symposium hosted by the International Centre for Comparative Criminological Research at the Open University entitled 'Resisting the Eclipse: An International Symposium on Prison Ethnography,' where prison ethnographers and researchers from across the globe came together to discuss prison research, eventually leading to the creation of the *Palgrave Handbook of Prison Ethnography* (Drake, Earle and Sloan, 2015). In this collection, particular efforts were made to try to include chapters from the global South to be more representative of the prison research experience across the globe – we engaged a lot with the Global Prisons Research Network (GPRN). Within this chapter, the importance of looking at prison research on a global scale will be discussed, both in terms of the research that is currently being done, and potential areas of study. I will also discuss the importance of looking comparatively between states and jurisdictions in order to learn more about our own practices, and to examine best practice by others. Through a global examination of the state of prison research, I *attempt* to identify *some* universal truths of prison research.

Ethnocentrism and Marginalised Voices

Ethnocentrism – 'assuming that what *we* do, our way of thinking about and responding to crime, is universally shared or, at least, that it would be right for everyone else' (Nelken, 2009: 291) – is a substantial problem when considering any form of academic research practice, both in terms of how that research practice is undertaken, and the implications later for policy. Indeed, in 1981, Wiarda noted that:

> the vast bulk of our social science findings, models, and literature, which purport to be universal, are in fact biased, ethnocentric, and not universal at all. They are based on the narrow and rather particular experiences of Western Europe (actually a much smaller nucleus of countries in central and northwest Europe) and the United States, and they may have little or no relevance to the rest of the world.
>
> *(1981: 163)*

Indeed, Boshoff (2009) found that, when looking at research collaboration within science in Central Africa, much research is produced in collaboration with partners from other regions, with such partners often having colonial ties. Where individuals were subsequently strengthened in their research skills, there was a tendency for those individuals to move 'away from the periphery and towards the core' (Boshoff, 2009: 430). As such, partnership development to empower those countries whose research practice is peripheral, rather than within the (arguably often Western democratic) core, is 'better accomplished through capacity building strategies that target institutions and networks, rather than individuals (Lansang and Dennis, 2004).' (Boshoff, 2009: 430).

Indeed, criminology as a whole has been subject to some quite scathing criticism for its imperialism and centring itself within the colonial. Agozino (the brilliant academic who describes criminology as 'obsessed with social control-freak domination over others in otherwise democratizing global communities' (2010: ii)), writes that

> given the crucial importance of (cultural) imperialism in the history of knowledge in all parts of the world (Said, 1993), one would need to explain why the field of criminology is dominated by scholars in former colonial centres of authority and how such colonialist domination of the field leads to theoretical underdevelopment through the concealment of the bloody legacy of colonialist criminology.
>
> *(Agozino, 2004: 350)*

The argument remains the same if for 'criminology' we substitute 'prison research,' which we need to work to address.

In addition, there is a clear lack of research being done by those actually from those under-researched regions – instead it is much more likely that researchers from the West will travel to research and 'report back.' Such research is invaluable in terms of gathering new information, but must be treated with care not to be imperialistic (i.e. coming from a Western perspective of what 'works' and is 'right'). It is also vital that we start to hear the voices of those *from* these global locations, and that greater respect is given to the variety of ways that such information can be gathered and reported: Western methodologies don't necessarily work in other jurisdictions, and it is important to consider 'decolonising methodologies' such as indigenous storywork (see Q'um Q'um Xiiem, Lee-Morgan and De Santolo, 2019) and the ways in which notions of time, space, and even 'native intellectuals' need to be given distinct consideration with respect to distinct societal, cultural, and historical contexts (see Tuhiwai Smith, 2021). Indeed, as Smith notes,

> [i]t galls us that Western researchers and intellectuals can assume to know all that it is possible to know of us, on the basis of their brief encounters with some of us. It appals us that the West can desire, extract and claim ownership of our ways of knowing our imagery, the things we create and produce, then simultaneously reject the people who created and developed those ideas and seek to deny them further opportunities to be creators of their own culture and own nations.
>
> *(Smith, 1999: 1)*

In addition to adjusting to a Covid-19 world, the globe has also been reacting to the death of George Floyd, killed by an American police officer in Minneapolis in May 2020. This horrific event, captured on social media, has led to worldwide protests, and, importantly in the context of this book, a serious discussion about the ethnocentrism of education, academia, and knowledge more generally. When teaching students, I try to point out to them that the majority of research that they are reading about is written by those from the English-speaking global North, taking on very particular epistemological and ontological perspectives about what is good/bad/worthy/ethical knowledge. For those of us researching from privileged positions, it is vital that we seek to interrogate our privileges within the field of prison research. Reni Eddo-Lodge makes an important point about the role of privilege-checking in her own discussions:

> I am university-educated, able-bodied, and I speak and write in ways very similar to those I criticise. I walk and talk like them, and part of that is why I am taken seriously. As I write about shattering perspectives and disrupting faux objectivity, I have to remember that there are factors in my life that bolster my voice above others.
>
> *(2017: 88)*

Even once we have checked our privileges, it is important for us to see the methodological inadequacies and deficiencies that those of us ensconced in the global North may suffer from by virtue of our colonial histories and traditions – termed '*epistemicide*, the murder of knowledge' (2014: 92) by de Sousa Santos:

> The global North is getting smaller and smaller in economic as well as political and cultural terms, and yet it cannot make sense of the world at large other than through general theories and universal ideas [...] The truth of the matter is that, after five centuries of 'teaching' the world, the global North seems to have lost the capacity to learn from the experiences of the world. In other words, it looks as if colonialism has disabled the global North from learning in noncolonial terms, that is, in terms that allow for the existence of histories other than the universal history of the West.
>
> *(de Sousa Santos, 2014: 19)*

The majority of well-known penal research has been situated within Western democracies and within the English language. This has resulted in considerable ethnocentrism within penal studies, as well as a lack of key voices – often those who have already been victims of forms of structural oppression through colonialisation. In addition to this, prison research often involves engaging with highly sensitive subjects (in both senses of the term) and marginalised groups whose voices go unrepresented. Serrant-Green's term 'Screaming silences' (2010), originally from the realm of public health, but also equally relevant – and already used with ex-offenders (Eshareturi, Serrant, Galbraith and Glynn, 2015) – is particularly useful:

> 'Screaming silences' are situated in the subjective experiences of individuals or groups (known as 'the listener') and the so-cial and personal contexts in which their experiences occur. The name 'screaming silences' reflects how an issue, as experi-enced by the listener, 'screams' out to them in relation to their health, because of its relationship or impact in their reality. Conversely, the same issue may be relatively 'silent' in the con-sciousness or experience of the greater majority in society, or

absent from the available evidence base where it fails to have wider impact on sharing aspects of health.

(Serrant-Green, 2010: 349)

In order to address this, Serrant-Green developed a 'Silences Framework' for investigating 'sensitive issues or marginalised perspectives' (2010: 351), containing four stages (with an optional fifth stage): 'Working in "silences"'; 'Hearing "silences"'; 'Voicing "silences," ' and 'Working with "silences"' (and the optional extra, which is 'particularly useful where the research outputs required are more applied and/or for those utilising existing studies to produce an action plan for service delivery or community action' (2010: 351–352): 'Planning for "silences."' Serrant-Green's work 'is closely aligned with anti-essentialist viewpoints, acknowledging the importance of situated views and the existence of power and inequality as contextualising features in society, research and researchers who seek to explore it' (2010: 358) – issues which need vital consideration in today's penal contexts.

International Prison Research Projects

As such, for a considerable period of time, the majority of prison research has been considerably ethnocentric in its approach, being situated predominantly within Western democratic jurisdictions. Indeed, even in a much more global contemporary academic landscape, the written academic situation is almost always in English. Yet of late, there has been an encouraging academic acknowledgment and recognition of the growing globalisation of prison research, with more and more countries' penal landscapes undergoing examination, and an increasing inclusion of the global South within penal discourse. An excellent resource for those planning on undertaking any international prison research is that of the Global Prisons Research Network (GPRN: https://sites.google.com/site/gprnnetwork/).

It is vital that anyone looking at research in any jurisdiction is keenly aware of the legal, social, cultural, linguistic, and penal idiosyncrasies of the jurisdiction in which that prison sits. Language is a key consideration when working in multiple jurisdictions, or when comparing prisons from across different countries. Sometimes linguistic idiosyncrasies can have implications for access (as Max Martin notes regarding his attempts to enter prisons in Myanmar, whereby the translated meaning of the word for 'reform' caused him barriers to accessing sites compared to the word for 'development' (Max Martin, 2019: 144)). Similarly, certain practices such as 'rehabilitation, remand or prison education carry different meanings, and comparing these quantitatively may not be the best way to describe the practices of imprisonment and illuminate their inherent social meanings' (Brangan, 2020: 609). Indeed, as I often say to students studying 'Criminal Justice Compared' with me, you need to make sure that what you are trying to compare is the same, rather than comparing apples and oranges.

Reflecting further about language, in 2022 I was invited to speak at a session on 'Sexualities and bodies in prison' at Maison des Sciences de l'Homme at Paris-Saclay (unfortunately, due to Covid-19, there was no trip to Paris for me!). This is, without a doubt, one of the best things I have ever done: my presentation was definitely not the best, but my participation made me suddenly realise the insular nature of the English-speaking research world. Apart from me, all the other contributors were speaking in French ... and I cannot speak French, at least certainly not to an academic standard. But the prison research community that I discovered there (who, fortunately for me, could in the main speak and understand English) was vibrant and engaging and really exciting to see. I know that I missed out on some incredible dialogue and discourse through my linguistic limitations, and the entire experience humbled me and made me think very differently about global research.

Similarly, I have also been privy to some discussions via another online collective that I follow: the Decolonial Critique Network Group (engaging with decolonisation in HE more broadly). The issues faced regard writing and publishing in English when this is not an individual's first (or even second) language, and the barriers this causes to those from jurisdictions that often go underrepresented within academic research publications. It is important to remember that language is often very specific to a cultural context, and certain words or terms in one language can mean something very different when translated, if they translate at all. This also raises the question of whether we *should* be translating everything into English, and what might be lost through the privileging of Western cultural publication stances (but that's another book entirely).

Jurisdictional differences can result in prison research processes differing hugely across the world, and the location within which a piece of research is undertaken can also have implications for how this research process is talked about in academic contexts. Speaking from a US perspective, Reiter suggests that 'there is not only a different attitude toward prison research generally in the United Kingdom and Europe, but a different attitude toward exactly how to talk about this research' (2014: 420). He goes on to suggest that this has led to an 'increasing *pixelation* of the US prison system' (2014: 420), whereby there are too few individual research projects being done to provide a clear overall picture of the US prison estate.[1]

Jurisdictional idiosyncrasies can have implications on matters of access and gatekeepers, for instance. Whereas in England and Wales, the requirements made from ethics committees, as well as the NRC and the institution itself can be bureaucratic and laborious, in other jurisdictions such hurdles may not be imposed upon the researcher (this does not mean that ethical principles do not need to be considered though!) – sometimes just knowing the right people can be your entry pass to a prison. Alternatively, the lack of familiarity with research; the issues of foreign researchers entering prison sites; and the potential distrust and secrecy that surrounds prisons, can have the opposite effect and require even greater diplomacy and bureaucratic procedure – some hurdles may be formally imposed, whereas others may require emotional and interpersonal work to be done to convince authorities to trust you as a researcher.

CZECH QUALITATIVE PRISON RESEARCH: KEY ROLE OF THE GATEKEEPERS

Lukáš Dirga

A popular method for assessing issues concerning the Czech prison environment is the qualitative methodology. This approach, however, has numerous pitfalls. Most importantly, there is the fact that

Czech prisons have the characteristics of total institutions, and due to inherent reasons, it is highly difficult to complete field research inside their facilities.

In this regard, a key role is played by so-called gatekeepers. In the case of Czech prisons, the most important gatekeepers are the governors, whose powers include approving research in facilities under their management. Thanks to experience gained during previous projects, I have discovered that making a request to carry out fieldwork inside a prison using a formal channel, such as a written request sent by mail, is highly ineffective.[2] Very likely, such a request will be rejected due to security reasons without being delivered to the prison governor. This is understandable because the primary task of a prison is to work with inmates and to ensure overall security. Moreover, many Czech prisons operate at the limit of their capacity and are overwhelmed by various requests for entry, including those made by students. Any presence of civilians inside a prison is demanding in terms of administration, time, and personnel. Moreover, a civilian presence presents significant security risks in consideration of the need to protect inmates, employees, and the entering civilians. Hence, the researcher's task is to convince the governor why the relevant risks should be taken. For these purposes, a written request is not a suitable instrument.

The solution I propose is informal interaction with individuals active in the prison environment, who are able to arrange communication with a key gatekeeper (governor) or his or her associates. As is the case with the entire process of qualitative research, personal contact is therefore the most important factor. To succeed, the researcher must be well prepared because, if fortunate, they will have only one opportunity to convince the governor to grant approval for the applicable project. Thus, fieldwork needs to start long before one's first steps within the prison walls. At the beginning of my career I was unable to devise strategies to the foregoing effect, and I paid the price by having numerous requests rejected.

It needs to be mentioned, however, that the situation has improved during the last decade, as cooperation between the academic world and the prison service in the Czech Republic has been strengthened. For that, stakeholders on both sides deserve acknowledgment and gratitude.

STUDYING EXPERIENCES OF IMPRISONMENT IN MYANMAR

Liv S. Gaborit

Doing fieldwork in Myanmar was significantly different to my previous experiences with prison research. In the Philippines I had conducted research in a context where I took part in frequent visits to various prisons and worked closely with prisoners who collaborated with the NGO I worked for. In Myanmar on the other hand, I came to a context where access to prisons was very limited, where even INGOs offering health support were stopped at the gate. I therefore commenced my research without knowing if I would ever gain access to prisons in Myanmar. For the first one and a half years of my research I collected data through alternative channels. I worked with former prisoners and realised that they had a freedom to report things to me they would likely not have had while imprisoned (Gaborit, 2019). After a year and a half I finally succeeded in gaining access to a Myanmar prison. It was the result of a long incremental process and a collaboration between DIGNITY – Danish Institute Against Torture – where I was based, the UNODC, who were an established actor in Myanmar, and of course the Myanmar Prisons Department. Through this slow incremental approach my colleagues and I had managed to build relationships and trust that were essential to successfully navigate the necessary bureaucratic process and become the first academic researchers ever to be granted access to Myanmar prisons.

In June 2018 I finally received the news that I had been granted access to visit Insein Central Prison and interview prisoners engaged in a meditation programme inside the prison (Gaborit, 2020). At the prison gate I was greeted by senior staff who were understandably wary at the thought of having a stranger visit their prison in order to write about it. The people who received me on the first day had not been part of the long process leading up to these visits and they were not familiar with me or my research. On the other hand, their familiarity with the reporting of critical human rights organisations and sensationalist media, caused fear. Thus on my first day I was respectfully chaperoned by two senior officials who were trying to figure out what my agenda was as we went through the day. On the second day of prison visits, things changed as I met with the two senior officials and their boss who had been involved in the process that led to my being granted access and with whom I had built a trusting relationship. When he saw me, he warmly welcomed me as a friend of the prison and put the fear of his wary officials at ease. After this meeting, the entourage that had chaperoned me was reduced from three to sometimes only one person and I gained more freedom that allowed me to visit more parts of the prison. Doing prison research in Myanmar has been an extremely challenging endeavour in which the incremental approach, patience, trust, and to gain human relations proved essential for gaining access even when working with a bureaucratic institution like a prison.

Even when one has got past the formal gatekeepers, there will be cultural and societal expectations and idiosyncrasies that require the researcher's consideration – not least when bringing gender and sex (and the associated power differentials that accompany these aspects of identity) into the equation. This is arguably a global phenomenon, but some cultural settings can be more complex than others.

UNDERTAKING PRISON RESEARCH IN LEBANON

Shereen Baz

Entering a prison to conduct qualitative research is difficult in any circumstance. Generally, it is difficult because individuals within prisons are considered 'high risk' or 'vulnerable subjects' who need protection, which in some cases 'hinders scientific inquiry' (Schlosser, 2008: 3). Within countries such as Lebanon (a small country located in the Middle East), which is by nature a Third World country, several other issues arise. Some of these issues faced by my study[3] included issues with gaining access, safety, gender, and in some circumstances, taboo.

As a researcher, I was not an agent of the Lebanese criminal justice system, nor a prisoner, and I was also a female in a male environment. Therefore, I did not have many things in common with the study's participants, especially since the participants were mostly male. It was because of my position as an 'outsider' that access to prisoners, as well as prison guards and police officers' openness to participate was at times a challenge. In relation to prison guards and police officers, being an 'outsider' meant that I was a threat, as from their point of view they were at risk of being reported and so were more cautious of what they were saying.

In addition, due to my gender and the prison guards and police officers being all male, patriarchy had some effects on my interactions with them in order to further establish my position as an outsider. Lebanon is a patriarchal society; this is especially true for corrections and criminal justice arenas. Women who enter these areas are usually given desk jobs and are very rarely granted access. Being a female and conducting research in a male dominated arena resulted in numerous comments and barriers to the study. Comments included 'why would a girl like you want to do such a research?' and 'this is not something you should be talking about.' These comments began from the start, i.e., when I was obtaining official permission to enter prisons to conduct my research, and ran through the whole research process. Direct comments occurred when, for example, a prison guard made me walk through the scanners several times upon trying to enter one of the prisons. This happened despite the walk-through metal detectors not indicating suspicion, and being subjected to a body search. When asked why I had to repeat the procedure, the prison guard replied, 'don't you know I like blondes?' Effects of gender were also experienced when participants expected to do most of the talking while I listened. Such occurrences affected the length of the interviews, and the power balance within the interviews.

With regard to personal safety within prisons, in Lebanese prisons, prisoners are not segregated according to their crimes. This means prisons are not classified into categories such as the United Kingdom's categories A, B, C or open prisons). Instead, prisons are composed of a mixture of criminals who roam around the prison grounds with little to no restrictions. Entering the prison entails walking alongside the prisoners and through their exercise yards and in general being in close proximity to them. The only 'guards' accompanying visitors are the head prisoners,[4] and only in extremely rare circumstances would prison guards be present. This meant that as a researcher, I was regularly left unattended amongst the prisoners. According to Schlosser (2008: 10), generally, before a researcher enters a prison, they 'will be advised of what to wear, with whom to speak, how to behave, what to disclose and where to go during entry.' This did not occur, and what little prison 'protocols' existed were something I had to learn along the way, mostly from the inmates themselves.

Additional research challenges within the Lebanese prison included the unstable situation within and outside of prisons which affected access, and the lack of prison guard control which meant that prisoners themselves would help me gain access to participants. There were also issues regarding the lack of space to conduct interviews and problematic attitudes with prison guards. For example, some of the guards mocked the study, stating that sex offenders 'are the only ones who should be innocent' and some even went as far as trying to prevent access into the cellblocks. In such situations, I used my connections to ensure I was granted access to the cellblocks.

In conclusion, in order to aid in the ethical completion of the research despite these issues, several steps were undertaken. These included: the use of connections, building good rapport and relationships with participants, acknowledging power relationships between the researcher and the researched, and following pre-existing ethical guidelines (such as the use of informed consent forms, information sheets, etc.). Following these steps helped ensure participants were comfortable and in turn more cooperative.

Notions of social proximity can actually add depth and humanity to the research interaction.

PRISON RESEARCH IN INDIA: REFLECTING ON THE CHALLENGES OF SOCIAL PROXIMITY

Madhumita Pandey

For my research, which explores the attitudes towards women and perceptions of culpability in convicted violent offenders, I chose Delhi Prisons (also known as Tihar Jail), which is situated in Delhi, India and is the largest prison complex in South Asia. Here, I briefly discuss the challenge of social proximity during prison research in India.

There is already a certain social distance between you and the participant with regard to them being imprisoned and you being a free agent. To add to that, the class polarization easily witnessed in India also finds its way into prison research. Most men I interacted with (both convicted rapists and murderers) hailed from villages outside Delhi. Furthermore, a large number had grown up in some of the poorest villages and districts of the country. As a researcher, while I did not share too many cultural dissimilarities with my participants, there was a certain social distance, as I had experienced a privileged urban life in India that provided numerous opportunities for me. Through this lens, before my participants' narratives could reflect a perception of 'self as victim,' somewhere I had already accorded them that status. I found myself on many occasions not only sympathising with their stories of childhood but also mesmerised by the new information and therefore felt the need to probe a lot. For instance, one of my participants convicted of murder explained,

> Our school was not like the schools they have in the cities. There were barely four rooms built with tin roofs at the edge of the village. We did not have a lot of classes as teachers seldom bothered to come and on days they came, they often just took attendance and left. All of us preferred playing outside than reading. There was hardly any money for stationary.

At this point, I asked numerous questions (some even unrelated to my overall research aim) regarding why parents or other village elders didn't complain about the teachers or ask why weren't there sufficient funds to run this public school, and so on, questions that my participant was kind and patient enough to answer. So, in hindsight, I realized two things: first, social proximity can make you go off track during an interview as you may seek more information from someone who is a part of a different social class, which can be a negative, particularly if prison permission is only granted for a limited amount of time; and second your participant may actually enjoy these 'extra' questions as it might may make them feel superior – the knowledgeable one. The latter can be a positive as it might help you bond well with the participant, but also quite challenging because the dynamics of the interview changes as the participant then controls the conversation (as they too can sense this social distance and the fact that you are taking a keen interest in their lived experiences which are significantly different to yours); thus it can be difficult to steer the conversation back.

In addition, access-based negotiations can also raise issues such as a 'tension between being a witness and being an accomplice' (Max Martin, 2019) to bureaucratic power.

DOING PRISON RESEARCH IN CANADA

Rosemary Ricciardelli

Prison research is about entering an enclosed society in itself, a society deeply shaped by the free world yet informed by the nuances of institutional living and the informal and formal rules governing all interactions. In Canada, federal correctional services fall under the jurisdiction of Correctional Services Canada and house prisoners sentenced to two years or more in prison. In addition, each of the 13 provinces and territories has their own correctional services, that hold remanded prisoners and those sentenced to a maximum of two years less one day, with few exceptions. Doing research in any system requires navigating the setting that is the prison space and its diverse meanings; prison is an involuntary home for many, a workspace for others, and a society within itself for all. Often understated about prisons is that staff and prisoners across institutions and services tend to know one another. Thus, as a researcher travels through institutions and organizations in Canada they will become a small part of that prison society in some way. As researchers, we do not leave those we encounter untouched and our presence in prison is even more pronounced because the prison is not a space where civilians can enter freely. As researchers, we are privileged to have access to such a society and we must remember that we are part of maintaining the social balance of the prison society – it is essential that the expectations of all those we encounter are kept in check. Research outcomes are slow and applied outcomes often feel even slower to come to fruition.

Particularly, in doing research with correctional services in Canada, there is a need to navigate access. Obtaining access can be a lengthy but rewarding process. The ability to do the research is very much rooted in the needs of the institution and one's ability to engage with staff or prisoners without drawing too significantly on resources. Although access is not always awarded for a multitude of reasons, despite best efforts by researchers throughout research proposal stages, but for those interested in prison research, we should not be dissuaded.

The totality of the prison society varies in light of many factors, for instance for some staff or prisoners the prison social world is consuming and impacts all corners of their lives, while others make efforts to differentiate between their life at large and prison living/working. How researchers approach prison research must respect and be considerate of both perspectives; recognizing that for some prisoners (or staff) a researcher is entering a private, personal space and, at times, a space laced with potential vulnerabilities. Moreover, in bearing witness to people's personal lives, either at work or in their temporary 'home,' prison research includes three interconnected components: ethnography, emotion work, and an ethical lens. The ethnographic component arises as a researcher learns to navigate the prison, observing, listening, and learning of the positives and hardships in the lives of staff or prisoners. In my experience, prisoners and staff are quite receptive to engaging in research, very open with their stories and insights. Of course, knowledge perpetuates the need for emotion work, to manage the seeming roller-coaster of emotions that underpin learning of the diverse experiences of all those encountered. The emotion work must be coupled with patience when doing research in Canada, as any instance within the institution can bring a halt to a research opportunity and understaffing can lead to delays in data collection. Moreover, the ethics of prison research must include recognizing that within the space of 'observation' in prison work, not all those encountered are consenting study participants – not everyone wants to be researched, included in a study, or even seen. Overall, key to doing prison research, in any country, is respecting the organizational processes, the staff, and the prisoners.

Some of the most impressive and inspirational research projects in prisons that I have read about have been in non Western jurisdictions, as you will have seen from some of the research reflections already included in this chapter. I don't know if doing research beyond England and Wales and the USA lends itself to more ambitious projects; whether other countries have a less restrictive prison research bureaucracy; or whether Brangan's argument about the Anglocentrism of the punitiveness versus penal exceptionalism debate (Brangan, 2020) means that moving beyond the 'Anglo' develops very different arguments and interpretations about punishment. Or even if it is just my point of view – the notion that something a bit 'different' about somewhere beyond my 'known realm' is inherently more complex and creative in my eyes. Whatever it is, there have been some astoundingly complex pieces of work across the world looking at various aspects of prisons.

It is, however, important to remember that international research is not, in and of itself, comparative. More often than not, these projects do not intend to be compared to the West – they are exploratory and develop knowledge distinct to that location, and are not intended to be compared to the more prolific body of knowledge from the USA and England & Wales. Yet, those of us situated within those Western realms often undertake our own comparisons as we read these studies – comparing the 'unknown' to the 'known.'[5] For those attempting comparisons, *huge* care must be taken – it is a much harder endeavour than it may initially appear to be.

Comparative Prison Research

A comparative research design is defined by Bryman as 'A research design that entails the comparison of two or more cases in order to illuminate existing theory or generate theoretical insights as a result of contrasting findings uncovered through the comparison' (2016: 698). International comparative research comes filled with challenges, particularly finding points of equivalence. Indeed, Cavadino and Dignan ask the question 'Is comparative penology possible?' (2006: 4). They note that finding standard measures (i.e. of punitiveness) across different jurisdictions is particularly challenging. Similarly, Nelken (2010) notes a host of issues with doing comparative criminal justice work, including deciding upon 'starting points' and 'units of comparison' (which can undergo change over time (2010: 71)); acknowledging cultural assumptions and structures of relevance, and choosing reference points for comparison. He notes that it is important to consider whether one is looking for similarities or differences when undertaking comparative work. As such, comparing from different starting points, with different legal and cultural languages around crime and punishment, and with different expectations, traditions, and research understandings, makes the undertaking anything but simple. As Brangan notes, there is a 'universalising tendency in the comparative sociology of punishment: the propensity to assume "that all societies are knowable, and that they are knowable in the same way and from the same point of view!" (Connell, 2006: 258)' (Brangan, 2020: 602). This may not, however, be the case, and needs to be given thought before attempting to undertake such a practice.

Nelken also encourages thinking around the purpose of comparative research: 'How far are we intending to learn more about our own system and its problems, and how far are we trying to understand another place, system or practice "for itself"?' (2010: 12). Such considerations can greatly shape the direction and process of the research project as well as the conclusions that are drawn, and may inform policy and practice. Acknowledging what is being looked at with regard to perspective becomes all the more important when one acknowledges the different approaches to punishment situated within different jurisdictions.

Brangan has gone on to critique the key notions of modern comparative penology – that being the Anglocentric nature of the discipline and the under-theorisation of penal exceptionalism in lieu of punitiveness (Brangan, 2020) – indeed, she states that 'exceptionalism serves Anglocentric concerns regarding punitiveness' (2020: 601), and goes on to suggest strategies to develop comparative penology further. The suggestion is to 'change where we compare' and look to a more diverse sphere of reference, as well as looking more 'within these exceptional fields' (2020: 606); 'rethinking the prison and penal politics' and looking 'in a way that accepts that the meanings and aims of other prison systems are not necessarily immediately perceptible' (2020: 608); and the need to recognise that 'culture is contingent rather than essential' (2020: 610), and requires more serious and detailed thought. Comparative penological practice can be very challenging, but also extremely rewarding in terms of knowledge development!

THE CHALLENGES AND POSSIBILITIES OF COMPARATIVE PRISONS RESEARCH

Abigail Stark[6]

Prison research entails many 'methodological landmines' (Schlosser, 2008: 1501), and my first experience of prison research was further complicated by its comparative dimension, exploring the meaning of citizenship for men imprisoned in the Republic of Ireland and England (Stark, 2019). Before fieldwork began, there was the challenge of determining suitable institutions for comparison, where – despite many 'basic similarities' (Sykes, 1958: xiii) – all prisons have their own character, culture, and social order. While I settled on sites of similar age, architecture, sentence-range and city location, it was never going to be possible to compare like with like, and thus cross-national comparison required sensitivity to how differences influenced both fieldwork and participants' experiences.

Practically, securing access was particularly complicated, requiring navigation of two systems, each with different requirements, forms and processes, in addition to managing gatekeeper concerns regarding any political implications of comparison. Practical, financial and time constraints also made it impossible to research concurrently in both jurisdictions, with fieldwork in Ireland taking place first. Thus, as a new prison researcher, I was also in an unfamiliar place, making the process one of learning about more than just the prison. I spoke with participants about national politics, and spent time learning Irish history in lessons at the prison school. Participants explained local colloquialisms, and differences in systems and terminology, as I sought to understand where 'functional equivalents' (Nelken, 2010: 45) existed. Fieldwork involved learning about, and being immersed in, a culture I knew little of beyond desk-based study. This resulted in a rich research experience, that encouraged constant reflection on context, similarity and difference, while requiring frequent enquiry of others to deepen my understanding of the country and system I was researching in.

Fieldwork experiences differed based on the gatekeepers facilitating my access – teachers in Ireland, and uniformed staff in England. This difference resulted in divergent assumptions about my positionality, inevitably influencing recruitment and interactions. While dependent on staff to escort me within the Irish prison, in

England I held keys and could move around independently, resulting in different practical, sensory and emotional experiences of the prison. I gained deeper understanding of the look, sounds, smells and feel of English prison wings, while in Ireland I was predominantly within the prison school, a space often viewed as an 'escape' from the landings. While the wings in England often brought feelings of sadness, anxiety or discomfort, the more relaxed environment of the Irish prison school made for a less oppressive research experience, with signs of joy – in an otherwise harsh environment – more frequently shared here.

My status as a foreign or native researcher also influenced individuals' framing of responses during interviews. Many participants in Ireland approached their involvement in the research as inherently comparative, explaining experiences in relation to their perceptions of English prisons, sometimes seemingly to amplify flaws in the Irish system. These contributions were challenging to unpick as I had not yet undertaken fieldwork in England, and sometimes required a re-direction of participants to their own situated experiences. This was less evident in England, suggesting my native status perhaps reduced the perceived necessity of comparative responses. Consequently, consideration of when experiences were described in relation to an envisaged comparator, or in the terms of one's situated experience, featured heavily during analysis.

Despite being practically, methodologically, and emotionally challenging, undertaking this comparative project provided experience and insights that strengthened my broader social research skills. It taught me the significance of national, local and institutional context both to the individuals' experiences and the research process, along with the importance of sensitive reflection on these contextual influences during analysis and writing. Although such reflection is perhaps most pronounced in comparative work, it is an essential dimension in seeking to understand any situated experience, whether considering local experiences or those further afield.

An Additional Punishment: Death Row

The existence of the death penalty in certain jurisdictions adds additional layers of complexity when undertaking prison research in those contexts. The incarcerative process which surrounds individuals awaiting capital punishment places distinctive dimensions on top of existing prison processes. In addition to the pains of imprisonment (loss of autonomy, security, heterosexual relationships, goods and services, and liberty) put forward by Gresham Sykes (1958), and added to by Crewe (2011) (namely 'the pains of indeterminacy, the pains of psychological assessment and the pains of self-government' (2011: 509), there is the additional pain of potential loss of life. Many individuals may be awaiting appeal hearings, so the loss of certainty associated with that is additionally painful. Such additional pains place additional ethical considerations upon the researcher's list: given the emotional and mental stresses such individuals may be experiencing – and the high potential for mental illness as a result – sometimes also referred to as 'death row syndrome' and 'death row phenomenon' (Harrison and Tamony, 2010), those researching such groups must take extra care when working with these individuals. It may be partly as a result of all these complexities that so little research is done with those on death row – there is very little empirical work out there on the subject that goes beyond the theoretical, and the majority of studies in existence are using demographic data, 'clinical' studies, and 'inmate institutional files and/or statistical analysis of violent prison disciplinary infractions' (Cunningham and Vigen, 2002: 194).

Despite there being huge complexities in undertaking such research, the empowerment that can come to highly controlled individuals being able to have their voices heard should not be dismissed. Maintaining a balance between these two issues revolves around notions of autonomy: giving participants actual free choice.

There are also access issues around research practicalities on death row. As would be expected, these are not easy to reach groups, so access can be very difficult to negotiate. A fascinating South Korean study[7] was undertaken by an individual who was assigned to work in the prison, and so was able to observe and interview death row inmates and staff (Byung Chul, 2015). Such 'insider access' can be invaluable with hard to reach groups, with advantages such as 'being able to screen for credibility, being able to deploy knowledge to identify salient issues for research and being able to establish rapport' (Bennett, 2015: 292). Other means of researching such individuals include the work of Professor Robert Johnson in the USA, who has been involved in numerous pieces of work looking at death row both empirically through 'in-depth, tape-recorded interviews during September 1978 with thirty-five of the thirty-seven men then confined on Alabama's death row' (1980: 546), as well as undertaking content analysis of three 'seminal' books on the subject (Chiapetta and Johnson, 2021), and analysing a selection of inmate blogs to understand mental health on death row (Johnson and Lantsman, 2021). In addition, Brown and Benningfield (2008) surveyed 40 prison officers working in a Midwestern prison housing a death row in the USA, using open and closed questions to unpick experiences, perspectives and attitudes of staff towards death row work; and others have analysed the last statements of death row prisoners from records (Eaton and Theuer, 2009; Eaton, 2014).

Pascoe, having undertaken fieldwork on the death penalty in Indonesia, Malaysia, Singapore, and Thailand, recommends some simple approaches to help understand the death penalty in more closed locations[8]: be clear on 'the definition of judicial punishment' (2016: 6); and overcome issues with lack of data through triangulation, 'the overlap of 1) first-hand or documentary sources; 2) secondary, interpretative materials and 3) interview-based information (Lilleker, 2003; Merriam, 1995)' (2016: 8).

As such, the employment of a range of different methodologies can help in overcoming some of the challenges of such a closed aspect of prisons.

THOUGHTS ON RESEARCH AT THE DEEP END OF THE PRISON EXPERIENCE

Robert Johnson

Over the last several decades, starting in 1971, I've studied hundreds of prisoners who were struggling to cope with the adversity posed by life at the deep end of the prison experience:

maximum-security prisons (think Attica or Sing Sing), various pu-nitive special housing units (euphemisms for solitary confinement, fittingly called 'the box' in many prisons), death rows (a species of solitary confinement fittingly called 'a living death' by many con-demned prisoners), and the death house, where my focus shifted to studying the experiences of execution team members who con-ducted executions by electrocution or lethal injection. The method of study across these subjects involved in-depth interviews in which the objective was to reconstruct the phenomenon at hand in terms that express what we now call the 'lived experience' of the person under study, however ironic that phrase sounds in the context of death sentences, whether we mean 'death by incarcera-tion' or 'death by execution' or even 'death of the spirit' in the existential wasteland that is forced solitary confinement.

I was trained by Hans Toch, who imparted many insights for which I remain grateful. One was respect and compassion for all fellow human beings, however heinous their behaviour might have been. There is always a back story; listen for it, and put your-self in the world of those you hope to understand. In the research context, this meant interviews in which one listened with care, probing gently, if somewhat relentlessly at times, to fully under-stand the experience of the person under study. A keen insight offered by Toch was to see the world as a fluid undertaking. This entailed thinking of persons and environments as inseparable, locked in endless transactions with one another, such that settings affected persons and persons, in turn, affected settings. As a result, even the prison world, obdurate and fixed from the outside, was, at bottom, a dynamic ecology of person-setting transactions. This view, in turn, bespoke the potential for variability and change in all of a prison's inhabitants – prisoners and their keepers – whose daily adaptations might open the door to personal growth and institutional reform.

Admittedly, the hopeful notion of a dynamic ecology as a recurring feature of prisons was greatly strained in my studies of life under sentence of death. Death rows are often settings of grim long-term isolation. This has been the case for most death rows in the last two centuries and remains true in many American states today, like Texas and Alabama, and in other states in which executions are carried out on a regular basis. The starkly and objectively dehumanizing features of those environments are salient in the minds of the prisoners, and those shared matters are often the ones prisoners broach in detail when one interviews them. But death rows do not give rise to completely uniform perceptions, and conditions of confinement under sentence of death do change and evolve. Today there are a few congregate death rows in which life in the prison pod or tier offers a variety of ways of living outside one's cell, much like a regular prison tier or wing. And even in the most repressive solitary-confinement death rows, one occasionally finds oases of care – impromptu group counselling offered by neighbours; earnest book discussions conducted cell-to-cell – that bloom in defiance of the expected protocol in a world lived in the shadow of executions. Essays and poems by death row prisoners can show how uniformly barren cells can be transformed into richly personal worlds uniquely tailored to the needs of the individual.

The final days and hours of the condemned prisoner are played out during what is called the death watch in a setting generally called the death house, culminating in executions in the death chamber. Here we see a total institution in the fullest sense of the term: surveillance is unrelenting, right up until the person is put to death before a carefully selected audience of civilians and officials (and researchers, in my case). I have had the unique opportunity to study these terminal environments and to describe those hidden worlds in ways I believe are true to the experiences of the persons I interviewed and, in the death house, also observed first-hand over the final hours of the execution process.

Looking back, I would not revise my work in any profound way, but over time, I've come to have a fuller sense of the fellow humanity of all the people I've studied – prisoners and keepers, condemned men and executioners – and of the tragic turns a life can take at the hands of the justice system. If I could do this research again, fifty-plus years older than when I first started my career, I would have a deeper sense of the loss and brutality that are so central to our prison systems, and a deeper sense of how harsh punishments seep insidiously into our personal lives and the larger society we all share.

Universal Truths for Prison Research

Similar to the suggestions made in Chapter Four (and in Sloan and Wright, 2015), there are some fundamental and universal truths for prison research that appear to transcend place and time:

1. There will always be ethical questions and challenges, although the checks and balances will differ depending on institutional and jurisdictional differences.
2. Relationship building and management is *vital* – the power of gatekeepers at all levels should never be underestimated, and your relationships with these people can make or break a piece of prison research, not least in terms of access.
3. No matter how strong you believe you are, you always need to make plans for some degree of support to maintain your own wellbeing. This may be formal or informal – it may be seeking help from others, or it may be making plans for self care. Research (in any context) is tiring and can be emotionally laborious, especially in sites of confinement. Look after yourself.
4. Every prison is different – never make any assumptions about what that setting 'will be like' – try to look at it without prior assumptions or notions of relativity (which can be challenging in itself!).
5. Power is inherent to prisons (and research and knowledge production[9]) – be aware of the power imbalances you see and feel, as well as your own power status in the research relationships you develop.
6. There will always be practical challenges to the research – try to remember that no research is ever perfect! The key is to try to think ahead as much as possible and, in the event of something cropping up during your research, (1) dont panic, and (2) take notes so that you can record, report, reflect, and learn!

Liebling noted one lesson that she had learned in the course of her research: 'Lesson one: how obliging staff and prisoners can be, and how open to interested outsiders' (1999: 155) – try to think positively! The words of Andrew Jefferson, an amazing international prison researcher, are particularly pertinent when trying to sum up the complexities of international (and domestic!) prison research (and how we explain this to our loved ones).

POSTCARD FROM THE EDGE

Andrew Jefferson

Dear Mum & Dad,

I know, even twenty years on, you are a bit baffled by all these journeys I make to far off places – to Nigeria, Sierra Leone, Tunisia, Jordan, the Philippines, Kosovo, Myanmar... Why? What for? What do I do there? Let me try and explain. You know, I've always been fascinated by enclosed spaces. I am still not sure why but what goes on in spaces where people are forced together, in often harsh, non-voluntary relations of power intrigues me. And everything I have seen and read over the years has reinforced the idea that societies are way too reliant on prisons and that the damage they do outweighs the service they are supposed to provide for society. Sticking plasters and cosmetic reforms have had relatively little success staunching the flow of people in and out of prisons with little change in their behaviour.

Anyway, back to my travels. Until quite recently – at least till the start of this century – most of the work on prisons has been about Western countries' prisons. Fieldwork-based studies of non-Western prisons was relatively rare and all we had was reports criticizing and condemning them which, not surprisingly, invited more resistance than progressive change. Early on I was puzzled by the idea of how we change something we know so little about. I wondered why we insisted on believing that confronting those responsible for prisons with their failures would inspire them to act differently.

My ambition was to try to help those committed to change to make sense of the places they wanted to change. I believed – and still do – that understanding the lives of prison staff, the rationales of harm-inducing institutions, the local histories of prisons and their relation to society is key to change. Prisons must be contextualized. They must be made sense of. My work then has been about sense-making, about understanding how prisons work and why. I have learned that prisons around the world are different, not the same, so different tactics will be necessary to change them or discourage their use.

I have also learned a lot about research methods because prisons are rather unique places to try to make sense of. Some scientists talk a lot about controlling variables (or the situation) to test a hypothesis. Prisons are notoriously difficult to control, at least in my experience. Almost the opposite is the case. In fact, the researcher is subject to the same controls – surveillance, searches, restrictions on mobility etc. – that prisoners are. I have learned to be a pretty good negotiator. In fact, this is one of the most important and perhaps least well understood aspects of doing prison research in non-Western settings (and maybe even Western settings too) – the art of negotiating boundaries. At every point in the research it is necessary to negotiate. At every point I have to make the best impression. At every point I have to gently persuade people to let me in, talk to me about their lives, and allow me to watch prison life unfolding. In many cases the prison authorities and then individual prison officers don't really understand why I just want to watch and listen. They are understandably suspicious and wary. Overcoming such resistance takes time and patience; it sometimes wears me out.

Sometimes being in the prison all day leaves me feeling dirty. I rush back to my temporary lodgings in the guest house or hotel and dive for the shower, desperately trying to wash away the impressions of the day, the images, the stories, the confrontations, and the righteous anger or petty annoyances that have filled the day. Prison research is a dirty business. To be honest I'm not sure it is a very healthy occupation. I am glad I have my colleague, Tomas, and the network of prison scholars we set up to keep an eye on me. But that's not always enough and there is not much they can do to help the family deal with my moodiness and the difficulties I have relating to so-called first world problems.

Is it worth it? I sometimes wonder. Does it make any difference? I am always in doubt. But I have learned to nurture and harness that doubt and put it to work when I am inside prison cells and corridors and exercise yards, when negotiating with officials for access, when analyzing the raw material collected and when writing those chapters and articles filled with the long words you so often remark upon.

Anyway, all for now. I hope this helps you make a little more sense of my strange professional world.

With love,

Andrew

Notes

1 I would argue that this is a global problem often dominated by the fashions and vagaries of gatekeepers and particular prison policies; and being drawn to 'sites of excitement' – closed, higher security institutions are undoubtedly seen to be more 'exciting,' and thus more researched, than the open prison estate in many instances.

2 See Dirga and Váně, 2020; Váně and Dirga, 2016; 2020; Dirga, 2017; Dirga, Lochmannová and Juřiček, 2015.

3 'The trajectory of sex offenders through the Lebanese criminal justice system: A tale of human rights violations.' A Ph.D. conducted by Dr Shereen Baz which examined the trajectory of sex offenders through the Lebanese criminal justice system by conducting interviews with imprisoned sex offenders, prison officers, police officers, judges, and lawyers.

4 Head prisoner: Prisoners who practically run the prison and do so either because they are selected by prison guards to do so or (in prisons where guards have little to no control) take on the role due to their powerful family, political, or religious ties.

5 Whatever it is to 'know' something, and if that is even possible.

6 This reflection is based on Ph.D. research completed while studying at the University of Sheffield, and funded by an Economic & Social Research Council +3 White Rose Doctoral Scholarship.

7 Written in Korean, but I attempted to read it through online translation services, and am *so* glad that I did.

8 In particular, he calls for more focus on 'the Islamic-majority states of the Middle East and North and East Africa' (2016: 4).

9 'But for the prisoners and former prisoners who would welcome an opportunity to engage in the production of knowledge about crime and punishment, the barriers to participation remain formidable, to say the least. The cost of attending conferences keeps those who do not qualify for travel grants from coming and making presentations. Announcements and calls for papers are posted where only those who

frequent universities or read professional journals will see them. If making successful submissions to journals and conference proceedings is not restricted outright to those with the appropriate credentials, there is always the acceptable form (e.g. "Manuscripts must be double-spaced and submitted in triplicate ...") to keep the non-professionals out' (Davidson, 1988: 3). Although some elements of academia have begun to change with regard to these opportunities, there are still incredible barriers to those who aren't classed as 'academic professionals,' even 35 years after Davidson made this statement.

References

Agozino, B. (2004) Imperialism, crime and criminology: Towards the decolonisation of criminology. *Crime, Law and Social Change*, *41*, 343–358.

Agozino, B. (2010) Editorial: What is criminology? A control-freak discipline! *African Journal of Criminology and Justice Studies*, 4(1), i–xx.

Bennett, J. (2015) Insider ethnography or the tale of the prison governor's new clothes. In Drake, D., Earle, R. & Sloan, J. (eds) *The Palgrave Handbook of Prison Ethnography*. Basingstoke: Palgrave Macmillan.

Boshoff, N. (2009) Neo-colonialism and research collaboration in Central Africa. *Scientometrics*, *81*(2), 413.

Brangan, L. (2020) Exceptional states: The political geography of comparative penology. *Punishment and Society*, *22*(5), 596–616.

Brown, K. L., & Benningfield, M. (2008) Death row correctional officers: Experiences, perspectives, and attitudes. *Criminal Justice Review*, *33*(4), 524–540.

Bryman, A. (2016) *Social Research Methods*. Oxford University Press.

Byung-Chul, Y. (2015) Qualitative study on the death-row syndrome. *Korean Journal of Criminology*, *27*(1), 163–188.

Cavadino, M., & Dignan, J. (2006) *Penal Systems: A Comparative Approach*. London: Sage.

Chiappetta, C., & Johnson, R. (2021) 'It's not gonna leave any scars': Trauma and coping among execution team members. *The Prison Journal*, *101*(4), 379–397.

Connell, R. (2006) Northern theory: The political geography of general social theory. *Theory and Society*, *35*(2), 237–264.

Crewe, B. (2011) Depth, weight, tightness: Revisiting the pains of imprisonment. *Punishment & Society*, *13*(5), 509–529.

Cunningham, M. D., & Vigen, M. P. (2002) Death row inmate characteristics, adjustment, and confinement: A critical review of the literature. *Behavioral Sciences & the Law*, *20*(1–2), 191–210.

Davidson, H. S. (1988) Prisoners on prison abolition. *Journal of Prisoners on Prison*, *1*(1), 1–4.

de Sousa Santos, B. (2014) *Epistemologies of the South: Justice against Epistemicide*. Abingdon: Routledge.

Dirga, L. (2017) Body as a project: The relationship Czech prisoners have to their bodies. *Sociológia/Slovak Sociological Review*, 49(6), 636–656.

Dirga, L., & Váně, J. (2020) Czech Republic: Religion and Czech prison – the history of an ambivalent partnership. In Martínez-Ariño, J. & Zwilling, A.-L. (eds) *Religion and Prison in Europe: A Contemporary Overview*. New York: Springer International.

Dirga, L., Lochmannová, A., & Juříček, P. (2015) The structure of the inmate population in Czech prisons. *Sociológia/Slovak Sociological Review*, 47(6), 559–578.

Drake, D. H., Earle, R. & Sloan, J. (eds) (2015) *The Palgrave Handbook of Prison Ethnography*. Basingstoke: Palgrave Macmillan.

Dresler-Hawke, E., & Vaccarino, F. (2010) The ethics of focus groups in correctional settings. *International Journal of Learning*, 16(12).

Eaton, J. (2014) Honor on death row: Apology, remorse, and the culture of honor in the US South. *Sage Open*, 4(2), 2158244014529777.

Eaton, J., & Theuer, A. (2009) Apology and remorse in the last statements of death row prisoners. *Justice Quarterly*, 26(2), 327–347.

Eddo-Lodge, R. (2017) *Why I'm No Longer Talking to White People about Race*. London: Bloomsbury.

Eshareturi, C., Serrant, L., Galbraith, V., & Glynn, M. (2015) Silence of a scream: Application of the Silences Framework to provision of nurse-led interventions for ex-offenders. *Journal of Research in Nursing*, 20(3), 218–231.

Gaborit, L. S. (2019) Looking through the prison gate: Access in the field of ethnography. *Cadernos Pagu*, no. 55, 1–25.

Gaborit, L. S. (2020) Visited by spirits: 'Betwixt and between' in meditation and solitary confinement in Myanmar. *Incarceration*, 1(1), 2632666320936431.

Harrison, K., & Tamony, A. (2010) Death row phenomenon, death row syndrome and their affect on capital cases in the US. *Internet Journal of Criminology*, 1, 1–16.

Johnson, R. (1980) Warehousing for death: Observations on the human environment of death row. *Crime & Delinquency*, 26(4), 545–562.

Johnson, R., & Lantsman, J. (2021) Death row narratives: A qualitative analysis of mental health issues found in death row inmate blog entries. *The Prison Journal*, 101(2), 147–165.

Lansang, M. A., & Dennis, R. (2004) Building capacity in health research in the developing world. *Bulletin of the World Health Organization*, 82, 764–770.

Liebling, A. (1999) Doing research in prison: Breaking the silence. *Theoretical Criminology*, 3(2), 147–173.

Lilleker, D. G. (2003) Interviewing the political elite: Navigating a potential minefield. *Politics*, 23(3), 207–214.

Max Martin, T. (2019) The ethnographer as accomplice: Edifying qualms of bureaucratic fieldwork in Kafka's penal colony. *Critique of Anthropology*, 39(2), 139–154.

Merriam, S. B. (1995) What can you tell from an N of 1? Issues of validity and reliability in qualitative research. *PAACE Journal of Lifelong Learning*, 4, 51–60.

Nelken, D. (2009) Comparative criminal justice: Beyond ethnocentrism and relativism. *European Journal of Criminology*, 6(4), 291–311.

Nelken, D. (2010) *Comparative Criminal Justice: Making Sense of Difference*. London, Thousand Oaks, New Delhi and Singapore: Sage.

Pascoe, D. (2016) Researching the death penalty in closed or partially-closed criminal justice systems. In Bosworth, M., Hoyle, C. & Zedner, L. (eds) *Changing Contours of Criminal Justice*. Oxford University Press.

Q'um Q'um Xiiem, J. A., Lee-Morgan, J. B. J., & De Santolo, J. (2019) *Decolonising Research: Indigenous Storywork as Methodology*. London: Zed Books.

Reiter, K. (2014) Making windows in walls: Strategies for prison research. *Qualitative Inquiry*, 20(4), 417–428.

Said, E. (1993) *Culture and Imperialism*. London: Chatto and Windus.

Schlosser, J. A. (2008) Issues in interviewing inmates: Navigating the methodological landmines of prison research. *Qualitative Inquiry*, 14(8), 1500–1525.

Serrant-Green, L. (2010) The sound of 'silence': A framework for researching sensitive issues or marginalised perspectives in health. *Journal of Research in Nursing*, 16(4), 347–360.

Sloan, J., & Wright, S. (2015) Going in green: Reflections on the challenges of 'getting in, getting on, and getting out' for doctoral prisons researchers. In Drake, D. H., Earle, R. & Sloan, J. (eds) *The Palgrave Handbook of Prison Ethnography*, pp. 143–163. Basingstoke: Palgrave Macmillan.

Smith, L. T. (1999) *Decolonising Methodologies: Research and Indigenous Peoples*. Dunedin, New Zealand: University of Otago Press.

Stark, A. D. (2019) 'Lived citizenship' from the perspectives of men imprisoned in the Republic of Ireland & England. Unpublished Ph.D. thesis, University of Sheffield.

Sykes, G. M. (1958) *The Society of Captives: A Study of a Maximum Security Prison*. Princeton, NJ: Princeton University Press.

Tuhiwai Smith, L. (2021) *Decolonising Methodologies*, 3rd edn. London, New York and Dublin: Bloomsbury.

Váně, J., & Dirga, L. (2016) The religiosity behind bars: Forms of inmate's religiosity in the Czech prison system. *Sociológia/Slovak Sociological Review*, 48(6), 641–663.

Váně, J., & Dirga, L. (2020) The prison chaplain as a part of penitentiary
care? Transformation of the Czech prison system after the fall of com-
munism. *Archives of Criminology*, 42(1), 253–269.

Wiarda, H. J. (1981) The ethnocentrism of the social science implications
for research and policy. *The Review of Politics*, 43(2), 163–197.

Nine

CHALLENGES AND 'CONCLUSIONS'

This chapter will bring together the key messages regarding the prison research process that have been raised throughout the book, and will offer some take-home points to advise and reassure those working in such areas. In addition, the importance of challenging the prison as an institution of control will be noted, as well as the importance of walking the tightrope between the different sides of the story when it comes to prisons and punishment.

Challenges for the Future

It is impossible to say what the future holds, but given the increasing penal populism in public discourse, and the increasingly immovable priority given to public protection in many of today's societies, it is unlikely that we will see a concerted move towards decarceration in the near future. For prison researchers, this promises a continuation of the field at least, sad as it is. When I started writing this chapter, I thought that its outlook was somewhat gloomy. Now, in the post-Covid-19 world that we live in, the mood drops further.

Covid-19

Just in case anyone has been living in a bubble (or if something dramatic happens and the world moves on and forgets 2020 – unlikely, but just for the sake of completeness), in early 2020 a new strain of coronavirus, resulting in the disease termed

DOI: 10.4324/9781315297217-9

Covid-19, emerged onto the global scene. The first publicised outbreak was in Wuhan, China, but even with the lockdown of a city of over 11 million people, the virus soon spread worldwide. The repercussions for everyday life were (and still are) huge – cities and countries under lockdown, not being allowed to meet with or hug loved ones, and a general sense of fear. Hundreds of thousands of people died, or contracted 'long covid' with implications that we can't even start to comprehend yet. Yet, there was hardly any general discourse comparing the hardships of lockdown to the hardships of incarceration. Perhaps this discussion will come in time – Fayter et al. discuss the Canadian context and the ways in which responses to Covid-19 'propelled carceral controls forward through a language of crisis management and risk. These trajectories of control reflect a much broader trend with dispossessed populations' (2021: 44), concluding that 'we must approach the pandemic context as an opportunity for radical and transformative social change, much of which can be modelled from solidarity and mutual aid supports found between prisoners' (2021: 54).

Within prisons, the implications were severe. Suhomlinova et al. (2022a) extended their existing use of correspondence methods for a project on transgender and non-binary prisoners in England and Wales to include questions about the experience of prison in a pandemic, finding stressors experienced around illness, 'job loss and financial insecurity,' 'difficulties accessing or acquiring necessities,' and 'social isolation and loneliness' (2022a: 6–10), and further exacerbations of Sykes' pains of imprisonment (Suhomlinova et al., 2022b; see also Maycock, 2022). Formal mitigation strategies varied across the world, from the suspension of visits and inter-prison transfers, and early release schemes in England and Wales (Suhomlinova et al., 2022b); the reduction of new prison admissions in Germany, Spain, and Romania; restriction on goods entering the prison; technological substitutions; and numerous other front-end, within prison and back-end strategies (Rapisarda and Byrne, 2020). Prison population reduction policies were a key feature used across the world, in countries including Nigeria, Columbia, Indonesia, Thailand, Poland, and the Russian Federation (Heard, 2020), and the use and impact of these policies has had implications for discussions around penal reform (Heard, 2020). In British Columbia, provincial correctional authorities took a 'health-informed rather than a justice-informed' (Murdoch, 2020: 1328) approach to respond to the pandemic, including ongoing education, screening, testing, induction units (quarantining), changing visitation (including the elimination of costs and restrictions on numbers of local and long-distance phone calls), cleaning, and physical distancing (Murdoch, 2020). Such approaches were not all successful or effective, and have been subject to criticism across the world (Brennan, 2020; Burki, 2020; Hummer, 2020).

The effects on prison research were also severe. In many cases, all face to face research stopped, prisons were closed to external visitors, and in England and Wales all empirical primary research projects were subject to a moratorium for an unknown duration in order to 'to ensure safety and reduce unnecessary burden on the prison and probation estate' (HMPPS, 2020: 3). Indeed 'Only applications involving secondary data analysis that did not pose a risk of potential harm to individuals and impact negatively on resources were considered' (HMPPS, 2020: 3). In the following months, research had to be made Covid-proof – in England and Wales, the HMPPS National Research Committee developed a medium-term plan which had to be complied with by any and all prison researchers (HMPPS, 2020) (see Chapter Three for details about the work of Hannah Gilman, who was trying to undertake research on whole life prisoners in England when the pandemic struck). Interestingly, some face to face research was actually undertaken in prisons in England and Wales: a thematic review by HM Inspectorate of Prisons was based on audio-recorded in-depth interviews with prisoners between 5 September and 5 November 2020 (HMIP, 2021: 28).

In discussions with other sociological researchers during the pandemic, something that fascinated me was the fact that the majority of challenges being faced by researchers were extremely similar to those experienced by many prison researchers as standard. Whilst many managed to overcome these in the main through the use of online technologies and phone interviews, I was struck throughout by the fact that none of the solutions suggested could easily be transferred to the prison context. Zoom, Skype,

Microsoft Teams only work if your prisoners have access to computers with the internet (which is rare in any instance, let alone in a private setting for a confidential interview), or phones that can be used in private spaces for sensible periods of time. Although some temporary secure phones were issued to all prisons that do not have in-cell telephony in England and Wales, these were subject to restricted use and surveillance, not to mention the extremely high costs of phone calls for the prisoner. Where video calls were available (and free during the time of coronavirus due to restrictions on prison visits), the restrictions in English prisons meant that calls were limited to 30 minutes, only one call was allowed a month, and only for those over 18 on the prisoner's friends and family list (although up to three additional people of any age could join the call if on the visitor list [https://www. gov.uk/staying-in-touch-with-someone-in-prison]). As such, this is not really an option for prison researchers in the majority of cases – it is unlikely that a prisoner would want to use their limited time, opportunities and funds to speak to researchers as opposed to friends and family (who also can play an important role in maintaining prisoner wellbeing and reducing reoffending in the long term). Asking individuals to give this time up for research feels somewhat less than ethical if it may jeopardize those relationships that will help upon release.

RESEARCHING PRISONS DURING COVID

Chris Kay

January 2020, I was finally ready to start a piece of research that was two years in the making: an evaluation of a sport-based rehabilitation programme across 13 prisons throughout England and Wales. Permissions had been obtained, prisons were on board, cohorts had been identified and so on. When you start doing prison research, one of the first lessons you learn is to expect the unexpected, and I tried to plan for most eventualities I could think of shy of a pandemic, but who plans for those anyway?

Nearly two years on (October 2021), I find myself in the exact same position I was in back then. The project is almost up and running again, and I am preparing to re-commence my prison tour of England and Wales. As research activity begins to trickle back into custodial settings it is important to remember that, as researchers, it is our responsibility to recognise the impact of broader contextual factors on the phenomenon under investigation. Covid-19 presents one hell of a contextual factor that needs to be considered.

Now, there are two ways we can look at this: empirically and epistemologically. Empirically, the pandemic introduced a new variable that I had to consider. Most of the original cohorts have, by now, been released. New participants could test positive and be unable to participate; I might test positive and be unable to undertake the work; an outbreak in the prison could cause a suspension in the programme. A larger concern, empirically at least, relates to the potential impact of Exceptional Regime Management Plan measures on the outcomes of the research. It is, after all, only logical that engaging in a sports-based rehabilitation programme with other people will be viewed more positively when you have spent nearly two years with only cell-based activity packs and the occasional video call.

When it comes to epistemology, I'm reminded of a paper by Liebling (1999) about the nature of prison research. She talks about the fact that while her research team entered their project with all the rigour of scientific methods, it was in fact their "judgement, intuition, creative instinct and various abilities to connect with others and [them]selves that steered [them] through" the project (ibid.: 159). While my project ultimately has remained the same in the sense that it is still an evaluation of a sports-based prison rehabilitation programme, the world in which that programme exists has changed from the one that existed two years ago, as have I along with it. My intuition, judgement, and ability to connect with people, which are at the core of my identity as a prison researcher, have all naturally been shaped by the pandemic, and will all significantly affect the ways in which I go about

> my future research. As such, it is imperative that I reflect upon my own position as a prison researcher (and a person) in a post-Covid prison environment as I go along if I am to understand what it is I am investigating. But I guess, all of that is part of the 'art of doing prison research' (ibid.).

There was some vital research being undertaken within prisons in the face of this global pandemic and the associated moratoria on research. Maycock, investigating the impact of Covid-19 on the Scottish prison estate, made use of 'a participatory correspondence methodology [...] enabling project participants to influence the direction of this project through suggesting research questions' (2022: 218), a method which is seen to be excellent for the exploration of sensitive topics and the promotion of reflection.[1] Issues were experienced practically – some letters within the sequence of letters sent were lost in the post or undelivered – and ethically in terms of concern regarding the wellbeing of participants (Maycock, 2021). Letter writing became a key way to 'enter' the prison ethically and legally, and provided vital reports from those incarcerated during the pandemic (see Suhomlinova et al., 2022a). In the USA, Pyrooz et al. undertook phone interviews in 'private attorney rooms' with 31 prisoners to gain perspectives from high security prisoners in the Oregon Department of Corrections in April and May 2020 (Pyrooz et al., 2020: 296). Research was done, but it was challenging.

Rising Prison Populations, Privatisation, and Punitive Policy Transfer

Penal populism and the retributive use of incarceration are on the rise in many societies today – indeed, those jurisdictions where prison populations are falling are fascinating by virtue of their exceptionalism (see Beyens and Boone, 2015). The capacity of the prison estate in many countries is being stretched, which has implications in terms of staff control, morale, and eventually turnover, and subsequently potentially impacts on prisoner wellbeing through the erosion of prisoner–staff positive relationships (see Liebling, 2004). The demands on all forms of resources – money, time, space – become intensified, which can have direct implications for the likelihood of gaining access to a prison site for research purposes: if a prison is struggling to enable prisoners to have meaningful time out of their cells, or the impact of overcrowding has negative implications for safety, then research projects may well be sidelined or delayed if they are not seen as a real priority. Even if access is achieved in such circumstances, the pressures placed on staff, as well as the lived experiences of prisoners sharing overcrowded spaces and having restricted options to leave their cells,[2] need to be taken into consideration.

There is also a move to greater use of privatisation within the penal estate in many jurisdictions. Privatisation can raise some interesting dimensions for the prison researcher, not least the fact that they may be run very differently, with different policies and priorities, in comparison to the public sector. Research shows staff inexperience and turnover to be even higher in the private prison estate (Liebling, 2004), which can have implications for researchers wishing to enter these sites. That said, there is a real dearth of literature on the different research experiences had in private vs public prisons[3] – certainly an area that would benefit from research in the future!

Privatisation is one of a number of policies that is increasingly transferring across national borders. Policy transfer – whether that be 'lesson drawing,' 'policy convergence,' 'policy diffusion' or full 'policy transfer' (Dolowitz and Marsh, 2000) – is not uncommon in criminal justice, particularly if one takes note of the importance of colonial histories in the development of state systems. That said, it is unlikely that there will be great success in the transfer of policy between states that hold fundamentally different penal outlooks and popular opinions on punishment: it is uncommon to see movement away from retributive punitivism in criminal justice policy in today's age of penal populism, particularly in Western neoliberal economies (see Cavadino and Dignan, 2006). Indeed, there is an increasingly punitive public discourse around crime and punishment: the notion of 'bad guys' and 'good guys' – in February 2018, following the mass shooting at Marjory Stoneman Douglas High School in the USA, President Donald Trump was quoted as saying 'We have to let the bad guys know that they are hardened' (*New York Times*, 2018).

The increasing notion of 'good guys' and 'bad guys' within public discourse can pose serious challenges to the prison researcher seeking funding, and for those who may come across other explanations for incarceration which don't align with public distaste for offenders and prisoners. After all, as prison researchers, we go home from the office and have conversations with non-specialists about our work – some of us teach the seemingly increasingly punitive student populations passing through our universities. It can be a hard sell to try to convince highly punitive people that prisoners' rights are of vital importance, and that perhaps retribution isn't the best way. Of course this viewpoint is distinct to certain jurisdictions: there are well known examples of more welfare-driven penal policies, and the prioritization of rehabilitation, especially within areas following the lead of Nordic Penal Exceptionalism (Pratt, 2008a; 2008b; Pratt and Eriksson, 2014). Yet, increasing punitiveness does play a part when competing for funding, as well as when trying to disseminate research and gain true impact. As such, researchers may need to look beyond the national policy landscape to see the source of some policies being integrated into the national prison system – if that information is even written down anywhere accessible.

That said, there are possible shades of light passing through the dark clouds:

More and More Prison Research and Researchers out there

As noted in Chapter Eight, in 2012, an international conference at the ICCCR was held which challenged the 'curious eclipse of prison ethnography' which Waquant (2002) posited. This was followed by an edited collection (Drake, Earle and Sloan, 2015), which showed that prison researchers and ethnographers *are* out there, and are out there in abundance, across the world. One of the common factors in prison research is the lack of community bringing us all together. Yet that too is changing, and at least the pandemic has shown us that connection and networking are not wholly dependent on being face to face. There are more and more online communities developing (the Global Prisons Research Network[4] and the Carceral Geography Working Group[5] as just two examples), and the move towards greater emotional openness in the prison research field has arguably opened up discourse around experiences of prison research much more. As such, there has definitely been an advance in the development of a prison research community.

The Development of a Prison Research Community

Within this growing research community, we are starting to see much more support from within – sharing experiences and challenges can be empowering, and allow us to see ways around our problems and ways to manage and understand our experiences better: the chapter that I wrote with Serena Wright about 'Going In Green' and the subsequent response to this is testament to this (Sloan and Wright, 2015). There is also a greater acknowledgment of the difficulties of undertaking prison research – people are becoming much more willing to share their challenges and achievements – as, I hope, this book shows. Sharing our negative experiences is not a sign of weakness – indeed, it can be an extremely important process in understanding ourselves and our work, and research has found that such expressions of negative emotions are 'associated with positive relationship outcomes, including elicitation of support, building of new close relationships, and heightening of intimacy in the closest of those relationships' (Graham, Huang, Clark and Helgeson, 2008: 394).

Such new communities open the door for much more wide-ranging forms of collaboration as advocated by Reiter: 'One way to gain access to prisons, and to encourage greater public accountability, is to collaborate methodologically and institutionally, to design new frameworks of analysis and build new networks of accessibility' (Reiter, 2014: 426) – in particular it would be prudent for us as a community to start looking beyond the

Western hegemony even more, and investing more collaborative efforts in more decolonised methodologies (Tuhiwai Smith, 2021; Q'um Q'um Xiiem, Lee-Morgan and De Santolo, 2019). Although, as we have noted, moving away from traditional methods is not always met with the support it deserves, such developments and collaborations can bring invaluable different information in different ways.

Greater Diversity within the Prison Research Community

The development of 'Convict Criminology' groups across the world is one such sign of hope. The inclusion of the ex-offender voice within the research process allows a different viewpoint to be gleaned, as well as providing much deeper insights into the prison experience. The prison research community has started to get much more diverse – in terms of participants' backgrounds and also with regard to interdisciplinarity. The inclusion of voices from an extensive landscape of disciplines such as architecture (see Fairweather and McConville, 2000), nursing (Norman and Parrish, 2008), education (Behan, 2014), etc. demonstrates the diversity in the prison research community – even if we may not meet together very often, if at all!

Increasing Attention Being Directed towards Victims of Structural Violence and Inequalities

Many of us in higher education in the West have become increasingly encouraged to engage with the developing discourses of decolonisation – the decolonised curriculum, decolonised methodologies, decolonised feminism (Verges, 2021) are just some of the developing discourses that are becoming more and more prominent and important. This inherently requires an engagement with notions of structural inequality, power imbalances, and marginalization – within the academic sector as well as the penal. Indeed, the process of decolonising has been said to involve 'actions that (1) center the epistemic privilege and political aspirations of colonised and subjugated peoples; (2) identify, dismantle and transform colonial systems and structures that marginalise; (3) advance and achieve the goals of *liberation, repair* and *radical equality*' (Abdelnour, 2022: 82). Such processes are essential in the prison context, where marginalisation and inequality are pervasive.

Increasingly Diverse Approaches Being Taken by the Prison Research Community

Exciting new methods and findings, as have been seen in Chapter Six in particular, are helping to develop the research being done in prisons in much more creative ways, and in ways that are capturing the lived experiences of those in prisons in much greater depth and detail. The increasing role of the voice of the participant in the development of research tools and projects – be that through appreciative inquiry, participatory action research, or convict criminology, is having the result of allowing the unseen and unheard to become much more likely to be seen or heard. That said, this is not a global phenomenon, and some prisons are still frustratingly closed to research scrutiny. Even so, compared to the start of the boom in prison research, the development from more 'traditional' methods of research, and the publication of work from an increasingly diverse range of jurisdictions, has been phenomenal in its diversity and creativity!

Conclusion

One thing that I have learned, from all my reading, teaching, and personal research experience (both regarding prisons and beyond) is the following key message: *no research is ever perfect* – be that on prisons or butterflies. As the Scottish poet Robert Burns once said, 'The best-laid schemes o' mice an' men gang aft a-gley' (Burns, 1785), or, for those not familiar with Scottish parlance – the best laid plans of mice and men often go askew/awry. You may not get to speak to the people or organisations you wanted to. You may not get access. You may not be allowed to do what you had initially hoped in your research proposal. You may have a bad interview where the conversation does not go to plan. The documents you want to look at may be embargoed or unavailable.

Don't lose heart. You will be able to research *something*, and that something may turn out to make a real difference to someone. Talk to other prison researchers and hear their stories and experiences – as I have tried to do with this book. Their insights and experiences will, if nothing else, help you feel more sane and less alone in the experience of researching prisons. And, hopefully, you will enjoy some – if not all – of the process (especially likely if you engage with strategies to develop and support your own emotional and mental wellbeing before you get started). I wish you all the very best – please look after yourselves! And Good Luck!

Notes

1 See also Chapter Six for more on the correspondence methodology.
2 For example, if an individual is having restrictions to leaving their cell due to resource pressures, at what point will the opportunity to leave their cells for a research activity be seen as an incentive that could undermine free consent to participate? Or, can it actually be argued that all such experiences – regardless of overcrowding – are actually incentives, in that they are a chance to do something different, and speak to someone new? Is that an issue?
3 Although interestingly there is work noting the risk of conflicts of interest between funding sources and private prisons being researched (Geis, Mobley and Shichor, 1999).
4 https://sites.google.com/site/gprnnetwork/
5 https://carceralgeography.com/

References

Abdelnour, S. (2022) What decolonising is not. *M@n@gement*, 25(4), 80–88.

Behan, C. (2014) Learning to escape: Prison education, rehabilitation and the potential for transformation. *Journal of Prison Education and Reentry*, 1(1), 20–31.

Beyens, K., & Boone, M. (2015) Mixing detention cultures: The Belgian–Dutch case. In Drake, D. H., Earle, R. & Sloan, J. (eds) *The Palgrave Handbook of Prison Ethnography*, pp. 479–498. Basingstoke: Palgrave Macmillan.

Brennan, P. K. (2020) Responses taken to mitigate Covid-19 in prisons in England and Wales. *Victims & Offenders*, 15(7–8), 1215–1233.

Burki, T. (2020) Prisons are 'in no way equipped!' to deal with Covid-10. *The Lancet*, 395, 1411–1412.

Burns, R. (1785) To a mouse. In *A Choice of Burns's Poems and Songs: Selected with an Introduction by Sydney Goodsir Smith* (1966). London: Faber and Faber.

Cavadino, M., & Dignan, J. (2006) *Penal Systems: A Comparative Approach*. London: Sage.

Dolowitz, D. P., & Marsh, D. (2000) Learning from abroad: The role of policy transfer in contemporary policy-making. *Governance*, *13*(1), 5–23.

Drake, D. H., Earle, R. & Sloan, J. (eds) (2015) *The Palgrave Handbook of Prison Ethnography*. Basingstoke: Palgrave Macmillan.

Fairweather, L., & McConville, S. (eds) (2000) *Prison Architecture: Policy, Design, and Experience*. London: Routledge.

Fayter, R., Mario, B., Chartrand, V., & Kilty, J. M. (2021) Surviving the pandemic on the inside: From crisis governance to caring communities. *Canadian Journal of Sociology*, *46*(4), 37–66.

Geis, G., Mobley, A., & Shichor, D. (1999) Private prisons, criminological research, and conflict of interest: A case study. *Crime & Delinquency*, *45*(3), 372–388.

Graham, S. M., Huang, J. Y., Clark, M. S., & Helgeson, V. S. (2008) The positives of negative emotions: Willingness to express negative emotions promotes relationships. *Personality and Social Psychology Bulletin*, *34*(3), 394–406.

Heard, C. (2020) Commentary: Assessing the global impact of the Covid-19 pandemic on prison populations. *Victims & Offenders*, *15*(7–8), 848–861.

HMIP (HM Inspectorate of Prisons) (2021) *What Happens to Prisoners in a Pandemic?* London: HM Inspectorate of Prisons.

HMPPS (2020) *COVID-19: The National Research Committee's Medium-Term Plan*. available at https://assets.publishing.service.gov.uk/government/uploads/system/uploads/attachment_data/file/917549/nrc-covid-19-medium-term-plan.pdf

Hummer, D. (2020) United States Bureau of Prisons' response to the COVID-19 pandemic. *Victims & Offenders*, *15*(7–8), 1262–1276.

Liebling, A. (1999) Doing research in prison: Breaking the silence? *Theoretical Criminology*, *3*(2), 147–173.

Liebling, A. (2004) *Prisons and Their Moral Performance: A Study of Values, Quality, and Prison Life*. New York: Oxford University Press.

Maycock, M. (2021) 'I do not appear to have had previous letters.' The potential and pitfalls of using a qualitative correspondence method to facilitate insights into life in prison during the Covid-19 pandemic. *International Journal of Qualitative Methods*, *21*, 1–11.

Maycock, M. (2022) 'Covid-19 has caused a dramatic change to prison life.' Analysing the impacts of the Covid-19 pandemic on the pains of imprisonment in the Scottish Prison Estate. *The British Journal of Criminology*, 62, 218–233.

Murdoch, D. J. (2020) British Columbia Provincial Corrections' response to the COVID-19 pandemic: A case study of correctional policy and practice. *Victims & Offenders*, 15(7–8), 1317–1336.

New York Times (2018) Trump suggests teachers get a 'bit of a bonus' to carry guns. Available at: https://www.nytimes.com/2018/02/22/us/politics/trump-guns-school-shootings.html

Norman, A. E., & Parrish, A. A. (eds) (2008) *Prison Nursing*. Chichester: Wiley.

Novisky, M. A., Narvey, C. S., & Semenza, D. C. (2020) Institutional responses to the COVID-19 pandemic in American prisons. *Victims & Offenders*, 15(7–8), 1244–1261.

Pratt, J. (2008a) Scandinavian exceptionalism in an era of penal excess: part I: The nature and roots of Scandinavian exceptionalism. *British Journal of Criminology*, 48(2), 119–137.

Pratt, J. (2008b) Scandinavian exceptionalism in an era of penal excess: part II: Does Scandinavian exceptionalism have a future? *British Journal of Criminology*, 48(3), 275–292.

Pratt, J., & Eriksson, A. (2014) *Contrasts in Punishment: An Explanation of Anglophone Excess and Nordic Exceptionalism*. Abingdon: Routledge.

Pyrooz, D. C., Labrecque, R. M., Tostlebe, J. J., & Useem, B. (2020) Views on COVID-19 from inside prison: Perspectives of high-security prisoners. *Justice Evaluation Journal*, 3(2), 294–306.

Q'um Q'um Xiiem, J. A., Lee-Morgan, J. B. J., & De Santolo, J. (2019) *Decolonising Research: Indigenous Storywork as Methodology*. London: Zed Books.

Rapisarda, S. S., & Byrne, J. M. (2020) The impact of COVID-19 outbreaks in the prisons, jails, and community corrections systems throughout Europe. *Victims & Offenders*, 15(7–8), 1105–1112.

Reiter, K. (2014) Making windows in walls: Strategies for prison research. *Qualitative Inquiry*, 20(4), 417–428.

Sloan, J., & Wright, S. (2015) Going in green: Reflections on the challenges of 'getting in, getting on, and getting out' for doctoral prisons researchers. In Drake, D. H., Earle, R. & Sloan, J. (eds) *The Palgrave Handbook of Prison Ethnography*, pp. 143–163. Basingstoke: Palgrave Macmillan.

Suhomlinova, O., O'Reilly, M., Ayres, T. C., Wertans, E., Tonkin, M. J., & O'Shea, S. C. (2022a) 'Gripping onto the last threads of sanity': Transgender and non-binary prisoners' mental health challenges during the Covid-19 pandemic. *International Journal of Mental Health*, 1–21.

Suhomlinova, O., Ayres, T. C., Tonkin, M. J., O'Reilly, M., Wertans, E., & O'Shea, S. C. (2022b) Locked up while locked down: Prisoners' experiences of the COVID-19 pandemic. *British Journal of Criminology*, *62*(2), 279–298.

Tuhiwai Smith, L. (2021) *Decolonising Methodologies*, 3rd edn. London: Bloomsbury.

Verges, F. (2021) *A Decolonial Feminism*. London: Pluto Press.

Wacquant, L. (2002) The curious eclipse of prison ethnography in the age of mass incarceration. *Ethnography*, *3*(4), 371–397.

APPENDIX

Prison Research Checklist

Before going in:

- Do you have ethical approval from (a) your institution, and (b) the relevant prison system bureaucratic process?
- Do you have permission to take electronic equipment/tools/supplies into the prison?
- Do you have spare batteries for any electronic equipment (if permitted)?
- Do you have any relevant (a) consent forms and (b) information sheets with you? (and spares!). Do you have somewhere safe to keep them upon completion of the work (i.e. not visible to others you may see outside the interview space)?
- Have you told an external contact where you are going?
- Do you have your ID documents with you?
- Do you have a notebook and pen?
- Have you locked away any personal items you dont want to/cant take in with you?
- Take three deep breaths.

When you leave the prison:

- Take three deep breaths. You may also want to ground yourself mentally outside the prison. Try to see a different thing from each colour of the rainbow; or work through all your senses: what can you see, hear, smell, feel, taste?
- Have you checked in with your external contact?

- Have you spent ten minutes writing down all the things you noticed/are now reflecting on that you couldn't at the time?
- Have you locked up your consent forms in a secure place?
- Have you uploaded your recordings onto a secure computer storage area?
- Dont forget to delete the files from the recorder so that you are taking a blank recorder into the prison next time.
- Remember to be kind to yourself and engage in self care. This may include debriefing with a colleague/supervisor. Eat, sleep and get into some fresh air. Do things that make you smile and give your mind space to decompress and process.[1] And most of all, be kind to yourself please.

Note

1 I used to come out of the prison, put all my research equipment away, and then go swimming. That hour of alone time, monotonously swimming lengths, allowed my mind to begin to process the day's work, as well as enabling me to emerge 'cleansed' at the end, ready to return to 'real life' of family, dinner and the life politics outside my research.

INDEX

Printed in Great Britain
by Amazon